Understanding UK Sport Policy in Context

The London Olympics of 2012 acted as a focal point for an examination of UK sport policy. Individual chapters from leading specialists in their fields focus upon the central components of the UK's 'model' of sport – for example elite, school and community sport and talent ID policies – and discuss what kind of 'legacy' 2012 is likely to leave on the sports landscape in years to come. The concept 'legacy' is a common theme running through all contributions which themselves stem from a wide variety of academic disciplines and sub-disciplines, including sport psychology, political science, sports studies, cultural studies and sociology. A wide range of topics and organisations are covered throughout the volume, including coaching, talent ID, school sports partnerships, PE and youth sport, participation in sport, the IOC and the Olympic Charter, the Olympic Movement and Islamic culture and, finally, issues of regeneration through sports mega-events.

This book was previously published as a special issue of the *International Journal of Sport Policy and Politics*.

Jonathan Grix is one of the UK's leading experts on sport politics and policy and has published widely in leading journals including *Public Administration* (2011), *Public Policy and Administration* (2011), *International Journal of Sport Policy and Politics* (2012), *Journal of Sport and Tourism* (2013) and *British Journal of Politics and International Relations* (2013).

Lesley Phillpots' research interests focus primarily upon policy for sport, school sport and physical education. She has recently published on the governance of sport, youth sport development and county and school sport partnerships, including in leading policy journals such as *Public Policy and Administration* (2011) and *Physical Exercise and Sport Pedagogy* (2012).

Understanding UK Sport Policy in Context

Edited by
Jonathan Grix and Lesley Phillpots

Routledge
Taylor & Francis Group

LONDON AND NEW YORK

First published 2014
by Routledge
2 Park Square, Milton Park, Abingdon, Oxon, OX14 4RN, UK

and by Routledge
711 Third Avenue, New York, NY 10017, USA

Routledge is an imprint of the Taylor & Francis Group, an informa business

British Library Cataloguing in Publication Data
A catalogue record for this book is available from the British Library

ISBN13: 978-0-415-59468-4

Typeset in Times New Roman
by Taylor & Francis Books

Publisher's Note
The publisher accepts responsibility for any inconsistencies that may have arisen during the conversion of this book from journal articles to book chapters, namely the possible inclusion of journal terminology.

Disclaimer
Every effort has been made to contact copyright holders for their permission to reprint material in this book. The publishers would be grateful to hear from any copyright holder who is not here acknowledged and will undertake to rectify any errors or omissions in future editions of this book.

Contents

Citation Information

The chapters in this book were originally published in the *International Journal of Sport Policy and Politics*, volume 5, issue 2 (July 2013). When citing this material, please use the original page numbering for each article, as follows:

Chapter 1
London 2012 and its legacies
Jonathan Grix (with Lesley Phillpots)
International Journal of Sport Policy and Politics, volume 5, issue 2 (July 2013)
pp. 163-164

Chapter 2
Understanding the impact of sport coaching on legacy
Patrick Duffy, Julian North and Bob Muir
International Journal of Sport Policy and Politics, volume 5, issue 2 (July 2013)
pp. 165-182

Chapter 3
'Scienciness' and the allure of second-hand strategy in talent identification and development
Dave Collins and Richard Bailey
International Journal of Sport Policy and Politics, volume 5, issue 2 (July 2013)
pp. 183-192

Chapter 4
An analysis of the policy process for physical education and school sport: the rise and demise of school sport partnerships
Lesley Phillpots
International Journal of Sport Policy and Politics, volume 5, issue 2 (July 2013)
pp. 193-212

Chapter 5
Physical education and youth sport in England: conceptual and practical foundations for an Olympic legacy?
Mark Griffiths and Kathleen Armour
International Journal of Sport Policy and Politics, volume 5, issue 2 (July 2013)
pp. 213-228

Chapter 6

The Olympic legacy and participation in sport: an interim assessment of Sport England's Active People Survey for sports studies research
Fiona Carmichael, Jonathan Grix and Daniel Palacios Marqués
International Journal of Sport Policy and Politics, volume 5, issue 2 (July 2013)
pp. 229-244

Chapter 7

Can viewing London 2012 influence sport participation? – a viewpoint based on relevant theory
Ian David Boardley
International Journal of Sport Policy and Politics, volume 5, issue 2 (July 2013)
pp. 245-256

Chapter 8

London 2012 Olympic legacy: a big sporting society?
Cathy Devine
International Journal of Sport Policy and Politics, volume 5, issue 2 (July 2013)
pp. 257-280

Chapter 9

The Olympic Movement and Islamic culture: conflict or compromise for Muslim women?
Tansin Benn and Symeon Dagkas
International Journal of Sport Policy and Politics, volume 5, issue 2 (July 2013)
pp. 281-294

Chapter 10

Policy transfer, regeneration legacy and the summer Olympic Games: lessons for London 2012 and beyond
Jon Coaffee
International Journal of Sport Policy and Politics, volume 5, issue 2 (July 2013)
pp. 295-312

Please direct any queries you may have about the citations to
clsuk.permissions@cengage.com

INTRODUCTION
London 2012 and its legacies

Binding this collection of papers is the focus on or around the 2012 London Olympics. The UK capital's third hosting of the world's greatest show on earth can be distinguished from 1908 and 1948 by virtue of its magnitude, international scope, commercialization, cost and emphasis on post-Games 'legacies'. Sports mega-events in the twenty-first century, especially the Olympics, are big business. In their search for the 'twin suns of prestige and profit' (Guttmann 2002, p. 175), states like the UK are willing to pay upwards of £11 billion of taxpayer's money to put on the Games. The reasons for wishing to stage a sports 'mega' are not always clearly articulated by governments, but in general, states increasingly promise event-related 'legacies' in return for such an investment. The papers that follow either explicitly or implicitly discuss the Olympics and their purported legacies. Pat Duffy *et al.* set out to show how sport coaching can itself impact on, and contribute towards delivering, legacy. Theirs is less a discussion of what the Games can do for sport coaching, but more a suggestion of how the field can be re-organized to maximize the momentum of the event, as well as suggesting the need for a more systematic approach to programmes that claim legacy and other policy objectives. Dave Collins and Richard Bailey, on the other hand, look to the increasing transfer of policy in elite sport development (in particular, talent identification) and effectively question the logic of following states like Australia, itself designed to a great extent on the jewel in the Eastern Bloc crown, East Germany. Talent identification is becoming increasingly important, as some states appear to be becoming more and more obsessed with their position on the final medal table.

From elite sport, we turn to school sport, where Lesley Phillpots traces the ups and downs of school sport partnerships (SSPs). If ever anyone remained in doubt about the link between politics and sport, the coalition Government put paid to that by scrapping, then partially re-instating, the highly successful network of SSPs. Their potential for ensuring a sporting legacy has been swapped for an emphasis on 'competitive' sport, a theme Mark Griffiths and Kathy Armour turn to in their piece on physical education and youth sport in England. Those familiar with sport policy will be forgiven for a sense of déjà vu, as the catalyst for a sporting legacy among children and youths now rests with the 'School Games', an Olympic-style event underpinned by the 'hope' that more competitive sport ('whether children like it or not', Griffiths and Armour 2012) will inspire others to become physically active. It is interesting to note how the 'School Games' appear to resemble the *Spartakiade*, an Olympic-style sports event used throughout the Eastern Bloc, most notably Russia and East Germany, as a forum to forge future sporting talent to represent the nation.

On the theme of inspiring others to become physically active, Fiona Carmichael and Jonathan Grix (with Daniel Palacios Marques) examine the usefulness of Sport England's Active People Survey for students of sport studies. While flagging up some of the drawbacks of the data, this paper concludes that independent analysis of the (raw) data collected can yield some interesting insights into sport participation and reaffirms the importance of the role of demographic variables (e.g. gender, class, employment status) in understanding participation trends. Ian Boardley, in his reflective paper, considers whether a 'demonstration effect' stimulated by the media coverage of London 2012 could influence the general public in their attitudes towards sport participation. He does this by introducing to sport politics and policy scholars theories drawn from sport psychology. Some may be familiar to readers, such as Bandura's self efficacy theory. Part of Boardley's purpose here is to make sport policy scholars aware of the conceptual armoury available to tackle pertinent questions such as sport participation. Sport policy is an area that is clearly under-theorized and scholars and students should look beyond sociology to other disciplines for ways with which to explain developments in the field.

In her piece on London's legacy, Cathy Devine crosses a number of disciplinary boundaries, drawing on law, policy studies, philosophy, ethics and political science. The argument here is that in order to align with the rights to sport set out in the Olympic Charter, the UK Government's sport policy needs to change from its focus on competitive sport (touched on above) to a more inclusive notion of sport, that is, a real policy of 'sport for all'. We remain with the theme of the ideals set out in the Olympic Charter in a thoughtful piece from Tansin Benn and Symeon Dagkas. Here, the actual *practice* of the Olympics is juxtaposed with the general principles of Olympism. The authors show how a commitment to universal human rights to participate in sport is hard to square with Olympic dress codes that effectively exclude Muslim women from taking part, given their religious requirements of covering the body. 2012 is unlikely to change this because Ramadan, the holy month for Muslims in which they fast, falls in the middle of the Olympics (as pointed out by Benn and Dagkas). Rounding off this collection is Jon Coaffee's analysis of mega-event policy transfer and the shortcomings associated with attempting to produce a legacy in the area of regeneration. Coaffee highlights the role of the IOC – a supranational and unaccountable body – in shaping 'models' of urban and other legacies expected of hosting nations. Such a 'one-size-fits-all' approach fails to take into account local contexts and specificities; what may be good for one city and nation may well not be good for another. How this plays out in London will be one of the key points of discussion in the future. London's East End, without a doubt one of the poorest areas of the city, has certainly been transformed by this predominantly publicly funded project. However, once the Olympic juggernaut has moved on to Brazil, the tangible Olympic legacies will be decidedly private. Whether Londoners will benefit more from the huge (Australian) Westfield Group-owned shopping centre or the Qatari Diar-part-owned Olympic Village than, say, investments and interventions to tackle inequality in health, gender relations and income differentials is debatable (see Grix 2012).

The variety of topics and themes covered in this collection highlight the fact that the concept of 'legacy' is 'elastic' and is used to cover the impact the Games is hoped to have on a wide range of factors. Whether it be more people partaking in physical activity and sport, or the (hoped-for) increase in inbound tourism, the trigger behind such legacies is said to be (by government) the sports mega-event itself. Hopefully this collection will assist students of sport politics and policy in their own reflections on London 2012, its impact on sport and sport policy in the UK and its possible legacies.

References

Grix, J., 2012. The politics of sports mega-events. *Political insight*, 3 (1), 4–7.
Guttmann, A., 2002. *A history of the modern games*. Chicago, IL: University of Illinois Press, 175.

Jonathan Grix (with Lesley Phillpots)

Understanding the impact of sport coaching on legacy

Patrick Duffy, Julian North and Bob Muir

Carnegie Faculty, Leeds Metropolitan University, Headingley Campus, Leeds LS6 3QS, UK

The creation of a legacy from the London 2012 Olympic and Paralympic Games has been articulated by government in the form of five promises, some of which have implications for coaching (Department of Culture, Media and Sport 2008, *Before, during and after: making the most of the London 2012 Games*. London: Department of Culture, Media and Sport). The *UK Coaching Framework* (sports coach UK 2008a, *The UK Coaching Framework: a 3-7-11 year action plan*. Leeds: Coachwise) makes the case that sport coaching has a role to play in delivering legacy and policy objectives through the systemic development of active, skilled and qualified coaches. The status of the UK Coaching Framework as a complex intervention to support policy and legacy objectives is addressed in this article. The analysis is referenced against seven criteria derived from the realist approach to impact evaluation (Pawson *et al.* 2005, Realist review – a new method of systematic review designed for complex policy interventions. *Journal of health services research and policy*, 10 (1), 21–34; Pawson 2006, *Evidence based policy: a realist perspective*. London: Sage), with an emphasis on programme theories. The programme theories of the Framework position sport coaching as a generative mechanism for outcome patterns in participation and performance sport. In order to maximize the impact of this mechanism, the Framework proposes strategic action areas that include participant and coach modelling; workforce analysis, recruitment and deployment; support and education; regulation as well as research. The Framework proposes to integrate these action areas into implementation chains throughout the United Kingdom, supported by the progressive alignment of resources. The programme theories recognize the agency and responsibility of the coach, as well as the volition of participants in different contexts, with implications for the way in which coaching roles are defined. It is concluded that the UK Coaching Framework is a complex intervention, which is amenable to realist impact evaluation. It is suggested that such evaluation will provide a more robust basis to understand the impact of sport coaching on legacy.

1. Policy context

Sport has assumed an enhanced role within government policy in the United Kingdom in recent years. Policy objectives have been articulated in participation and performance-oriented sport in each of the home countries (Sport Scotland 2007, Department for Children and Schools 2008, Sport England 2008, UK Sport 2008, Sports Council for Wales 2009, Sport Northern Ireland 2009). Recent analyses have suggested that the driving force for sport policy in different countries is related to its cultural significance, its malleability to deliver non-sport objectives for government and its multidimensionality (Bergsgard *et al.* 2007). The varied policy aspirations for the role of sport coaching in the United Kingdom support this analysis (e.g. Department of Culture, Media and Sport (DCMS) 2002).

The economic and cultural significance of sport was evident in the bid to host the London 2012 Olympic and Paralympic Games, reflected in two pledges: 'to inspire a generation of young people through sport' and 'to transform the heart of East London' (DCMS 2008, p. 43, 36). These pledges were subsequently translated into five legacy promises, which included the creation of a world leading sporting system with high-quality clubs, coaches and facilities (DCMS 2008).

Coaching, therefore, is perceived to have a role in delivering a legacy from the Olympic and Paralympic Games. However, the mechanisms by which such a legacy contribution would be delivered and evaluated were not detailed (DCMS 2008). This reflects a wider challenge to quantify the potential role and benefits of coaching, supported by robust data relating to its efficacy in delivering policy objectives. In this context, the need for a more systematic approach to impact evaluation in coaching will be addressed in this article, with a particular focus on its contribution to legacy.

Despite a relatively recent and fragmented policy pedigree (Houlihan 1997, Bergsgard *et al.* 2007), the role of sport coaching in support of policy and legacy objectives has begun to consolidate in recent times. This process of consolidation commenced with the publication of the *UK vision for coaching* (UK Sport 2001), which proposed the establishment of coaching as a profession by 2012. Although the overall directions outlined in this publication had been signalled 10 years earlier in *Coaching matters* (Sports Council 1991), little progress was made in the intervening period in the absence of a wider policy impetus for coaching.

The policy context began to change following the publication of *Game plan* (DCMS 2002), where the need for a more systematic approach to the development of sporting talent was highlighted. Government also sought to enhance school sport and to increase social inclusion in and through sport. Following on from this, the requirement for a stronger policy focus on sport coaching was identified and a task force was established. The subsequent report (DCMS 2002) made a number of recommendations with a view to create a more effective coaching system. These recommendations formed the basis of 'the Coaching Project' and included provision for the employment of 3000 community sports coaches, the United Kingdom Coaching Certificate (UKCC), 45 coach development officers and research (North 2010). These initiatives led to new investment of £28 million for the period 2003–2007 and contributed to an evolving landscape within coaching, the composition of which was charted in workforce terms for the first time in 2004 (MORI 2004).

This landscape also included an increased policy focus on coaching in all four home countries, with a particular emphasis on the implementation of the UKCC. By 2005, combined expenditure on sport coaching across the United Kingdom exceeded £60 million annually (sports coach UK 2006a), and a process to establish a long-term plan for coaching was initiated leading to the publication of *The UK Coaching Framework* (sports coach UK 2008a). By this time, data on the coaching workforce suggested that 1.11 million adults were involved in coaching, with 76% classified as volunteers, 21% part-time paid and 3% full-time paid. Of the coaching workforce 53% reported that they had some form of coaching qualification (North 2009).

2. The role of coaching in support of policy and legacy outcomes

Although many of these advances marked important progress in coaching policy, there remained a need by 2005 to articulate a long-term programme for the development of coaching across the United Kingdom. This need was amplified by the success of the London 2012 bid. Increasing clarity in the strategic objectives of the lead agencies across the United Kingdom also provided the challenge of more clearly articulating the policy contribution of sport coaching. These policy and legacy objectives were echoed a year later in the declaration of the first UK Coaching Summit. The summit called for an action plan for coaching in three phases (sports coach UK 2006b).

The resultant document, entitled *The UK Coaching Framework: a 3-7-11 year action plan*, proposed coaching as a mechanism to deliver sport policy, and by extension, legacy objectives (sports coach UK 2008a). Although there has been considerable debate over the role of coaching in supporting the achievement of policy objectives in participation (North 2008), repeated policy statements attest to its importance (Sport Scotland 2007, Sport England 2008, UK Sport 2008, Sports Council for Wales 2009, Sport Northern Ireland 2009). The framework took a positive view of the policy role of coaching and set out a vision of creating a 'cohesive, ethical, inclusive and valued coaching system where skilled coaches support children, players and athletes at all stages of their development and is world leading by 2016' (sports coach UK 2008a: Executive Summary).

A key feature of the UK Coaching Framework was the initiation of core strategic action areas that included participant and coach modelling; workforce analysis, recruitment and deployment; support and education; licensing and registration; research and development. Notably, a shift was proposed in the classification of coaching roles away from a solely performance-oriented paradigm to more strongly reflect the needs of participants in children's sport, participation and talent development as well as high performance.

The proposed implementation chain included a central role for governing bodies of sport, operating within the context of UK and home country sport policy and investment programmes. The Framework was formally recognized by key stakeholders as the reference document for the development of the UK coaching system up to 2016. Four resource pillars were identified for successful implementation: employment and deployment of coaches; education and professional development of coaches; governing body coaching infrastructure; coaching infrastructure within policy and other support agencies.

The UK Coaching Framework was, therefore, positioned as a strategic and operational change intervention for improving the quality and quantity of coaching to support policy and legacy objectives. Making the case that coaching plays a key role in guiding sports participants at all stages of their development, the Framework positioned itself as 'the backbone' of the coaching legacy (McGeechan and Duffy 2008). This case was made on the basis that the creation of a world-leading coaching system would provide a sustainable vehicle through which policy objectives in both participation and performance would be enhanced. The document also recognized individuals (participants and coaches) and organizations (such as governing bodies, sports councils, UK Sport, Skills Active, Youth Sport Trust, local authorities, schools and clubs) as central to the change and legacy-building process.

The coaching workforce required to deliver on the vision of the Framework was quantified in three potential scenarios (North 2009), while the elements of the proposed coaching system were laid out in detail (sports coach UK 2008a). This quantification was significant in that one of the risks associated with legacy pledges and promises is their intangible nature. In the case of coaching, which was not explicitly highlighted in the London 2012 bid, the future planning perspective generated following the announcement of the games, created the conditions in which a long-term and quantifiable programme such as the Framework might be contemplated. Although the detailed objectives and targets associated with the Framework were outlined, the ongoing process and methodology for the evaluation of progress was not fully defined (sports coach UK 2008a).

Despite the fact that the Coaching Task Force (DCMS 2002) had earlier initiated a strand of ongoing research, there has been an absence of impact analysis of coaching policy interventions. Indeed, there has not been a strong tradition in sport where the systematic and evidence-based evaluation of programmes informs policy. This is a limitation in other policy areas, leading Pawson (2006, p. 7) to observe 'There are precious few examples of it (evaluation) leading to actual decisions to "retain, imitate, modify or discard programmes". Evaluation research, in short, has reached industrial proportions but remains feudal in its capacity to create change'.

This article focuses on the status of the Framework as a complex intervention, with a view to the ongoing evaluation of its impact on policy and legacy objectives. This analysis uses a set of criteria that have been drawn from the realist approach to evaluation (Pawson and Tilley 1997, Pawson *et al.* 2005) and has been informed by the wider consideration of the potential contribution of a critical realist approach to the study of coaching (North in press). Prior to examining these criteria as they relate to the Framework, it is first necessary to consider recent trends in programme evaluation and their implications for impact assessment with particular reference to the UK Coaching Framework.

3.   The evolving field of programme evaluation

3.1   *Experimental, pragmatic, constructivist and pluralist evaluation*

The evaluation of policy-related interventions has been subject to a variety of approaches since its beginning alongside social programmes of the United States in the 1960s. Pawson and Tilley (1997) have summarized these into four main categories: experimental, pragmatic, naturalistic and pluralist. They provide a comprehensive overview of the strengths and limitations of each, the detailed analysis of which is beyond the scope of this article (Pawson and Tilley 1997, Pawson *et al.* 2005, Pawson 2006). In the context of this article, the relative merits of each approach have been summarized, with a view to identifying a suitable methodology to apply to the evaluation of the UK Coaching Framework.

The first of these approaches, the experimental, places a strong emphasis on control and causation, with the express desire to 'exclude every conceivable rival causal agent from the experiment so that we are left with one, secure causal link' (Pawson and Tilley 1997, p. 5). In the case of the UK Coaching Framework, with many strands and a wide-reaching agenda, such a tightly controlled method of evaluation is problematic. For example, it would not be possible to chart direct causal links between the allocation of resources to coaching and the achievement of success in participation or other sport policy objectives. In addition, the tightly controlled methodology is not easily applied to the diverse range of sports and contexts within the coaching landscape.

The pragmatic approach is the second method outlined by Pawson and Tilley (1997) and highlights the importance of linking the programme and its evaluation to the objectives of policymakers. A limitation of this line of attack is the potential narrowness of focus and 'the more explicit the policy mandate, the more compressed and purely technical the researcher's role' (Pawson and Tilley 1997, p. 17). In the context of the current analysis, the danger would be to solely focus on the set of stated policy objectives relating to participation, performance and creation of a legacy through coaching. Many of the coaching-related objectives, such as the recruitment, education, support and quality assurance of coaches, would be marginalized in such analysis. In addition, the focus within the Framework on the creation of a sustainable system and process in coaching would likely take a back seat to the more pressing issues associated with the production of policy outcomes.

Pragmatic evaluation is at a very different place to the third perspective under consideration, that of constructivism which is at the heart of the naturalistic school of programme evaluation. To its credit, constructivism recognizes the complexity of human interaction and understanding the world, with a consequent focus on processes rather than outputs. This approach also claims to empower those engaged in the evaluation process, as part of consensus building. However, one of its key limitations is eloquently expressed by Pawson and Tilley (1997, p. 21): 'Since on this view there is no single objective reality to report upon, hermeneutic dialectic circles (not surprisingly) go round in circles, rather than constituting a linear advance in the truth'. This limitation is further compounded by 'the inability to grasp those structures and institutional features of society which are in some respects independent of the individuals' reasoning and desires' (Pawson and Tilley 1997, p. 23).

In the context of the UK Coaching Framework, the constructivist emphasis would likely be on the identification of meaning for the multitude of actors involved in the intervention. Although such an approach has its merits through the provision of rich insights and individual empowerment, it does little to build the kind of robust conceptual framework required for systemic change, impact evaluation and the ongoing creation of more effective structures for coaches and the participants with whom they work. Sport- and country-specific differences, coaching domains and participant categories and strategic action areas provide important organizing concepts that require analysis taking into account wider social and economic influences. Thus, while it is recognized that many of the concepts used in the UK Coaching Framework have emerged from an intensive process of interaction and the creation of shared meanings within the coaching community, the constructivist approach does not offer the perspective or full range of tools required to evaluate such a multifaceted intervention.

Pawson and Tilley (1997) identified the pluralist approach as the fourth category of programme evaluation, which is also referred to as comprehensive evaluation. This approach includes analysis and synthesis of initial concepts and design, monitoring implementation and assessing the utility of the programme. Although the strengths of this approach are acknowledged, particularly the emphasis on impact, the intimidating resource implications to 'research everything' have rendered this approach impracticable. Within coaching, a landscape that includes over a million coaches, more than 70 formally recognized governing bodies and 4 home countries, the feasibility of conducting a comprehensive impact evaluation is beyond reach. Like the other approaches above, comprehensive evaluation has much to offer. However, the need to seek alternatives to these methods became apparent in order to fully address the range of policy and implementation issues that were signalled in the UK Coaching Framework.

3.2 *Realist review*

Realist review has drawn from the lessons of the approaches outlined in the previous section and looks upon 'interventions as whole sequences of mechanisms that produce diverse effects according to context, so that any particular intervention will have its own particular signature of outputs and outcomes' (Pawson 2006, p. 171). Recognizing the key building blocks of social science 'such as the nature of causation, the constitution of the social world, the stratification of social reality, the emergent nature of social change', Pawson (2006, p. 18) emphasizes the 'open system' nature of the social world where historical and institutional forces play a strong role. It is for this reason that he speaks of interventions as 'complex systems embedded in complex systems'. Although recognizing these historical, social and institutional influences, Pawson (2006, p. 18) notes that 'behavioural regularities are, of course, also influenced by the volition and choices of the people who act them out' noting that 'a ceaselessly changing complexity is the norm in social life'. Crucially for coaching, this approach recognizes the salience of the choices and actions of coaches and participants in the front line.

Recognizing the complexity of social interventions, the essence of realist review is its focus on what works through the application of a generative model of causation. Its trademark is 'to look for causal powers within the objects or agents or structures under investigation' (Pawson 2006, p. 21). The building blocks of this approach are outcome patterns, generative mechanisms and contextual conditions. Outcome patterns recognize the limitations of attempting to impose regularity, suggesting that 'It is the totality of outcomes – successful, unsuccessful, bit of both – that may act as the initial empirical guide for future optimal locations' (Pawson 2006, p. 22).

The strength of this approach for coaching is that it recognizes that there will be a varied range of outcomes in the multitude of different contexts within which coaching occurs. For example, the delivery of coach education programmes may work well where there exists a cost-effective model that is accessible to and meets the needs of coaches on the ground. However, even where such a system exists, sport-specific and local circumstances are likely to become manifest and the realist approach seeks and recognizes these nuances. Notably, the delivery of the UKCC has been subject to a very wide range of sport-specific, national and regional influences, which have made it difficult to assess the optimal model for delivery and the consequent impact on coaches.

Within the realist methodology, generative mechanisms are used to explain the propensity of systems to make certain things happen: 'the rhythms and associations of natural and even social science are constant enough that we can navigate our way through them …. We rely on mechanisms to tell us why interconnections occur' (Pawson 2006, p. 23). Crucially, it is argued that programmes only work 'if people chose to make them work' and 'the development of cumulative knowledge about "what works" requires sustained investigation of the generic mechanism, namely the operation of choices under the inducement of programme resources' (Pawson 2006, p. 24). The achievement of the vision of the UK Coaching Framework relies on increasing numbers of coaches making choices to further develop their skills and qualifications. The Framework also assumes greater accessibility to quality coaching by participants. It is posited that the combination of the strategic action areas, operating as part of a coordinated system, will create the conditions to motivate and support coaches, employers and participants to act in a way that enhances the quality and quantity of sporting experiences.

One of the strengths of realist review is its commitment to provide explanation of what works in given contexts. There is an inherent recognition that contextual constraints will have a bearing on implementation because 'interventions, by definition, are always inserted into pre-existing conditions' (Pawson 2006, p. 24), with recognition that there will be successes and failures in every programme. In this context, Pawson (2006) refers to a process of 'enlightenment' as a result of realist review. The realist has a modest opinion of the role of the research in gathering definitive evidence. In the case of a complex programme, the research process is seen as 'producing a sort of highway code to programme building, alerting policy-makers to the problems that they might expect to confront and some of the safest measures to deal with them' (Pawson 2006, p. 170). The nuances associated with this approach also pose challenges within the policymaking process, where clear-cut and less complicated solutions are sought by politicians (Pawson 2006).

3.3 Application of realist review to coaching

It is for these reasons that the realist review methodology, already applied within the health sector (Pawson *et al.* 2005), would appear to hold merit for application to sport policy in general and coaching in particular. The essence of this methodology is that it seeks to provide 'an explanatory analysis of what works for whom, in what circumstances, in what respects and how' (Pawson *et al.* 2005, p. 22). This involves making the programme theories of the intervention explicit, as well as the assumptions about how it should work and the expected impacts.

Evidence is then collected to 'populate this theoretical framework, supporting, contra-dicting or modifying the programme theories as it goes' (Pawson *et al.* 2005, p. 1). The review then seeks to combine the theoretical and evidence-based components and focuses 'on explaining the relationship between the context in which the intervention is applied, the mechanisms by which it works and the outcomes which are produced' (Pawson *et al.* 2005, p. 1). Decision-makers are thus provided with the opportunity to more fully understand the intervention and the ways by which it can be made to work more effectively.

Pawson *et al.* (2005) outline seven defining features of complex interventions to include: the existence of a theoretical basis, the active input of individuals, the length of the intervention journey, the non-linear nature of implementation, fragility and social context, proneness to leak and borrowing and finally the intervention as an open system that feeds back on itself. The application of these criteria to the UK Coaching Framework provides a useful basis for an assessment of its status as a complex intervention. This is an important first step in moving to a more systematic and periodic review of the Framework in the context of legacy and sport policy objectives. The scope of this article does not allow for exhaustive treatment of each of the criteria, so particular emphasis has been placed on the programme theories.

4. The UK Coaching Framework as a complex intervention

The publication of *The coaching workforce* (North 2009) demonstrated the value of quanti-fiable data in charting progress in coaching at a system level. However, such data are primarily descriptive and predictive at this stage and will not provide the level of precision and understanding of what is working, for whom, in what circumstances and why. Clearly, there is a need to study the experiences of participants, coaches, administrators and other key stakeholders in a range of coaching contexts. Such research will provide a robust analysis of the impact of an intervention such as the UK Coaching Framework.

As seen in the previous section, the application of realist review methodology to coaching is seen to hold significant potential, given its focus on outcome patterns, mechan-isms and context. A further strength is the recognition of human volition as an ingredient in considering the successes and failures of interventions. By emphasizing the significance of context and explanation rather than uniformity and solutions, realist review provides an appropriate method for the evaluation of the complexities associated with the coaching landscape. In the United Kingdom, this landscape consists of over 1 million coaches, 2.75 million guided sport hours per week, 8 million regular sports participants, 70 UK-wide governing bodies, 4 home countries and a multitude of delivery agencies in school, club, local authority, further and higher education and other environments (North 2009).

The current analysis, therefore, seeks to establish the status of the UK Coaching Framework as a complex intervention that is amenable to ongoing review using realist evaluation methodology. The seven defining criteria for complex interventions that follow have been drawn from Pawson *et al.* (2005) and Pawson (2006) for the purpose of this analysis, with the strongest emphasis on programme theories.

a.   The UK Coaching Framework is based on the theory that coaching is a mechanism to generate sport policy outcome patterns. This mechanism is optimally activated through the sport-specific development and implementation of participant and coach development models which form the basis for action within five strategic action areas. Implementation should occur within a delivery chain where the roles of governing bodies, central and other organizations are defined

The underlying theories of the UK Coaching Framework were derived from previous policy documents, literature reviews, research, consultation with the sport coaching industry and reference to emerging international trends (sports coach UK 2008a). Although the theories underpinning the document were not explicitly labelled as such, there exists considerable documentation from which a retrospective analysis and key theories can be drawn (sports coach UK 2006a, 2007, 2008a,b, North 2009).

At a macro policy level, the UK Coaching Framework drew its origins from a theory that sport coaching itself is a mechanism that generates outcome patterns in both participation and performance-oriented sport. Although some evidence exists to support this theory (North 2008), its application at national programme level remains to be tested in a concerted fashion. Much of the demand for a more coherent and sustained approach to coaching emanated from the policy documents referred to earlier, which expressed a need for coaching for children; teenage and adult participants; talented, high-performance and elite athletes (Sport Scotland 2007, Sport England 2008, UK Sport 2008, Sports Council for Wales 2009, Sport Northern Ireland 2009). Discussions on investment in the Framework involved the alignment of coaching with the policies and programmes of the key agencies, thus formaliz-ing the theory that coaching is a generative mechanism (Duffy 2009). Figure 1 provides an example of this alignment process in England.

The UK Coaching Framework was also based on the theory that the provision of skilled, active and qualified coaches on a sustained basis to the front line would best be achieved through governing bodies of sport, working within the context of the policies and investment programmes of UK Sport and the home country sports councils. This theory positions governing bodies as pivotal to the implementation chain for the intervention. There were a number of caveats to this theory, the first of which related to willingness, capability and resource alignment. Although most governing bodies attest to the importance of coaching, the internal policy, organizational and resource conditions were found to be varied. A further caveat to the lead role of the governing bodies of sport was the recognition that a large proportion of the 1.11 million coaches that are active throughout the United Kingdom do not operate with close or any links to such governing bodies (North 2009). Indeed, it was recognized that just slightly over half of all those who classify themselves as coaches hold some form of governing body coaching qualification.

This relatively weak position in terms of 'market penetration' was broadly accepted by the governing bodies themselves, and agreement was reached in the first year of full operation of the Framework on the need for coaching support networks within each of the home countries. Such networks consist of organizations other than governing bodies that play a role in identifying, communicating with and supporting coaches (e.g. local authorities, county sports partnerships, educational institutions, regional and national agencies that have reason to come into contact with coaches). The Framework further posited that there is a

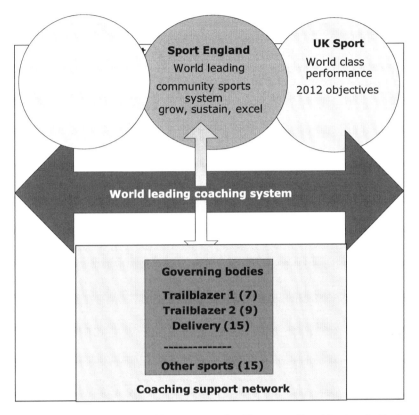

Figure 1. Alignment of the UK Coaching Framework with sport policy objectives in England.

range of actions and services required to act interdependently to develop a cohesive coaching system.

The Framework also proposed the theory that for sustained and effective implementation, there was a need for strategic and policy leadership. The creation of a Coaching Strategy Group was proposed, notably to replace the previous Coaching Steering Board, which had been set up to oversee the expenditure of the £28 million new investment in coaching following the Coaching Task Force report. The purpose of this strategy group was 'to coordinate coaching policy within the UK' with representation from each of the home countries, UK Sport and the governing bodies (sports coach UK 2008a).

The document assigned the strategic leadership function to sports coach UK, recommending that the 'mission, structure, operation and funding of the organisation should reflect this leadership and system building role' (sports coach UK 2008a, p. 32). The Framework also placed the requirement on sports coach UK that 'The operating structures and business plans of the sports coach UK Group (sports coach UK and Coachwise) will be revised in line with directions (sic) of the UK Coaching Framework and reflected in a new strategy for the Group' (sports coach UK 2008a, p. 32). The creation of stable and long-term systems, terminology and ways of working, with a system-building emphasis was a key finding in the consultation process associated with the development of the Framework. Equally, the development of robust models, underpinned by appropriate theory and research, was called for by governing bodies, with the plea that such models (and the associated implementation) should not be arbitrarily changed or set aside.

One of the key interventions proposed was the creation of participant and coach development models based on the needs of each sport, adapted from core principles and guidelines developed through the specialist and coaching advisory groups convened by sports coach UK (Duffy 2009). This approach was based on the theory that participant need and development should be at the centre of a guided process of improvement within coaching. Consequently, a participant development model was drawn up, informed by the perspectives of the stakeholders and integrating some of the strongest features of the model of long-term athlete development (Balyi and Hamilton 1995, Stafford 2005) and the developmental model of sports participation (Côté and Fraser Thomas 2007). A sport-specific interpretation of this model is outlined in Figure 2 (Duffy 2009).

A key feature of the model is that it challenges the conventional practice of viewing coaching within a high-performance-oriented paradigm. In focusing on participant need, the Framework suggested a diversification in the way coaching roles are described, supported, rewarded and certificated. The result has been the production of a coach development model that has become known (unofficially) as the '4 × 4' (Duffy 2009). As the name suggests, there is a need for an expanded breadth and depth of coaching roles across four key coaching domains (children, participation, performer development, high performance as outlined in Figure 3), reflecting emerging research and practice on the nature of coaching roles and expertise (Lyle 2002, National Coaching and Training Centre 2003, Côté et al. 2007, European Coaching Council 2007, Côté and Gilbert 2009).

The Framework proposed that the implementation of the strategic action areas across a critical mass of governing bodies in each of the home countries would provide the basis for creating a world leading coaching system by 2016. The essence of this programme theory was that active, skilled and qualified coaches would make a significant contribution to policy

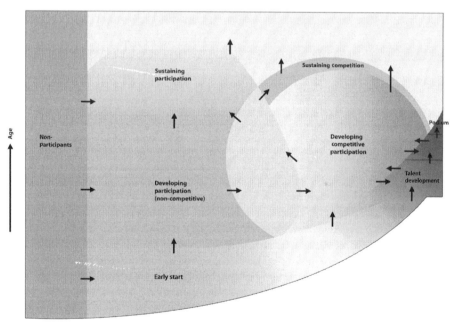

Figure 2.   Participant development model (sample gymnastics application of core model).

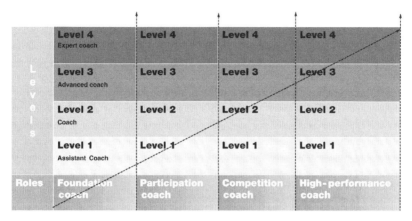

Figure 3.   Coach development model.

objectives in children's sport, participation, talent development and high performance. In order to maximize the recruitment and development of these coaches, clear participant and coach development models operating within sport- and country-specific coaching systems were deemed as essential building blocks. These models 'for' the sport challenge each sport to clarify and refine their own programme theories and lay the basis for sport-specific application of the wider set of principles outlined in the Framework.

b.   Participants, coaches, governing bodies and others are active in applying, adapting or ignoring the principles of the Framework

Realist review recognizes the significance of agency by all stakeholders in any complex intervention. Thus, although the originators of an intervention operate on the basis of stated intentions and outcomes, there is a process of interpretation and adaptation among those responsible for implementation at various levels. Recognizing the significance of agency, a key theory within the Framework is that the delivery of quality coaching is primarily the responsibility of the coach. This theory recognizes the professional responsibilities and decision-making of coaches, operating within a social and organizational context.

Reflecting the ecological perspective of Bronfenbrenner (1979) and later adapted into a sport context by Carlson (1988, 1993), a series of layered interactions were identified within the overall coaching system as part of the process to develop the UK Coaching Framework. Although the theoretical terms were not made explicit in the document itself, these include the participant and the coach (the micro system), the immediate environment within which the coach and participant operate such as clubs and schools (the endosystem) and the wider system of regional and national agencies (the exosystem). Notably, this approach has a strong resonance with the contextual layers identified by realists: individual capacity of the key actors, interpersonal relationships supporting the intervention, the institutional setting and the wider infrastructural system (Pawson 2006, p. 31).

At the different levels of the coaching system, the Framework suggested that effective decision-making would be promoted, informed by the needs of participants, guided by coaches of varied skill level and motive in the four coaching domains and operating within organizational structures at local, regional and national level as appropriate. This represents one of the greatest challenges of the Framework, in that it at once seeks to establish a common reference point for the development of the coaching system, while recognizing that high-quality coaching is situation, context and sport specific. This approach leaves much to the perception, interpretation and actions of all of the actors and stakeholders throughout the coaching system. Pawson *et al.* (2006, p. 22) note that 'we should expect that, in tracking the successes and failures of interventions, reviewers will find at least part of the explanation in terms of the reasoning and personal choices of different actors and participants'.

Governing body personnel were assigned a particularly significant role in applying the methodologies and models of the Framework to their sport-specific contexts. The decisions made within each sport relating to their needs, current context, participant and coach development models, resource allocation and delivery mechanisms have a critical bearing on the effectiveness of their coaching systems. In turn, the front-line arrangements that are in place for the recruitment, deployment and support coaches have an impact on whether the coaches themselves have the opportunity to apply participant-centred practices in the context of their own coaching philosophy and capabilities.

c. There is a long spatial, temporal and organizational journey in the application of the Framework to the needs of participants, coaches, governing bodies and others

Pawson *et al.* (2005) highlight the organizational, spatial and temporal journeys of complex interventions. The origination of the UK Coaching Framework itself was a long journey, with the process taking over 2 years in total and including three UK Coaching Summits between 2006 and 2008. The process also involved extensive engagement with governing bodies, home country sports councils, UK Sport, Youth Sport Trust, Skills Active and other stakeholders. In order to maximize the integrity of implementation and to oversee the translation of core models into practice, the need for coordinated action and aligned resources was emphasized. Three key layers were identified: strategic/policy level, programme/management development and implementation. The core roles of each of the main agencies were defined. Pawson *et al.* (2005, p. 22) emphasize that one of the functions of a review process should be to 'explore the integrity of the implementation chain, examining which intermediate outputs need to be in place for successful final outcomes to occur, and noting and examining the flows, blockages and points of contention'.

The length of the journey for the successful implementation of the Framework has substantial organizational, spatial and temporal components. As outlined earlier, the intervention seeks to impact at all levels of the coaching system, ultimately to enhance the quality of the experience of the participant at the front line. Spatially, the implication is that the Framework will ultimately seek to impact all corners of the United Kingdom, reaching over 1 million coaches and creating a sustainable infrastructure for the recruitment, deployment, support, development and quality assurance of the coaches. The potential dilution of the message within the overall organizational journey has also been signalled in evaluation reports of one aspect of the Framework, the UKCC (Lyle 2007).

Short-, medium- and long-term targets were established within the Framework as part of the 11-year plan. Clearly, given the various 'distances' to be travelled by the initiative the need for clarity of function, effective leadership and coordination, appropriately resourced and committed governing bodies and support agencies are all central to the creation of an effective implementation chain. In a policy and legacy context, the length of the implementation journey highlights the need for a combination of consistency, adaptation and resilience in the application of the programme theories over time.

d. The implementation chain is non-linear and can even go in reverse

Experience from other domains highlights the non-linear nature of interventions (Pawson *et al.* 2005), suggesting that top-down initiatives can become bottom up in the course of implementation. The UK Coaching Framework recognizes the need for top-down intervention on the one hand and the central role of the sport and the coach in responding to participant need on the other. Inherent in this recognition is that many of the solutions advocated by the Framework are already evident to varying degrees. Many coaches demonstrate excellent practice on a daily basis and have no great need for further support or interest in policy interventions. Furthermore, even before the emergence of the UK Coaching Framework, governing bodies, funding and other agencies were demonstrating elements of best practice. It is evident therefore that while the Framework sought to provide a methodology for the creation of sustainable coaching systems, the emergent process will be subject to constant refinement and adaptation based on the circumstances and needs of the governing bodies and others involved in implementation.

Notably, Pawson *et al.* (2005) suggest that the shape of interventions is influenced by the power of the different agencies. A key implication for policy and legacy objectives is the recognition that the final outcome may not look like that which was first anticipated. In addition, the role of organizations in mediating and influencing the initiative means that there is likelihood that more influential organizations will shape the initiative to suit their interests. Where there is congruence between these interests and policy or legacy objectives, this may not be problematic.

The corollary is that there may be a conflict between the intentions of the originators of the intervention and powerful vested interests. Tensions may emerge between conservative forces seeking to retain the status quo and transformative forces seeking to pursue change. One example of this phenomenon is the difficulties associated with achieving a meaningful realignment of the UKCC with the core principles of the Framework and the coach development model. Pawson *et al.* (2005, p. 23) suggest that the review process should examine 'how the relative influence of different parties is able to affect and direct implementation'. Over time, such analysis will provide a perspective on the 'force field' and competing interests operating within policy (Rose 1973) and across coaching contexts (Jones *et al.* 2005).

e. The intervention is fragile and embedded in multiple social systems

It should not be expected that interventions will be applied in the same way in all contexts. What works, for whom, in what contexts and why are central to the required analysis, recognizing that 'rarely, if ever, is a programme equally effective in all circumstances because of the influence of context' (Pawson *et al.* 2005, p. 23). The UK Coaching Framework has taken account of the need for unique solutions to emerge in face-to-face coaching interactions as well as in the different contextual layers within and between each sport and home country. As stated, it is already apparent that the impact of the initiative to date is varied across sports and countries. Even within sports and home countries, there are significant variations, in line with the realist observation that differences exist between 'policy timing, organizational culture and leadership, resource allocation, interpersonal relationships, and competing local priorities and influences' (Pawson *et al.* 2005, p. 23).

f. The intervention is leaky and prone to be borrowed

Regardless of the level of clarity and detail provided in interventions, dialogue among those responsible for its implementation is both desirable and inevitable. Pawson *et al.* (2005,

p. 23) observed that 'we should expect the same intervention to be delivered in a mutating fashion shaped by refinement, reinvention and adaptation to local circumstances'. This will particularly be the case when snags occur and in the interpretation and application of labels. A feature of the development and early stages of the Framework was the high level of interaction between governing bodies with a view to identifying priorities, sharing best practice and identifying optimal solutions to some of the implementation issues that have occurred.

Pawson *et al.* (2005) also suggest that reviewers take account of 'label naiveté' (Øvreteit and Gustafson 2002) where the programme theory will carry titles that do not necessarily reflect the experiences or language of practitioners or managers, or the outcomes of empirical studies. The issue of labelling is of particular salience to the UK Coaching Framework, as the consultation process highlighted the need for a more common language to describe key elements of coaching and the coaching system. Time will only tell if the concepts and labels have a resonance with those responsible for implementation.

g.   The intervention is an open system that feeds back on itself

'As interventions are implemented, they change the conditions that made them work in the first place' (Pawson *et al.* 2005, p. 23). Within the context of the UK Coaching Framework, the process itself brought about early changes in the way policy agencies and governing bodies in sport interacted. There was also a substantial level of discussion and engagement around participant and coach development models, much of which has resulted in activation by governing bodies around their sport-specific versions. As mentioned earlier, this work raised significant questions about the nature, delivery and cost issues associated with the UKCC, with the need for further enhancement of the technical basis of the certificate also being identified with a closer focus on participant need and coaching domains (sports coach UK 2008a). The recent amendments to the National Occupational Standards (Skills Active 2011) do not appear to have taken the directions set out in the Framework fully on board, particularly in relation to the different coaching domains, while concerns about the costs associated with the UKCC, particularly for volunteers, have endured.

A key implication for the programme and for sport policy and legacy objectives is the need to incorporate open and ongoing feedback mechanisms, as well as recognizing the fluid and changing nature of the initiative. The UK Coaching Framework has made provision for systematic reviews and adjustments at the end of each of the three main phases, albeit without a clear specification of how this should happen. The work of Pawson *et al.* (2005) suggests that ongoing and responsive interaction will be necessary to reflect the openness and fluidity that is inherent in an initiative such as the UK Coaching Framework. An evident implication for policy and legacy objectives is that at the very least adaptation of the methods and processes of the Framework will be required, as well as adjustment to programme and policy objectives along the way.

It is apparent from the foregoing analysis that the application of a realist approach to programme evaluation provides fertile ground for the assessment of the impact of the UK Coaching Framework on policy objectives and on the quality of coaching over time. Given the range of sports, coaching domains and home country contexts the seven criteria reviewed here suggest that not only is the Framework amenable to such review, but it will benefit significantly from the associated rigour and precision.

5. Summary

This article has suggested that the role of coaching within wider sport policy objectives in the United Kingdom has begun to consolidate in recent years. This policy position, which is still at an early stage, has focused on the contribution that coaching makes to core sport objectives, such as participation, performance and the creation or extension of opportunities for children in school and/or community contexts. Within this canvas, the emergence of legacy policy objectives since the success of the London 2012 bid in 2005 has placed further expectations on coaching as part of a macro sport policy agenda (DCMS 2008).

Although sport coaching is referenced in the high-level policy statements associated with the London 2012 legacy pledges, the integration of actions into the detail of the five legacy promises has been shown to be less specific. Notably however, coaching is referred to in the context of the creation of a world leading sport system (DCMS 2008). The nature of this contribution is not defined and it has been left to the UK Coaching Framework to map out a plan to maximize the impact of sport coaching up to 2016 (sports coach UK 2008a). Coaching would also appear to have an implicit role in other legacy promises such as inspiring a generation of young people and promoting inclusive, positive attitudes towards and active participation of disabled people in sport (DCMS 2008).

A key challenge from this emerging scenario is evaluating the impact of coaching as part of the sport policy agenda and in support of legacy objectives. The analysis outlined in this article suggests that the UK Coaching Framework is a complex intervention that is amenable to analysis using a realist review methodology (see Figure 4). There is a clear need for such review, in order to chart the progress of this sport coaching policy programme and to identify what works, for whom and in what circumstances and why. Realist review offers discipline and structure to the evaluative process, by placing an emphasis on outcome patterns, mechanisms and context. In seeking to explain rather than solve problems, it offers a

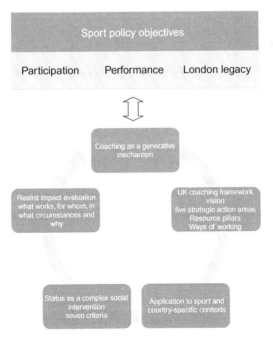

Figure 4.   Application of realist methodology to the review of the UK Coaching Framework.

discriminating and sophisticated toolkit to get closer to the pulse of what makes coaches, participants and the coaching system tick.

Much of the legacy discourse relating to the London Games (and indeed other major games) has focused on the direct and observable impact on elements such as economy, infrastructure and regeneration. A feature of the London legacy promises has been the prominence of longer term agendas that offer the prospect of linking with sport development and system-building objectives. This longer term focus, which has the potential to be quite intangible, begs several questions in terms of programme evaluation and efficacy at a general level and specifically in relation to sport coaching. Realist review provides a robust methodology for charting progress over time, taking into account the initial policy and legacy aspirations, the stated intentions of the UK Coaching Framework and the perspectives of the wide range of stakeholders in the conception, delivery and consumption of the intervention.

6. Conclusion

The realist approach to programme evaluation provides the basis for a firmer analysis of the mechanisms that generate outcome patterns in coaching and in the development of high-quality coaching systems. Realist review provides the basis for studying these and other emergent mechanisms across the wide range of contexts found in the four main coaching domains, sport-specific delivery and each of the home countries. The commissioning of such reviews remains an open question, as there has not been a history of systematic impact evaluation to date.

In providing a methodology that can be applied to the analysis of impact in different sports, coaching domains and countries, the realist sensitivity to the significance of context is congruent with the core aspirations of the UK Coaching Framework. Although the vision of the Framework speaks of the creation of a world leading coaching system, it is the recruitment, development and deployment of skilled coaches to the front line in a diverse range of sports, coaching domains and contexts that rests at the heart of the intervention. The realist focus on what works, for whom, in what circumstances and why holds out the possibility of providing an analysis that has the capability of interrogating the core programme theories and their impact at the front line, as well as applying this methodology at the macro level. There is also a need to further research the impact of the intervention within specific sports and in each of the home countries.

It has been argued that there is a sound basis upon which the UK Coaching Framework should be viewed as a complex intervention that is amenable to the application of realist review. Realist review provides a robust basis for the evaluation of such an intervention and can assist in more clearly ascertaining the role of coaching as a mechanism to support the delivery of legacy objectives in a range of contexts. In the case of legacy objectives for London 2012, it will mean that in sport coaching at least, longer term legacy pledges and promises can be subjected to the foil of rigorous analysis and impact evaluation.

References

Balyi, I. and Hamilton, A., 1995. The concept of long-term athlete development. *Strength and conditioning coach: the official magazine of the Australian Strength and Conditioning Association*, 3 (2), 5–6.

Bergsgard, N., *et al.*, 2007. *Sport policy: a comparative analysis of stability and change*. Amsterdam: Elsevier.

Bronfenbrenner, U., 1979. *The ecology of human development: experiments by nature and design*. Cambridge, MA: Harvard University Press.

Carlson, R., 1988. The socialization of elite tennis players in Sweden: an analysis of the players' backgrounds and development. *Sociology of sport journal*, 5, 241–256.

Carlson, R., 1993. The path to the national level in sports in Sweden. *Scandinavian journal of medicine and science in sports*, 3, 170–177.

Côté, J. and Fraser-Thomas, J., 2007. Youth involvement in sport. *In*: P. Crocker, ed. *Sport psychology: a Canadian perspective*. Toronto, ON: Pearson.

Côté, J. and Gilbert, W., 2009. An integrative definition of coaching effectiveness and expertise. *International journal of sport science and coaching*, 4, 307–232.

Côté, J., *et al.*, 2007. Towards a definition of excellence in sport coaching. *International journal of coaching science*, 1 (1), 3–16.

Department for Children and Schools, 2008. *Physical education and sport strategy for young people*. London: Department for Children and Schools.

Department of Culture, Media and Sport, 2002. *The coaching task force-final report*. London: Department of Culture, Media and Sport.

Duffy, P., 2009. Opening address. *UK Coaching Summit*, 28–29 April, Glasgow.

European Coaching Council, 2007. *Review of the EU 5-level structure for the recognition of coaching qualifications*. Koln: European Network of Sport Science, Education and Employment.

Houlihan, B., 1997. *Sport, policy and politics: a comparative analysis*. London: Routledge.

Jones, R., Armour, K., and Potrac, P., 2005. *Sports coaching cultures: from theory to practice*. London: Routledge.

Lyle, J., 2002. *Sports coaching concepts*. London: Routledge.

Lyle, J., 2007. *United Kingdom coaching certificate impact study*. Leeds: sports coach UK.

McGeechan, I. and Duffy, P., 2008. Foreword. *In*: sports coach UK, ed. *UK Coaching Framework: a 3-7-11 year action plan*. Leeds: Coachwise.

MORI, 2004. *Sports coaching in the UK*. Leeds: sports coach UK.

National Coaching and Training Centre, 2003. *Building pathways in Irish sport: towards a plan for the sporting and health well-being of the nation*. Limerick: National Coaching and Training Centre.

North, J., 2008. The role of coaching in increasing participation. Unpublished sports coach UK document.

North, J., 2009. *The coaching workforce 2009-16*. Leeds: sports coach UK.

North, J., 2010. Using 'coach developers' to facilitate coach learning and development: qualitative evidence from the UK. *International journal of sports science and coaching*, 5 (2), 239–256.

North, J., in press. *A critical realist approach to theorising coaching practice. Handbook of sports coaching*. London: Routledge.

Øvreteit, J. and Gustafson, D., 2002. Evaluation of quality improvement programmes. *Quality and safety in health care*, 11 (3), 270–275.

Pawson, R., 2006. *Evidence based policy: a realist perspective*. London: Sage.

Pawson, R. and Tilley, N., 1997. *Realistic evaluation*. London: Sage.

Pawson, R., *et al.*, 2005. Realist review – a new method of systematic review designed for complex policy interventions. *Journal of health services research and policy*, 10 (1), 21–34.

Rose, R., 1973. Comparing public policy. *European journal of political research*, 1 (1), 1.

Skills Active, 2011. *National Occupational Standards* [online]. Available from: http://www.skillsactive.com/skillsactive/national-occupational-standards/level-2/item/3169/3169 [Accessed 30 June 2011].

Sport England, 2008. *Sport England strategy 2008-11*. London: Sport England.

Sport Northern Ireland, 2009. *Strategy for sport and physical recreation for Northern Ireland*. Belfast: Sport Northern Ireland.

Sport Scotland, 2007. *Reaching higher – building on the success of Sport 21*. Edinburgh: Sport Scotland.

sports coach UK, 2006a. *Targets and resources in coaching*. Leeds: sports coach UK.

sports coach UK, 2006b. *Declaration of the first UK coaching summit*. Grantham: sports coach UK.

sports coach UK, 2007. *The UK action plan for coaching: consultation document*. Leeds: sports coach UK.

sports coach UK, 2008a. *The UK Coaching Framework: a 3-7-11 year action plan*. Leeds: Coachwise.

sports coach UK, 2008b. *Declaration of the third coaching summit*. Coventry: sports coach UK.

Sports Council, 1991. *Coaching matters: a review of coaching and coach education in the United Kingdom*. London: Sports Council.

Sports Council for Wales, 2009. *Corporate plan 2009-2012*. Cardiff: Sports Council for Wales.

Stafford, I., 2005. *Long-term athlete development*. Leeds: sports coach UK.

UK Sport, 2001. *UK vision for coaching*. London: UK Sport.

UK Sport, 2008. *UK Sport 2007 annual review*. London: UK Sport.

'Scienciness' and the allure of second-hand strategy in talent identification and development

Dave Collins[a,b] and Richard Bailey[c]

[a]Institute of Coaching and Performance, University of Central Lancashire, Lancashire, UK; [b]Grey Matters Performance, Stratford upon Avon, Warwickshire, UK; [c]RBES Ltd, Sheerness ME12 3LL, UK

In searching for the next edge or the magic ingredient, policymakers in sport are increasingly drawn to seemingly uncritical copying from other systems. Some of the constructs seem attractive, holding an apparent validity that promotes their adoption but, on closer scrutiny, can appear to be based more on rhetoric than evidence. In this article we propose the new term of 'Scienciness' to describe this apparent but erroneous validity, offering an exemplar of its harmful impact through the import into the United Kingdom of features from apparently successful systems in talent development, namely, the former Eastern Bloc and Australia. This article identifies some characteristics of Scienciness constructs, together with some procedural and systemic recommendations for the avoidance of its worse excesses.

Introduction

As pressures rise in international sport, optimizing the identification, recruitment and development of performers has an ever-increasing importance. In the face of such pressures, sports systems have been under continual pressure to generate new approaches, and whilst some of these are more-or-less 'home-grown', many more have their origin elsewhere. The 'global sporting arms race' (De Bosscher *et al.* 2008), and the subsequent pressures to be seen to succeed on the world stage, has led to a drive towards the exchange or transfer of principles and practices between sporting nations (Bloyce and Smith 2010).

The discussion of this phenomenon in sport often borrows from the constructs of public and social policy and, in particular, the concepts of 'policy learning', 'lesson drawing' and 'policy transfer' (Houlihan and Green 2008). Whether or not these terms ought to be considered interchangeable or not is a matter for another occasion. Suffice to say, they all describe a process in which knowledge about policies, practices and institutions in one time and/or place is used in the development of policies, practices and institutions in another time and/or place (Dolowitz and Marsh 1996, Rose 2005). This language is useful in part because it does not presume the relationship between the different time/place frames to be inter-dependent, as do some sports policy writers (Bloyce and Smith 2010). Indeed, an underlying theme in this article is that the exchange of information between sporting nations is rarely reciprocal or bidirectional. On the contrary, policy transfer in sport seems to have the character of a sort of role modelling, in which certain nations that are judged to be successful, whether absolutely (in terms of total medals won, e.g. the former Eastern Bloc, China and United States), or relative to their size or resources (e.g. Australia, Jamaica and Sweden), are selected as the target for an often uncritical reproduction in the home environment.

A further theme relates to the type of information that is transferred. Elite sport is, by definition, an extremely competitive endeavour. Sporting systems are continually searching the global marketplace for practices that might add a competitive advantage. The sport policy literature has tended to presume implicitly that these practices are the results of rigorous scientific testing and that the most significant obstacle to their implementation is the inherent difficulty of translating ideas and strategies from one context into another (Green 2003, 2007, Houlihan and Green 2008, Bloyce and Smith 2010). We would like to suggest that there is another barrier to successful policy learning and transfer that has barely been acknowledged in the literature, which we call 'Scienciness'. According to Green and Houlihan (2008, p. 189), 'the prevalence of policy learning is most common in areas of greatest uncertainty'. Systemic approaches to elite sports performance with their combina-tion of short history and extremely high expectations might be considered a paradigm case of such uncertainty. However, there is another aspect of the context of elite performance that might also warrant uncertainty, namely that the scientific principles behind any comprehen-sive sports system are highly technical and specialist. As a further complication, elite developments are by definition 'cutting edge' and thus, de facto, are often lacking in the usually accepted standards of underpinning evidence. Effective transfer of such principles from one setting to another assumes that the drivers of such change really understand these nuances and know what they are talking about; unfortunately, experience shows that this is often not the case.

Scienciness refers to the illusion of scientific credibility and validity that provides a degree of authority to otherwise dubious ideas. Scienciness is conveyed through, for example, esoteric language and complex statistical representations, and supplemented by association with an apparently successful foreign system. Our use of this new term was inspired by the American political satirist Stephen Colbert (2005), who talked about 'Truthiness' which is the conviction that something is true, despite there being absolutely no evidence in favour of it. Scienciness follows the same logic. It is essentially a rhetorical devise to attribute the authority of science to methods and ideas possess little or no under-pinning evidence or theoretical base.

Tracing the history of influence

Scienciness is particularly apparent in many of the UK's recent policy directions in elite performance. Such approaches have seemed to follow the old adage that 'the truth is out there already, and just needs to be discovered', so (the argument goes) the inspection of successful national systems must yield the answer. In the early stages, the methods of the former Eastern Bloc countries were seen by many as an effective underpinning for British systems (Riordan 1980). Acceptance encompassed diverse aspects such as the (purportedly) empirically rigorous approach to training and the (apparently) efficient conversion of young potential to world class. Dissonant dismissals included the 'it's just the drugs' explanation or even the selective recognition that the sociopolitical environment may play a part. Nonetheless, the Eastern Bloc influence was substantial and persists today in many con-structs such as the widespread use of periodization (Bompa 1999) and early specialization and hothousing of talent (Kozel 1996, Wiersma 2000, Baker 2003).

Driven by *Sport: Raising the Game* (Department of National Heritage 1995) and Prime Minister John Major's (1995) focus on (re)establishing UK sport as a world beater

(Theodoraki 1999), the influx of all things antipodean represented a move away from the by then ethically discredited Eastern Bloc states as the role models of choice. The Australian Institute of Sport was seen as the world-leading model and, consequently, these ideas flooded into many of the major leadership and support roles across sport. (Substantial anecdotal evidence around the foundation of the UK Institute, coupled with a consideration of the staff demographics of various organizations such as the English Institute of Sport, should attest to this statement.) Key features of this influx were the prescription of multisport support practitioners as the most effective way for Institutes of Sport to operate and the adoption of anthropometric and performance measures as a means for identifying and directing talent (Hoare 1995). Once again, in common with the Eastern Bloc perspective, early selection was seen as a key component of the way forwards.

More recently, the search for the next answer has diversified geographically and socio-politically to embrace ideas from across the world, including Canada, China, Jamaica, Kenya and the United States. The importing of these concepts has often been covert, driven by the appointment of foreign specialists (coaches, scientists, etc.) who bring with them a package of constructs and theories that they apply through their practice. Wherever the ideas originate, however, we believe that critical reflection on the adoption of ideas is instructive and may lead others to more carefully consider what is to be borrowed and why. Accordingly, whilst this article will take a largely historical focus on the old Eastern Bloc and the Australian systems, we hope that this will also offer a lesson in the dangers of ill-considered copying. In short, without careful thought, the 'lessons we learn' can often be the wrong ones and the mistakes made are destined to be repeated. We pursue this idea through a specific focus on talent development methodology or at least what is perceived or perhaps *believed* to have happened. The Talent Identification and Development focus reflects our own interests, but also represents an area where, we contend, the employment of second-hand strategy is particularly rife.

Examples of positive transfer

Just to show that we are not uncritically dismissive of idea import (which would itself also be Scienciness), we start by considering aspects of positive transfer, albeit that many have been insufficiently adopted. In many ways, the Eastern Bloc system was ahead of its time; ideas such as over-speed work using downhill run-ups have only just re-emerged as means to train physically and to offer an experience of future potentialities (by use in Pole Vault, e.g. to help athletes get the feel of greater heights from faster approach before they are sufficiently powerful to accomplish this unaided). The opposite idea using uphill run-ups to mentally condition against in-event variability (due to wind, nerves, etc.) is another excellent example. Finally, the Australian Institute of Sport originated a number of ideas that represent a third exemplar of positive transfer, such as reverse periodization in swimming (literally training at race pace at the start of the training phase, as opposed to the more traditional periodized approach of gradual build-up). All these ideas are well founded empirically and theoretically and represent the antithesis of Scienciness, namely *science, per se*. One might expect such concepts to be rapidly recognized, considered and adopted by acquisitive coaches, both because of their rational basis and because they clearly work.

Other exemplars for positive transfer can be seen in the approach to coaching and talent identification and development. The Eastern Bloc system was clearly coach led, but meta-leadership was provided by a cohort of highly trained sport specialists, supported by an array of scientists who were fully incorporated into the total support team. The existence of degree-level training for coaches was an acknowledged and positive feature of the Eastern Bloc. In contrast, the United Kingdom has only very recently pushed the possibility of coaching as a profession (SportscoachUK 2010), although even its aspiration falls short of a graduate profession. Moreover, many coaches (from a variety of sports and levels of experience) resist this encroachment and interference of sport science into coaching. Whilst scientific support now plays a widespread role in UK sport, the integration and impact are far from uniform due, it seems, to a misunderstanding and suspicion on all sides (Collins 2008a, 2008b).

Finally, it is interesting to contrast the overt long-term orientation towards talent identification and development that characterized both Eastern Bloc and early Australian systems with the short-term focus that has traditionally characterized the UK approach (Abbott *et al.* 2002, Bailey *et al.* 2010). In both the Eastern Bloc and Australian contexts, age group medals were seen as useful but not essential waymarks on a path that was completely focused on senior success. This type of focus has only recently been established in UK sport, and sports are now starting to realize the wisdom of the long-term view, inspired to a large degree by policy and funding pressures associated with the London 2012 Games.

Our central point is that not all imported, second-hand ideas are problematic. The ideas we have discussed are all well founded scientifically, rational and easily operationalized to enable a strong audit of progress. Unfortunately, however, the United Kingdom has been slow to pick up on such ideas, albeit that they are now starting to be incorporated.

Negative transfer: Scienciness as the main driver in talent development

In contrast to these well-founded initiatives, the UK sports system has been quick to seize on some prime exemplars of Scienciness. Indeed, so pervasive have these ideas become, and so strongly promoted, that even a scientific, empirically based refutation has trouble in making an impact.

First, consider the Long Term Athlete Development (LTAD) model (Balyi and Way 1995, 1998, Balyi and Hamilton 1996, 2000, 2003, 2004, Balyi 2001, 2002), an approach explicitly grounded in the Eastern Bloc philosophy, which has been and largely remains the fundamental driver for Government, sporting organizations, quangos, trusts and coach education in the United Kingdom, as well as Ireland, Canada and elsewhere (National Coaching and Training Centre and Irish Sports Council 2003, Canadian Sports Centres 2005, Stafford 2005). This drive has encompassed a broad swath of policy and consumed a substantial amount of resource. In the current climate, which stresses the need for evidence-based practice, one would expect such a pervasive policy to be strongly supported by scientific rigour. We and several other authors suggest that this is not the case (Bailey *et al.* 2010, Ford *et al.* 2011). The approach incorporates much face-valid and simple advice, guidance that is so fundamental and sound that it is almost irrefutable (the progression of 'learn to train' through to 'learn to compete' stages, etc.). However, these same systems also include a veneer of Scienciness that covers several more questionable statements. Consider as an example the concept of critical periods, which are described as developmental phases that, if not fully exploited at that time, will prevent an individual *ever* achieving his/her genetic potential (Balyi and Hamilton 1996, Balyi 2001, 2002). Empirical evidence for this principle is somewhat lacking (Bailey *et al.* 2010, Collins *et al.* in press), and few of the source papers cited in support of LTAD seem to be peer reviewed. Furthermore, to our knowledge, no empirical evaluation of the impact of LTAD has been commissioned by the agencies that have promoted the approach.

This offers some interesting speculations on how high-scienciness constructs get a hold and why they seem so pervasive and persuasive. Perhaps, once an agency has invested a lot of money and other resources for a construct, it is difficult to evaluate it impartially; after a certain level of investment, one becomes committed to being committed! Whatever the reasons (and our speculations are just that), such reluctance represents another characteristic of Scienciness constructs and their often-stifling perpetuation.

A similar though less pervasive impact can be discerned from the Talent Search Programme (Hoare 1995) and its various spin-offs. As introduced earlier, this elaborate and apparently empirically grounded tool proffered a means to identify not only high potential for a particular sport or group of sports, but also an indication of which activities would offer the best return for investment for each youngster. The tools were purchased and deployed with great fanfare across the United Kingdom despite the lack (to the best of our knowledge) of any empirical evidence in support of the method or even its general approach. Not only did the programme prove ineffective with children, it also produced a series of anomalous results. In Scotland, for example, the first delivery of the programme saw some more than 20 children identified as having world-class potential in High Jump, but none in Curling (Abbott *et al.* 2002). Subsequent results speak against the veracity of this suggestion, such gold medals at World and Olympic levels in curling, yet none in High Jump! The application of the same anthropometric-based techniques to visiting athletes at the Sydney 2000 Olympics also produced some questionable outcomes:

> Before Sydney, on the Gold Coast there was a project going on in Australia where they were going round the teams, measuring their physical attributes. They wanted to have your seated height and I wasn't even on the bottom of the scale so physically I wouldn't have made it [selection into rowing] ... You could select a lot of people who are potentially good at it [rowing] but actually they haven't got the correct mental attributes.

> (British Rower (who won a medal at that Games), cited in MacNamara *et al.* (2010))

Careful consideration of the mechanics of the tests, notably the items used and the weightings applied, revealed several basic flaws; for example, it was discovered that some relatively marginal measures were given far greater regard than central constructs like hand–eye coordination (Abbott and Collins 2002, Abbott *et al.* 2002). Such basic procedural shortcomings, covered by a veneer of glossy presentation and computer programs, provided another Scienciness project. This approach was later dropped, but only after securing, and wasting, substantial amounts of funding from central sports agencies. The basic tenets persist, however, and many coaches and administrators, inspired by the promise but not the reality of Talent Search, still talk wistfully of the holy grail of talent identification and development: a simple test that will reveal an individual's latent talent for sport in general or a particular sport. Like the Holy Grail, itself, we have reason to believe, and a good deal of research evidence to suggest, that no such secret test actually exists!

Overcoming Scienciness – accentuating positives (and avoiding negatives)

Given the scope and expense of Scienciness-induced errors, it would seem worthwhile considering why these mistakes occur and how decision-making on future initiatives may be strengthened. At the simplest level, scienciness reliance on a pair of relatively well-established features of human decision-making: we are overly influenced by claims couched in technical language; we find it extremely difficult to distinguish between genuine science and pseudoscience (Shermer 2003, Tavris and Aronson 2007). To be clear, we are not in any way suggesting that proponents and adherents of sciencey ideas are unintelligent or scientifically illiterate. In fact, some research studies show that intelligence and education can actually correlate with the acceptance of pseudoscientific beliefs, and moreover 'high intelligence ... makes one *skilled at defending beliefs arrived at for non-smart reasons'* (Shermer 2003, p. 73; emphasis in original).

Neither physiological constructs like critical periods nor practices like Talent Search are obviously mistaken. It is perfectly reasonable for sport scientists and practitioners to generate and propose new ideas. However, the heart of the scientific method does not lie in the plausibility or appeal of theories, but in their *testing*. This was a point made most famously by Karl Popper in 1933 (translated into English in 1959, p. 317):

> I think that we shall have to get accustomed to the idea that we must not look upon science as a 'body of knowledge', but rather as a system of hypotheses; that is to say, as a system of guesses or anticipations which in principle cannot be justified, but with which we work as long as they stand up to tests, and of which we are never justified in saying that we know they are 'true' or 'more or less certain' or even 'probable'.

Whatever critiques of Popper's views have come subsequently, this central point has remained valid: science is fundamentally about testing, criticism and attempted falsification. Scienciness falters not because its ideas are inherently silly or mistaken; they are not. The problem lies in the lack of testing. In the context of sport, untested ideas usually result in wasted time and energy on the part of the players who choose or are forced to adopt them. However, our concern in this article has been with ideas that have drawn substantial amounts of government funding (and it always needs to be remembered that money invested in one area is always money taken away from another).

With these points in mind, we offer three tentative proposals. First, we need to consider the personal characteristics of the decision-makers and major consumers of any new initiative. The ease with which sciencey projects, such as those described above, have been uncritically adopted suggests the need for a critical education and the universal application of evidence-based practice. This does not necessarily mean that central agencies' employees need research degrees, although this would parallel requirements in other areas of government. At least there would be a huge benefit from breaking down the evident barriers between, for example, central agencies like sports councils and universities. In any case, however, programmes need to be researched and developed accurately, both before commencement and at the pilot stage. This is hardly a costly task: for example, Abbott *et al.*'s (2002) analysis of Talent Search took 18 months and cost less than £43,000; the costs for the project itself were more than £1,000,000.

Our second proposed step relates to the need for scientific influence in the policy system of all relevant bodies, and for this influence to be recorded as a key strand of all new initiatives. The fact that the underpinnings of LTAD were developed externally and imported into the United Kingdom with no socially specific setting or modification (Toms *et al.* 2009), and were not first circulated for comment to interested UK scientific parties is surely, at the very least, surprising. The fact that no empirically based projects have been sponsored to evaluate its veracity is also a systemic failure.

Our third step is largely focused on the governmental level. The talent identification and development process, if led in an inclusive and evidence-based manner, has the potential to make significant contributions to a number of levels of participation and performance (Bailey *et al.* 2010). There are gains to be made in elite performance, sport participation, lifelong physical activity/health *and* even general achievement (Collins *et al.* in press). Unfortunately, the artificial segregation of these agendas into distinct and seemingly uncooperative sections of the government machine acts to prevent the strong symbiosis that is there to be had. Such a lack of joined-up-ness may be an inevitable feature of current systems. However, the potential for waste through duplication is comparatively small compared to the 'Type 2 error' (thinking something does not work when it does) associated with talent identification and development and its related constructs.

Accordingly, we suggest government policymaking must consider these factors in its policy setting and execution. This aspirational but powerful goal, plus accepting the ultimate responsibility for the direction, leadership, monitoring and refinement of talent identification and development to maximize exploitation against public (and positive) targets, will make the 2012 legacy a more realistic and positive target.

Conclusions

Elite sport often involves acts of remarkable speed, power or grace. Athletes performing at their best can appear superhuman to the rest of us. It is not surprising, then, that talent identification and development has leant itself to scienciness: the exceptionality of great sport seems to be beyond everyday measures and practices. This may account for the uncritical reception shown to exotic imports like LTAD and Talent Search. These ideas look appropriately complex, opaque and sciencey.

That such practices have become central elements in the UK's talent identification and development strategy serves to underline the fact that sport policymaking, whether it is framed as 'evidence based' or not, is inherently rhetorical (Fischer and Forester 1993, Young *et al.* 2002):

> The selection and presentation of evidence for policy making, including the choice of which questions to ask, which evidence to compile in a synthesis and which syntheses to bring to the policy making table, should be considered as moves in a rhetorical argumentation game and not as the harvesting of objective facts to be fed into a logical decision-making sequence. (Greenhalgh and Russell 2006, p. 34)

Our claim is that, in the world of elite sport policy, this rhetoric has come to rely on face validity and the appearance of rigour, rather than the scientific method.

Does it matter? Well, yes it does, not least because the UK's sport system and its countless constituent parts invest millions of pounds in seeking to identify, recruit and develop the champions of the future. This investment is premised to success, and success is far more likely to follow science than non-science. Perhaps what is needed is a more humble version of the National Institute of Clinical Excellence that offers expert evaluation of state-funded sports initiatives. This need not be costly; indeed, it seems likely that many sport science researchers would be eager to become involved. This group would not replace evaluation; it would precede it by asking a small number of very basic questions: 'Has the idea been tested empirically and the results published in peer-reviewed journals?' 'Has the idea been trialled in a relevant context?' In other words, 'What is the evidence?'

Acknowledgements

We thank Jonathan Grix, Matthew Reeves, Jennifer Leigh, Gemma Pearce, Dave Morley and the three anonymous reviewers for valuable comments on an earlier version of this article. None of them are responsible for its arguments.

References

Abbott, A. and Collins, D., 2002. A theoretical and empirical analysis of a 'state of the art' talent identification model. *Journal of High Ability Studies*, 13 (2), 157–178.

Abbott, A., *et al.*, 2002. *Talent identification and development: an academic review*. Edinburgh: sportscotland.

Bailey, R.P., *et al.*, 2010. *Participant development in sport; an academic review*. Leeds: Sportscoach UK.

Baker, J., 2003. Early specialisation in youth sport: a requirement for adult expertise? *High Ability Studies*, 14, 85–94.

Balyi, I., 2001. Sport system building: long-term athlete development in British Columbia. *In: Pathways to success – good coaching for children, players and athletes, a report of the National Centre for Training and Coaching's 6th National Coaching Forum*, 8 June 2001 Limerick, Ireland.

Balyi, I., 2002. Long-term athlete development: the system and solutions. *Faster, Higher, Stronger*, 14, 6–9.

Balyi, I. and Hamilton, A., 1996. Planning for training and performance: the training to win phase. *BC Coach (Canada)*, 3 (1), 9–26.

Balyi, I. and Hamilton, A., 2000. Key to success: long-term athlete development. *Sport Coach (Canberra, Australia)*, 23, 10–32.

Balyi, I. and Hamilton, A., 2003. Long-term athlete development update: trainability in childhood and adolescence. *Faster, Higher, Stronger*, 20, 6–8.

Balyi, I. and Hamilton, A., 2004. *Long-term athlete development: trainability in childhood and adolescence. Windows of opportunity. optimal trainability*. Victoria: National Coaching Institute British Columbia and Advanced Training and Performance Ltd.

Balyi, I. and Way, R., 1995. Long-term planning for athlete development: the training to train phase. *BC Coach (Canada)*, 2 (2), 2–10.

Balyi, I. and Way, R., 1998. Long-term planning for athlete development: the training to train phase. *Faster, Higher, Stronger*, 1, 8–11.

Bloyce, D. and Smith, A., 2010. *Sport policy and development*. London: Routledge.

Bompa, T.O., 1999. *Periodization training for sports*. Champaign, IL: Human Kinetics.

Canadian Sports Centres, 2005. *Canadian sport for life: long-term athlete development*. Vancouver, BC: Canadian Sports Centres.

Colbert, S., 2005. *The Colbert report* [online]. Available from: www.colbertnation.com/the-colbert... 2005/the-word—truthiness [Accessed 10 November 2011].

Collins, D., 2008a. Where from here? Reflections on being. *In: BOA invited keynote, British Association of Sport and Exercise Sciences annual conference*, 2 September, Brunel University.

Collins, D., 2008b. Strange bedfellows: WHY sport AND exercise psychology? *In: Invited keynote, inaugural British psychological society DSEP conference*, 11 December, London.

Collins, D. *et al*. Unpublished manuscript. No further details available.

De Bosscher, V., *et al.*, 2008. *The global sporting arms race*. Aachen: Meyer and Meyer Sport.

Department of National Heritage, 1995. *Sport: raising the game*. London: Department of National Heritage.

Dolowitz, D.P. and Marsh, D., 1996. Who learns what from whom: a review of the policy transfer literature. *Political Studies*, 44 (3), 343–357.

Fischer, F. and Forester, J., 1993. *The argumentative turn in policy analysis and planning*. Durham, NC: Duke University Press.

Ford, P., *et al.*, 2011. The long-term athlete development model: physiological evidence and application. *Journal of Sports Sciences*, 29 (4), 389–402.

Green, M., 2003. An analysis of elite sport policy change in three sports in Canada and the United Kingdom. Unpublished doctoral thesis. Loughborough University.

Green, M., 2007. Policy transfer, lesson drawing and perspectives on elite sport development systems. *International Journal of Sport Management and Marketing*, 2 (4), 426–441.

Green, M. and Houlihan, B., 2008. Conclusion. *In*: B. Houlihan and M. Green, eds. *Comparative elite sport development: systems, structures and public policy*. Amsterdam: Elsevier, 272–293.

Greenhalgh, T. and Russell, J., 2006. Reframing evidence synthesis as rhetorical action in the policy making drama. *Healthcare Policy*, 1 (2), 34–42.

Hoare, D., 1995. Talent search. *The National Talent Identification & Development Program*, 13 (2), 10–12.

Houlihan, B. and Green, M., 2008. *Comparative elite sport development: systems, structures and public policy*. Amsterdam: Elsevier.

Kozel, J., 1996. Talent identification and development in Germany. *Coaching Focus*, 31, 5–6.

MacNamara, A., Button, A., and Collins, D., 2010. The role of psychological characteristics in facilitating the pathway to elite performance. Part 1: identifying mental skills and behaviours. *The Sport Psychologist*, 24, 52–73.

National Coaching and Training Centre and Irish Sports Council, 2003. *Building pathways in Irish sport*. Limerick: Ireland National Coaching and Training Centre and Irish Sports Council.

Popper, K.R., 1959. *The logic of scientific discovery*. London: Hutchinson.

Riordan, J., 1980. *Soviet sport: background to the Olympics*. New York: Columbia University Press.

Rose, R., 2005. *Learning from comparative public policy*. London: Routledge.

Shermer, M., 2003. Why smart people believe weird things. *Skeptic*, 10 (2), 62–73.

SportscoachUK, 2010. Available from: www.sportscoachuk.org/index.php?PageID=2&sc=5 [Accessed 5 January 2012].

Stafford, I., 2005. *Coaching for long-term athlete development*. Leeds: sports coach UK.

Tavris, C. and Aronson, E., 2007. *Mistakes were made (but not by me): why we justify foolish beliefs, bad decisions, and hurtful acts*. Orlando, FL: Harcourt.

Theodoraki, E., 1999. The making of the UK Sports Institute. *Managing Leisure*, 4 (4), 187–200.

Toms, M., Bridge, M., and Bailey, R.P., 2009. A developmental perspective of sports participation in the UK: implications for coaching. *In: International council for coach education conference*, 14 November, Vancouver, BC, Canada.

Wiersma, L.D., 2000. Risks and benefits of youth sport specialization: perspectives and recommendations. *Pediatric Exercise Science*, 12, 13–22.

Young, K., *et al.*, 2002. Social science and the evidence-based policy movement. *Social Policy and Society*, 1, 215–224.

An analysis of the policy process for physical education and school sport: the rise and demise of school sport partnerships

Lesley Phillpots

Department of Sport Pedagogy, University of Birmingham, Birmingham B15 2TT, UK

This article examines the policymaking process for physical education (PE) and school sport (PESS) through an examination of the creation and recent demise of the ground-breaking 'school sport partnerships' (SSPs) initiative using Sabatier's advocacy coalition framework (ACF) model (1988, An advocacy coalition framework of policy change and the role of policy oriented learning therein. *Policy Sciences*, 21, 129–168). The central premise of this socio-economic model of policy analysis is that policymaking occurs through the dynamic interplay of policy brokers and interest groups who compete to influence the course of policy selection. The controversial and widely criticized decision in October 2010 by the new coalition government to abandon its funding of SSPs in favour of a new School Games framework for competitive school sport highlights the highly politicized nature of policymaking for PESS. It is argued that the successful bid for the London 2012 Olympic and Paralympic Games provided an ideal opportunity to formally and systematically embed the work of SSPs in order to inspire a generation of young people in England to engage in sport and physical activity. Drawing upon empirical data, it is argued that there is evidence to support Sabatier and Jenkins-Smith's (1993, *Policy change and learning: an advocacy coalitions approach.* Boulder, CO: Westview Press; 1999, *The advocacy coalition framework: an assessment.* Boulder, CO: Westview Press) contention that the major policy change (the creation of SSPs) was the consequence of lobbying by an emerging advocacy coalition led by the Youth Sport Trust (YST). However, the model's acknowledgement of the role of significant individuals and the weakness of the advocacy coalition working on behalf of PESS is more helpful in explaining the coalition government's recent decision to end the funding of SSPs.

Introduction

The launch of the national Physical Education (PE), School Sport and Club Links (PESSCL) strategy in 2002 through a joint Department for Education and Skills (DfES) and Department for Culture Media and Sport (DCMS) Public Service Agreement (PSA) target represented a major political and financial commitment by the Labour government to the creation of a ground-breaking infrastructure for school sport. Its rationale was that 'all children, whatever their circumstances or abilities, should be able to participate in and enjoy physical education (PE) and sport' (DfES/DCMS 2002, p. 1). At the heart of the plan was an ambitious PSA target to

Enhance the take-up of sporting opportunities by 5 to 16-year-olds so that the percentage of school children in England who spend a minimum of two hours each week on high quality PE and school sport within and beyond the curriculum increases from 25% in 2002 to 75% by 2006 and to 85% by 2008, and to at least 75% in each School Sport Partnership by 2008. (DfES/DCMS 2002)

Schools had a pivotal and central role to play in enhancing the engagement of young people in sporting opportunities by pooling and linking their resources with sport and community providers such as specialist sports colleges (SSCs) and school sports coordinators (SSCos), thus positioning themselves as key, structural components in a new 'dynamic infrastructure for physical education and school sport' (DCMS 2001, p. 13). School sport partnerships (SSPs) acted as the central backbone of the strategy and involved families of schools whose role was to enhance the sporting opportunities for young people. The partnerships were based upon local networks of schools that typically included an SSC, approximately 8 secondary schools and 45 primary schools clustered around them (DfES 2003). Each partnership received a grant of just over a quarter of a million pounds to provide funding for infrastructure posts to support the work of PE and school sport (PESS) and to boost sports opportunities in the locality. The programme's key objectives were wide-ranging and involved strategic planning, primary liaison, school and community links, coaching and leadership and raising standards. These outcomes represented a mixture of education, sport and community objectives and underlined the challenges posed to all the delivery agents in a set of overlapping outcomes that blurred the boundaries of their work.

This article primarily examines the rise of SSPs (and also provides an update on their demise) through the use of the advocacy coalition framework (ACF) (Sabatier and Jenkins-Smith 1993) as a theoretical tool to analyse policy stability and change in PESS. The ACF provides a useful framework as it focuses upon the role of agency (e.g. policy actors) and structures (e.g. value systems, policy subsystems, administrative arrangements and resource dependencies) whilst also acknowledging the centrality of ideas in the policy process. It offers what Houlihan and Green (2006) suggest is one of the more fully articulated and internally coherent frameworks which complements and extends existing policy analysis literature. The starting point for the empirical research acknowledged the requirement, emphasized by Sabatier, in particular, to examine the policy context over a time period of a decade or more in order to deliver a more reliable account of the process of policy change (see Weiss 1982, Sabatier 1988, Sabatier and Jenkins-Smith 1999b). This approach therefore rejects the notion of policy change as short-term decision-making, in favour of one that acknowledges the process of 'policy learning' that occurs as a consequence of changes to the belief systems of individuals and/or coalitions over time (Sabatier 1991). As a consequence, the article begins with a chronological account of the emergence of PESS as an increasingly key political policy concern in England from the 1990s onwards. The article also draws upon empirical data from an unpublished PhD thesis (Phillpots 2007) that analysed policy change for selected aspects of the PESSCL and PE and Sport Strategy for Young People (PESSYP) strategies and in particular a case study that focused upon the creation of SSPs. The article also provides an update on the coalition government's decision in 2010 to end the funding of the SSP initiative in favour of the creation of a new School Games framework for competitive school sport in order to deliver the youth sport legacy promises of London 2012 (DCMS 2007).

Background and context

Physical education and school sport: raising the game

The Conservative government from 1990 to 1997 oversaw an array of educational reforms that included the introduction of a national curriculum for schools, the appraisal of teacher performance and the publication of school league tables. Evans and Penney (1995) argue that the Conservative government used the forum of the National Curriculum generally, and PE specifically, to promote its political ideologies and initiate a return to core societal values and traditional ways of teaching. This viewpoint is reinforced by Fisher (1996, p. 140) who highlights that

> The pressure for a greater emphasis on traditional competitive team games in the school curriculum … can be seen as a feature of a political context in which tradition, order, stability and accountability are important.

The publication of the Conservative government sport policy document *Sport: Raising the Game* in 1995 established youth sport and sporting excellence as two government priorities and in the preface to the document, the Prime Minister John Major espoused the values underpinning sport as a binding force between generations and a defining characteristic of nationhood and local pride (Department of National Heritage 1995). Significantly, it placed a 'twin emphasis on school sport and excellence', with teachers 'identified as key agents for realising successful policy implementation' (Houlihan 2000, p. 174). As a sport policy document, it laid the foundations for new sporting structures and partnerships, in which schools played a crucial role in administering and delivering the Conservative government's agenda for sport.

Henry (1993) and Houlihan (1997) argue that there was a marked political change in the British government's approach to sport post-1991. An important factor was John Major's personal interest in sport and his personal advocacy undoubtedly led to renewed political interest in the area. His particular vision and policy ideas for PESS privileged and focused upon the values of elite and competitive sport and the discourse of traditional competitive team games within schools. His personal advocacy secured a higher political and policy profile for sport and within this supportive context of renewed interest in youth sport policy initiatives, New Labour came to power in 1997.

The Labour government's strategy document *A sporting future for all* (DCMS 2000) announced a number of national initiatives that would change the way in which PESS was resourced and administered. In a joint press release by the DfES and the DCMS on 11 January 2001, the government outlined its commitment to 'giving children a sporting chance' by offering them access both during and after school, to high-quality coaching and the opportunity to take part in competitive sports within and between schools. The government set out its plan to raise standards of PESS through a five-point plan that focussed upon investing in school sport facilities, the creation of 110 SSCs, extension of sporting opportunities beyond the school day (through an allocation of £240 million), the establishment of 600 SSCos linked to an SSC and access for talented 14- to 18-year-olds to coaching support. These arrangements signified an investment in, and change to, the resourcing of PE and heralded fundamental amendments to the way in which school sport was staffed, administered, delivered and funded.

Specialist schools

The Blair government promised to commit substantial funding to schools in order to improve the country's economic performance and achieve its broader sociopolitical agendas

(Giddens 1998). Significantly, the Labour government chose to develop the specialist schools initiative that had been established by the Thatcher government in 1988 (Chitty 2004). These schools were allowed to specialize in subjects such as sports, arts, modern languages or technology and were expected to engage in thorough audits, plans and targets for whole-school improvement through their chosen subject. Specialist schools were required to work with named partner schools and local community groups, in order to benefit young people within and beyond their school boundaries. Specialist status was intended as a catalyst for educational innovation and to help schools sustain and accelerate the pace of whole-school improvement (Morris 1998). The programme was partly financed through private sector sponsors, with matched government funding per pupil, each year, for a period of 4 years. In addition to this capital grant, each school was required to target one-third of its funding on sharing resources and expertise in its specialist subject area with partner schools and the wider community. In acquiring specialist status, schools were made directly accountable to government and their political demands and agendas (Penney 1994).

Specialist sports colleges: the hub sites of PE and school sport policy change

A fundamental objective for SSCs was to raise standards of teaching and learning in PESS. SSCs were required to provide expertise and resources for PESS to local schools and the wider community in order to strengthen their links with private and/or charitable sponsors and to extend the range of opportunities available to children. Houlihan (2000) has highlighted the inherent difficulties and challenges faced by SSCs which were positioned at the intersection of these multiple political policy agendas. Their broad responsibilities included raising academic standards, educationalists' concerns with the learning needs and achievements of all children and the concerns of the national governing bodies (NGBs) of sport for sport development and the identification of sporting talent. For SSCs, this meant that agencies with an interest in youth sport such as the Youth Sport Trust (YST), the DCMS, the DfES, the New Opportunities Fund, Sport England (SE) and the NGBs of sport were all now actively involved in the delivery of the government's PESS policy objectives.

The government viewed schools as central hubs for their policy objectives because of their potential to unite the threads of broader policies for youth sport: sport in education, sport in the community and the development of talent. Schools were also in a unique position as they provided access to all young people, placing them at the centre of pathways for the delivery of youth sport and broader education policy outcomes. The growing involvement of sports coaches, NGBs and sports development officers in the provision of sporting activities in and around the school context arguably resulted in a blurring of the policy boundaries surrounding sport and PE (Flintoff 2003). McDonald (2002) also questioned how such administrative arrangements, enforced alliances and the diverse beliefs and values of such a range of policy actors would eventually shape the outcomes of this policy initiative.

A new infrastructure for school sport in England: the PESSCL strategy

The national PESSCL strategy was launched in 2002 with a joint DfES and DCMS PSA target to

> Enhance the take-up of sporting opportunities by 5 to 16-year-olds so that the percentage of school children in England who spend a minimum of two hours each week on high quality PE and school sport within and beyond the curriculum increases from 25% in 2002 to 75% by 2006

and to 85% by 2008, and to at least 75% in each School Sport Partnership by 2008. (DfES/DCMS PSA Target 2002)

Sub-targets were set by the Prime Minister's Delivery Unit and HM Treasury and included the creation of 400 SSCs by 2005 (subject to high-quality application), 400 SSCo partnerships, 3200 SSCos in secondary schools and 18,000 primary or special school link teachers by 2006. Targets also included improvement to the quality of teaching, coaching and learning in PESS and an increase in the proportion of children guided into sports clubs from SSPs. The strategy was an over-arching initiative that initially included eight work strands made up of: SSCs; SSPs; a gifted and talented programme; the Qualifications and Curriculum Authority (QCA) PE and school sport investigation; Step into Sport; school to club links; professional development; and swimming. Delivery of the strategy was administered through a board of representatives that included the PE professional associations, head teachers, the Office for Standards in Education (Ofsted), the QCA, SE, DCMS, DfES and NGBs. Ofsted was responsible for monitoring and evaluating the impact of each of the programmes to ensure that the strategy made a difference to the quality of PE in schools.

School sport partnerships

SSPs were a significant element of the new PESSCL strategy and involved families of schools whose role was to enhance the sporting opportunities for young people. As mentioned above partnerships were based upon local networks of schools that typically included an SSC, approximately 8 secondary schools and 45 primary schools clustered around them (DfES 2003). Each partnership received a grant of just over £250,000 to fund infrastructure posts and to boost sport opportunities for young people in the locality. The programme's key objectives were wide-ranging and involved strategic planning; primary liaison; school and community links; coaching and leadership; and raising standards. These outcomes represented a mixture of education, sport and community objectives and underlined the challenges posed to all the delivery agents of these overlapping outcomes that blurred the boundaries of their work.

At the outset, the SSP programme's key outcomes focussed upon the following:

- Increased participation amongst school age children, in particular girls and young women, black and ethnic minorities, disabled young people, and young people living in areas of socio-economic disadvantage
- Improved standards of performance by children across a range of sports
- Improved motivation, attitude and self-esteem, resulting in increased personal and social development in all aspects of school life
- Increased numbers of qualified and active coaches, leaders and officials in all schools and local sports clubs/facilities. (IYS 2004, p. 1)

The YST had responsibility for managing and supporting the work of SSPs. The trust through its substantial financial backing from Sir John Beckwith and the dynamic leadership of its CEO Sue Campbell was ideally positioned to contribute to and champion successive governments' agendas for PESS. It had developed direct links with schools initially through its successful TOP programmes in primary schools and its vision was to create opportunities for all young people to receive a quality introduction to PESS through a number of activity-based programmes. The DfES, DCMS, YST and local education authorities (LEAs) were actively involved in the work of SSPs, alongside an increasing range of national and local sports organizations such as sports clubs, County Sport Partnerships (CSPs), local authorities (LAs) and NGBs.

The explicit role of SSCs was to raise sporting and academic standards in schools and local communities and to play an active role in establishing and driving partnerships amongst schools, the private sector and the wider community (Evans *et al.* 2002). The expectation was that specialist schools should be outward looking and through innovative, consultative and collaborative practices work to improve the quality of provision with local and national partners (DfES 2003). The overall success of SSPs was recorded annually in a number of reports by the Institute of Youth Sport (IYS 2011). The PSA target (2008) of 85% participation was exceeded by 5 percentage points (IYS 2008) and the *Active England Programme Report* (Sport England 2008) reported that the PESSCL strategy had increased participation in sport and physical activity amongst 636,000 young people in England.

The *Playing to win: a new era for sport* strategy (DCMS 2008a) announced the restructuring and rationalization of sport provision in England and the transition from PESSCL to a new strategy named PESSYP. Whilst its policy objectives to improve the quantity and quality of PE and sport undertaken by young people aged 5–19 in England ostensibly remained the same, it introduced new work strands and received a further investment of £755 million in government funding over 3 years to deliver a change in PSA target 22 'Indicator 5'. The Labour government's new ambition was that 'All children and young people aged between 5–16 years should have the opportunity to participate in five hours of sport per week by 2011 (including two hours of high quality PE and sport at school)'. Crucially, SSPs were required to develop new administrative and structural arrangements in order to create more opportunities for young people to participate in a further 3 hours each week of sporting activity in partnership with voluntary and community providers. Through more than £2.2 billion investment over its duration, the Labour government aimed to create a world-class system for PESS for all young people who would stimulate, increase and sustain their participation in sport.

In order to analyse such marked policy change for PESS since 1990, Sabatier's ACF (1988) is adopted as the theoretical tool for analysing policy change.

The theoretical approach

The advocacy coalition framework

This theoretical approach is derived from a growing body of sport policy research that adopts theoretical models for policy analysis used in other policy domains (e.g. Coalter 1990, Henry 1993, 2001, Houlihan 1997, 2000, 2002, Green 2002, Houlihan and White 2002, Houlihan and Green 2006). Sabatier's ACF (1988) is an increasingly popular theoretical model for the analysis of policy change and, since its emergence in 1986, has been applied, assessed and revised on several occasions (Sabatier 1991, 1998, Sabatier and Jenkins-Smith 1993, 1999b). It has also proved to be one of the most promising theoretical approaches to the analysis of policy processes (Parsons 1995, Schlager and Blomquist 1996, Eberg 1997, Grin and Hoppe 1997). The ACF (Sabatier 1991, 1999) is predominantly a model in which power is invested in policy agents and structures including values, subsystems, resource dependencies and administrative arrangements provide the cement of policy coalition groups and their ideas. The ACF suggests that policy change is a function of the interaction of competing advocacy coalitions within policy subsystems and policy change is a dynamic and continuous process, in which policy is formulated, implemented, contested and reformulated (Sabatier 1988).

A key element of the ACF is its focus on the policy process as a whole and in particular 'policy networks' and 'policy communities' (Heclo 1974, Kingdon 1984). The framework refers to a competitive policy context in which rival coalitions of policy actors hold certain values and views about policy problems and their solutions (Sabatier and Jenkins-Smith 1993, Sabatier 1998). Schlager and Blomquist (1996) describe a policy area in terms of a number of subsystems of groups and individuals (i.e. interest groups, academics, researchers, journalists and government actors at all levels) who are involved in the creation of 'policy ideas'. Members of these subsystems regularly seek to influence the course of public policy within a particular issue arena and tend to cluster into competing coalitions that advocate distinct policy viewpoints (Wildavsky 1987). Whether the beliefs and policy positions of these elites change in any significant way will depend partly upon the degree of conflict within the subsystem. Sabatier (1988) suggests that when there is a serious threat to the fundamental beliefs of a policy subsystem, conflict will be intense and organizational elites become less willing to change their policy positions and beliefs. In periods of extreme conflict, stable coalitions are sustained over extended periods of time and any change to the membership of coalitions arises as a direct consequence of political events exogenous to the subsystem. Advocacy coalitions consist of actors who specialize in particular policy issue areas and who follow and seek to influence the course of policy development in that area (Heclo 1978).

In fully developed policy subsystems, competing advocacy coalitions fight to translate their belief systems into public policy by mobilizing political resources through the assembly and analysis of information in order to support their own belief systems and attack those of the opposing coalitions (Jenkins-Smith 1990). Exponents of the ACF focus much of their attention upon the inner world of individuals and the structure and content of their belief systems (Jenkins-Smith 1988, Sabatier 1988, Sabatier and Jenkins-Smith 1993). Members of coalitions act collectively on the basis of these belief systems in order to 'manipulate the rules of various government institutions to achieve shared goals' (Sabatier 1991, p. 153). In order to operate effectively, advocacy coalitions use information to persuade decision-makers to adopt the policy alternatives espoused by their coalition. They attempt to manipulate the choices of decision-makers by active support of those public officials who hold positions of public authority and who share similar values. Whilst a number of coalitions may compete for control over public policy, there is often one that is dominant. Sabatier (1998) suggests that whilst power sharing can exist amongst coalitions, it is more likely to occur when coalition parties recognize that continuation of the status quo is unacceptable or sharing is mediated through a 'policy broker' who is respected by all parties.

Sabatier and Jenkins-Smith (1993) argue that a vital factor in policy change is the role of the policy broker, who plays an important entrepreneurial function in the process of policy change. The policy broker may be part of or outside government and retain an elected or appointed position as part of an interest group or a research organization. What defines a policy broker is their willingness to invest their time, energy, reputation and, on occasions, their money in the hope of future returns (Sabatier 1999, p. 122). The role of the policy broker is a crucial one, prompting important people to pay attention to specific policy solutions, whilst managing coalition conflict within acceptable boundaries.

The use of the ACF allows the researcher to investigate the policy process through a particular focus upon key variables that include a policy broker and the involvement of competing coalitions. The policy links between government departments responsible for sport and education within England suggest that the ACF should prove to be an appropriate model for analysing policy change in the field of PESS. There is also a growing body of research which suggests that the ACF can make a contribution to the analysis of policy for sport (Houlihan and White 2002, Green 2005).

Methods

Interviews

In order to acknowledge Sabatier's (1999) demands for a medium-term view of the policy process, 23 interviewees were selected from a range of government, sport and education agencies who had been involved in the PESS policy area for at least 5 years. Initial contact was secured with a range of interviewees through purposive sampling and these respondents were asked to recommend other individuals (snowball sampling) capable of delivering an informed account of the PESS policy area. The selection process necessitated the identification of interviewees whose social characteristics and close association with the research topic made them well suited for interview (Devine and Heath 2002). Sabatier also advocates the engagement of politicians and individual actors in close contact with the political arena and who possess specialist knowledge of procedures and policymaking.

Semi-structured interviews were chosen for their relative flexibility and potential to provide insights into the perceptions, beliefs, values and experiences of key actors close to the heart of policymaking in PESS. Whilst other methods are certainly capable of providing insights into the nature of policy change, the use of semi-structured interviews provides a more 'agent'-informed understanding of the historical developments and processes associated with this policy context.

Documentary analysis

Documentary analysis represents an 'integrated and conceptually developed method, procedure and technique for locating, identifying and analysing documents for their relevance, significance and meaning' (Altheide 1996, p. 2). Documentary evidence can take the form of official and private documents, personal letters or memos and researchers must consider carefully the origins and authors of documents and texts, the purpose for which they were written and the audience they were intended to address (Grix 2004). Documentary analysis allows researchers to gather data in an unobtrusive fashion, quickly and inexpensively, and May (2001) also stresses the benefits of the use of documents that have the capacity not only to reflect the facts but also to construct social reality and generate versions of events. As documents can be interpreted in different ways, Bell (2005, p. 113) suggests that researchers need to consider the type of document, who produced it, what its purpose was and the circumstances in which it was produced. Policy documents represent an important source of data and were used in this study in order to gather data unobtrusively and to supplement that gathered through semi-structured, in-depth interviews.

Data analysis

The data generated by a qualitative study of this nature demand a systematic approach to analysis. Patton (1990) suggests the adoption of inductive and/or deductive content analysis for information gathered from interviews and documentary material. Whilst inductive analysis involves the collation of data, such as NGB annual reports or a range of documentary evidence, deductive analysis often arises from the insights provided by theoretical frameworks such as the ACF. Both inductive and deductive content analyses were adopted in order to deliver a robust account of policy change for PESS. Ten-Have (2004) advocates a two-stage data analysis process: first, open coding of data in which their reduction and simplification into themes helps sharpen the focus of the analysis, then a second phase involving refinement and conceptual elaboration of the data established in the first phase of the process.

Interview transcripts and documentary evidence were analysed and coded into the themes suggested by the ACF. As the ACF (Sabatier and Jenkins-Smith 1999b) highlights the importance of explaining policy change through an examination of the role of lobbying and interest groups, key individuals and policy brokers and the role of changing beliefs and value systems, the discussion is structured using these central themes. Although the article and empirical data primarily focus upon the development of SSPs, the discussion also provides an update on the policy decision made by the coalition government to cut its funding for SSPs.

Discussion

Lobbying and interest groups

The involvement of a number of groups or power elites that included DfES, DCMS and the YST in determining policy for SSPs was clearly evident within this work strand of the PESSCL strategy. The Labour government's willingness to invest in SSPs was ostensibly an investment in school sport in order to raise academic standards. It was also indicative of what Sabatier and Jenkins-Smith (1999b) describe as policy-oriented learning in which invest-ment in the school sport policy area was partly explained through an increasing alignment of the core and secondary values of a dominant coalition of policy actors. The YST and Sue Campbell were both powerful agents in persuading DfES and DCMS that SSPs were capable of contributing to and supporting government in achieving its own policy objectives. Sue Campbell described how the YST had lobbied on behalf of PESS and

> had brought in good people. We have the ability to make things happen, to turn a statement by government into a practical thing on the ground, it makes a difference and gains you a reputation. (Interview: Sue Campbell, 12 May 2006)

As the ACF suggests, and this case study in particular reveals, the YST lobbied on behalf of school sport and was capable of managing and shaping a policy initiative and its delivery through a working coalition between DfES and DCMS.

The central role played by these agencies in determining policy and policy delivery for SSPs was set against the marginal contribution of organizations such as LEAs, LAs, NGBs, Ofsted and Association for PE (AfPE). These circumstances meant that Sue Campbell was able to capitalize upon her position as non-political advisor for PESS and the YST's role in managing SSCs to lobby on behalf of PESS. A senior manager of the YST described how Sue Campbell had used this opportunity to skilfully create an advocacy coalition comprised of the YST, DfES and DCMS. In describing the creation of the PESSYP strategy and SSPs she suggested that

> so we had somehow to try and say, we don't need a parallel system in which school sport partnerships are separate from schools, we need a single comprehensive system in which sports colleges are at the heart of a partnership of schools. (Interview: senior manager YST, 6 July 2006)

The empirical evidence from this case study highlighted the role and use of power in determining the policy process for SSPs. In particular, the empirical data illustrated the involvement of state actors such as DCMS, DfES and the YST in dominating policy for SSPs, whilst subduing the voices and active contribution of others. The action of these policy actors in shaping the agendas for SSPs was evident in their capacity to impose a set of stringent policy conditions upon other policy actors involved in its delivery. The participation and contribution of sports clubs, NGBs, LAs and LEAs to policy formation was limited and implementation was framed by tight delivery targets and fiscal conditions set by the government. These agents also found themselves increasingly subject to the policy demands of a dominant coalition of policy actors. Whilst SE had attempted to reassert some degree of control over policy for SSPs, it was evident from the empirical data that whilst DCMS, DfES and the YST retained close control over policy agendas in this work strand, LEAs and PE professional groups remained marginal to policymaking for SSPs.

Key individuals

Whilst there is some evidence to support Sabatier and Jenkins-Smith's (1993, 1999a) contention that major policy change is a consequence of the lobbying of an active and dominant coalition, their acknowledgement of the role of significant individuals in determining policy change provides a more powerful explanation. The advocacy and support for PESS given by Prime Minister John Major provided a catalyst and a source of momentum for policy developments within school sport. Sue Campbell was active in seeking support for the work of the YST in primary schools and in articulating to politicians a clear vision for school sport. Campbell's broad and passionate vision for PESS, when combined with her technical expertise and long-standing involvement in sport, undoubtedly resonated with and captured the interest of a number of influential politicians. Within the ACF, the concept of power is described through the possession of technical information within policy communities and policy subsystems. One senior civil servant described how as a

> non-political advisor Sue was able to convince Estelle at a very early stage that this was a runner. The National School Sport Strategy brought two government departments together so we were able to agree an approach and move forward quickly. (Interview: 16 June 2006)

Another civil servant also described how the whole of the PESSCL strategy was based upon the vision provided by Sue Campbell and the YST (Interview: civil servant, 12 July 2005). Sabatier and Jenkins-Smith's (1993) framework also suggests that political actors are seldom able to retain a majority position through the exercise of raw power and, instead, must convince other actors of the unassailability of their position in defining policy problems and feasible policy alternatives. In seeking support for her ideas for school sport, Sue Campbell described how

> Estelle Morris (Secretary of State for Education) was a huge player in all of this and so was Kate Hoey (Minister for Sport) and since then Richard Caborn (Minister for Sport) has taken over and he has carried it on. So Ministerial support in trying to get this mission accomplished was key. It wouldn't have happened otherwise. (Interview: 12 May 2006)

The arguments and plans for PESS were technically feasible and engaged a number of key politicians who were convinced of the robustness of these arguments. The commitment and involvement of Estelle Morris as Minister for Schools and later Secretary of State for

Education and that of Kate Hoey as Minister for Sport meant that two senior political figures in key positions had an interest and the power to secure investment for school sport. Campbell was able to align the value systems of these senior politicians with those of her vision for PESS and, most importantly, to secure funding for SSPs by embedding them within Exchequer provision.

The policy broker

Sabatier (1999) highlights the crucial role of policy brokers in influencing policy change and prompting important people to pay attention to particular policy solutions. Brokers are individuals who may be part of or outside government, retain an elected or appointed position or be part of an interest group. The definition of a policy broker is an individual who is willing to invest their time, energy and reputation in the hope of future returns and who plays an important role in managing coalition conflict within acceptable boundaries (Sabatier and Jenkins-Smith 1993). Sue Campbell's success in brokering an agreement between DfES and DCMS to design and operate a new national strategy for PESS was testament to her abilities. There was no evidence of any coalition actively opposed to her policy ideas for school sport and the successful collaboration of two government departments to deliver the PESSCL strategy was a ground-breaking policy at that time. A senior civil servant involved in managing the DfES/DCMS involvement in the PESSCL strategy described how, as joint advisor to both secretaries of state for DfES and DCMS, Sue Campbell had already done a lot of background work in bringing the two departments together (Interview: 12 July 2005). Furthermore, a senior member of the PE profession outlined how Campbell had used a window of opportunity to skilfully position PESS at the centre of education and sport policy agendas:

> I doubt whether the government would of its own accord have made the connections between PE and school sport, and its capacity to deliver on a number of agendas including raising educational standards in schools and improving pathways to elite sport. (Interview: 19 July 2006)

A senior manager of the YST also described the 'Hoey, Morris and Campbell triangle as a very powerful piece of fusion' (Interview: senior manager YST, 6 July 2006), which had led to the creation of the national infrastructure for PESS. A number of key policy actors bore testament to the personal qualities of Sue Campbell and the skilful political role she played in harnessing the interest of government ministers. A senior HMI (Her Majesty's Inspectorate) described Sue as a lobbyist, who was

> highly influential, articulate, knowledgeable and sensitive to catching the moment, the thing about lobbying is that you have got to catch the Minister's eye. Sue understood this, and her great strength was her quality of thinking, her commitment and the fact that what she said made sense. (Interview: senior HMI, 19 October 2006)

A senior head for SE also explained how she had

> a vision and packaged it for civil servants so they could then sell it to Ministers. Because if government can't see milestones in their project plans, they aren't going to sign it off. (Interview: 30 June 2006).

Her political ability and clarity of thought were also combined with what a senior manager of the YST described as a total and relentless advocacy for PESS. A member of the AfPE attested to her 'skilful policy entrepreneurship, her ability to persuade, her commitment, her workaholism, her total single-mindedness' (Interview: 19 July 2006), whilst a senior staff member of the YST believed there were few individuals like Sue Campbell with the capacity to gain access and deal effectively with politicians and civil servants.

Changing beliefs and values

There is little evidence to support the ACF's explanation of policy change as the outcome of changes to the belief systems of coalitions within the policy subsystem. Empirical data suggest that the policy context for PESS has been characterized by ongoing and acrimonious debates about the nature of PE and whether its purpose should serve education or sport outcomes. These problems have been compounded by the apathy of successive governments towards PESS (Kirk 2002). At the crux of the dissonance have been debates between politician, the media and the PE profession and also within the PE profession about the distinctive purpose and practices of PESS. For Penney and Evans (1999, p. 43) these arguments have focused upon whether the rationale for PE should be

> children's physical, mental and social development, as distinct from a view of physical educa-
> tion as essentially about performance in specific activities (sports and particularly team games)
> achieved through the attainment of specific skills.

What emerges is the strength of traditional, hegemonic beliefs about the value of team games and sport's character-building qualities and its capacity to influence policy for PESS to the present day. The view of PE which privileges competitive sport and games and the promo-tion of excellence, discipline and moral fortitude successively dominates those who argue for the broader educational potential of PE to engage all pupils (see Evans 1990, Kirk 1992, 1993, Penney and Evans 1995, 1999). The enduring failure of politicians to understand the arguments presented by some educationalists of the distinction between sport and PE was reinforced by Sue Campbell who in describing her conversations with politicians and civil servants describes how 'they found it difficult to grapple with what physical education is' (Interview: 12 May 2006). She believed that securing government support for the PESSCL strategy required a clear articulation of the benefits of PESS that resonated with politicians' beliefs and values of PE as traditional, competitive sport.

The relative detachment of LEAs, AfPE and Ofsted from the PESSCL strategy and SSPs can, in part, be explained by the retention of a set of beliefs that have remained relatively impervious to change even to the more fundamental 'secondary aspects' of policy. Sue Campbell explained that in her negotiations with government the pure message of PESS had not got PE the resources and profile it needed (Interview: 12 May 2006). Organizations such as AfPE, LEAs and Ofsted have retained what Sabatier describes as their 'core belief systems' and a strong commitment to the educational values of PE. The empirical evidence reveals how arrangements for SSPs positioned LEAs and AfPE at the margins of the policy context partly as a consequence of their initial failure to embrace a vision of PE that was not consistent with their own value systems.

The policy context in which the PESSCL strategy exists is still maturing and evolving, yet there is growing evidence of a dominant advocacy coalition involving the YST, DfES and DCMS in arrangements that have been brokered by Sue Campbell. SE, NGBs, SSPs, CSPs sports colleges and sports clubs all appear to be 'insiders' who are actively involved in, and who share, a commitment to the values of the PESSCL strategy. Their relationships appear to be predicated upon what Sabatier and Jenkins-Smith (1993) describe as a sharing of 'policy beliefs'. There are, however, those agencies, such as AfPE, LEAs and Ofsted, who appear to remain relative policy 'outsiders' and whose views and values appear to differ to those of the dominant policy coalition.

A senior civil servant working within the PESSCL strategy was extremely positive in their support for the contribution of SSPs, which they believed represented 'an increasingly mature network which was driving change, driving virtually everything we are doing, driving the high quality agenda by showing good practice' (Interview: senior civil servant, 16 June 2006). It is evident that SSPs have provided the structural arrangements and connections that had not previously been established within this policy sector. A senior official at the QCA suggested that the establishment of SSPs had 'Provided the opportunity for agents and agencies to work together to the same outcomes but maintain separate although increasingly similar objectives' (Interview: QCA senior official, 13 June 2006). Indeed, there was widespread endorsement for the work of SSPs from a number of agents involved in the PESSCL strategy, an endorsement that was supported by the Annual Monitoring and Evaluation Report (IYS 2005), which claimed that

> partnerships are rapidly establishing themselves as an important element in the sports infra-structure of communities, integrating their activities with those of sports clubs and the local community. (IYS 2006, p. 39)

A senior manager of the YST suggested that SSPs provided the conditions for proper and effective collaborative working, whilst also removing the competitive element between schools (Interview: senior manager, 10 July 2006).

There appeared to be a generally held consensus amongst the actors and agents involved in the delivery of the SSP initiative that it had brought together a disparate and often competitive assortment of organizations to work together in order to achieve a broad set of mutually shared outcomes.

The demise of SSPs

Building on the impetus of growing political and popular interest in sport, the bid for London 2012 focused upon using the Olympic Games as a vehicle to endorse and promote sports participation for all social groups (London Organising Committee of the Olympic Games (LOCOG) 2007a,b). On securing the bid for the Olympic Games, PSA Target 22 aimed to 'deliver a successful Olympic and Paralympic Games with a sustainable "legacy" and get more young people taking part in high quality PE and sport' (NAO 2010, p. 5). The candidate file asserted that the London Olympics would be the first time that Games and 'legacy' planning will work hand in hand (BOA 2004). The Labour government's Olympic Legacy Action Plans *Before, during and after: making the most of the London 2012 Games* (DCMS 2008b) outlines the priorities for the long-term benefits of the 2012 Games and one of its five promises *to inspire a generation of young people*. It also established a Programme Board to oversee and assure delivery of the legacy promises and the PSA to 'deliver a successful Olympic Games and Paralympic Games with a sustainable legacy and to get more children and young people taking part in high quality PE and Sport' (DCMS 2008b, p. 12) by offering all 5- to 16-year-olds in England 5 hours of high-quality sport a week and all 16- to 19-year-olds 3 hours a week by 2012.

The election of a new coalition government in May 2010 provided the opportunity to consolidate the work of SSPs in order to achieve the London 2012 Olympic legacy promises (DCMS 2007). However, exogenous shocks such as the global economic banking crises led to times of economic austerity and financial repercussions for all policy areas. In October 2010, the new Secretary of State for Education, the Right Honourable Michael Gove, wrote an open letter to Baroness Sue Campbell (the Chair of the YST) informing her that the DfE would no longer provide ring-fenced funding for SSPs:

> After seven years and £2.4 billion investment from the Government and Lottery, the Department expects all schools to have embedded the good practice and collaboration developed over this time and to continue providing two hours a week of PE and sport. I can confirm therefore that the Department will not continue to provide ring-fenced funding for school sport partnerships. I am also announcing that the Department is lifting, immediately, the many requirements of the previous Government's PE and Sport Strategy, so giving schools the clarity and freedom to concentrate on competitive school sport.

As Griffiths and Armour (forthcoming) argue in this special issue, the decision signalled the intention of the new coalition government to make significant political and ideological changes to the configuration of PESS policy. They suggest that this new policy approach had two clear aims, to introduce more traditional competitive sport into schools (despite evidence that SSPs had increased the number of children engaged in competitive sport and extended the range of sports available) and to allow schools to decide on the amount of PESS offered (despite compelling evidence that curriculum time for PE declines when schools are free to determine its allocation) (Griffiths and Armour forthcoming). The new Schools Secretary, Michael Gove, stated that the DfE would end the £162 million PESSYP strategy in order to give schools the time and freedom to focus on providing competitive sport. In an article written by Simon Hart, in the Daily Telegraph (2010), he criticized this decision by accusing the government of making a mockery of the commitment to provide a sporting legacy as a consequence of the 2012 Olympic Games. The coalition government also experienced an unprecedented backlash against the proposals to abandon the PESSYP strategy led by Olympians, sports bodies, sports journalists and volunteers. The decision to abandon the PESSYP strategy led to several Commons debates on 'school sport' and on 13 December 2011, Gerry Sutcliffe Labour MP highlighted that

> It has been more than a year since the Government first announced their intention to dismantle the sports infrastructure .... It had a clear structure—the Youth Sport Trust was set up to deal with school and youth sport; Sport England was set up to deal with community sport through national governing bodies; and UK Sport was set up to deal with the elite level—and it was renowned around the world. It has also been more than a year since the Government announced that they were ending funding for school sports partnerships .... Next Tuesday will be the first anniversary of the partial U-turn on school sport, when the Government were forced to introduce a hastily cobbled together package of funding.

The School Games competition

In an attempt to reframe the role of government and unleash entrepreneurial spirit, the flagship policy idea *Big Society* was evident in Michael Gove's announcement that the DfE's approach to policy for PESS

> differs fundamentally from that of the last Government. . . . The best way to create a lasting Olympic legacy in schools is to give them the freedom and incentives to organize it themselves, for themselves, rather than imposing a centralized government blueprint. (Gove October 2010)

These fundamental policy changes required different structural and administrative approaches to the delivery of the Olympic legacy to those originally approved and planned by the previous Labour administration (Woodhouse and Fielden 2010). The decision under-lined the coalition government's intention to abandon what it perceived as the overly bureaucratic PESSYP strategy (despite Gove's admission in the letter that there was 'evidence that the network had helped schools to increase participation rates in the areas targeted by the previous Government').

The letter to Sue Campbell announced the introduction of a new Olympic style competition to create a lasting legacy in schools. A new competitive 'School Games' with funding from the DCMS and the National Lottery was introduced to improve the numbers of young people taking part in competitive sport across the country (YST 2011). Commencing in September 2011, the School Games is a celebration of competitive sport

> with funding support from the DCMS and the Department of Health to pay for 450 new roles to work three days a week as School Games Organisers . . . supporting as many schools as possible to set up intra- and inter-school competitions and link schools to clubs. (YST 2011)

Whilst there is evidence that the retention of these games organizers has been a response to vigorous lobbying within the media and from many elite sports people as a consequence of the demise of ring-fenced funding for SSPs, there is no intention by the coalition government to formally reinstate these partnerships and the PESSYP strategy.

The announcement of a new youth sport policy document *Creating a sporting habit for life: a new youth sport strategy* (DCMS 2012) represented an attempt to reinvest in selected elements of school sport policy, despite a 60% reduction in government spending. The introduction of a School Games competition sought to provide a framework for competitive school sport as part of a lasting legacy for London 2012. Its rationale was based upon a year-round sporting calendar that included 30 sports that were designed to get young people competing at intra-school and inter-school levels and culminating in local, regional and national events. Whilst many of the ideas and structural components of the strategy appeared similar to selected elements of the PESSYP strategy, Jeremy Hunt, the Secretary of State for Culture, Olympics Media and Sport, announced that the strategy would

> bring a sharper sense of direction and purpose across the entire sporting family through payment-by-results: a collective discipline of building on what works, and discarding what doesn't. The most successful organisations will be rewarded; and those which don't deliver will see their funding reduced or removed. (DCMS 2012, p. 2)

Its publication highlighted the highly politicized nature of policy for PESS and the government's intention to drive policy delivery through tightly managed structural arrangements and fiscal control.

Conclusion

The ACF (Sabatier and Jenkins-Smith 1999b) highlights factors such as the role of belief systems, key individuals, policy entrepreneurs and interest groups in explaining policy change. The involvement of a number of groups or power elites that included DfES, DCMS and the YST in determining policy for SSPs was clearly evident within this work strand of the PESSCL strategy. The Labour government's willingness to invest in SSPs was ostensibly an investment in school sport in order to raise academic standards. It was also indicative of what Sabatier and Jenkins- Smith (1999b) describe as policy-oriented learning in which investment in the school sport policy area was partly explained through an increasing alignment of the core and secondary values of a dominant coalition of policy actors. The YST and Sue Campbell were both powerful agents in presenting SSPs as a network that was capable of contributing to and supporting government in achieving its own policy objectives. As the ACF suggests, and this case study in particular reveals, Sue Campbell acted as an effective policy broker who was capable of managing and shaping a policy initiative and its delivery through a working coalition amongst DfES, DCMS and the YST.

What characterized the period before the launch of SSPs was the lack of a coherent vision or ideas about how PESS could be harnessed in order to address policy concerns. The ACF's focus upon the role of ideas and information as a major force for change proved useful in mapping the ideas that have framed the SSP initiative and of the changing values and belief systems of the policy actors involved. The ACF's particular focus upon the process of enlightenment and the reorienting of ideas helped to provide a framework which accounted for changes in government disposition towards school sport and also described how these changes impacted upon the relationships and networks of SSPs, CSPs, LEAs and NGBs.

A central assumption of the ACF is that 'coalitions', rather than individual decision-makers, are involved in the design of 'policy ideas'. The extensive and detailed accounts of coalition behaviour that emerged from the empirical data identified the growing influence of a dominant advocacy coalition centred upon the DfES, DCMS and the YST. In addition, the ACF's attention to the role of coalitions suggests that consideration should be given to those coalitions within the policy subsystem who are 'outside' policymaking processes. The contested nature of value changes amongst the coalitions involved in the work of SSPs highlighted the positioning of education agencies such as Ofsted and LEAs (whose belief systems remained at odds with those of the dominant coalition) at the margins of this policy initiative. The ACF also emphasized the role of the policy broker and their involvement in managing the activities of coalitions in order to seek policy solutions. Sue Campbell's capacity to broker and handle the relationship between two government departments and sport and education agencies was indicative of her capacity as an outstanding policy broker.

One of the main weaknesses in adopting the ACF as a theoretical framework for this study was the model's failure to address the role of power in favour of an account of the role of ideas and policy-orientated learning. John (1998), in particular, is critical of the advocacy coalition's failure to pay sufficient attention to the role of institutions and structural concerns within the policy process. It is acknowledged that within this study this framework failed to sufficiently account for the institutional arrangements and formal structural mechanisms that currently frame public policy in England. The role of government-imposed PSA targets and the privileged position of agencies such as the YST and SE were arguably not adequately addressed and acknowledged by this framework. Indeed, the empirical evidence from the case study illustrated how the government was able to exercise its power and control (often through quangos) over all aspects of the policy process.

This article concludes that PESS is a highly politicized policy area that has been particularly vulnerable to the ideologies of successive governments and the influence of powerful politicians over the past three decades. Whilst it is acknowledged that all policy areas are politicized, it is argued that organizations such as the YST appear to exercise power in policymaking for SSPs; however, their position is vulnerable due to their heavy reliance upon government funding and ministerial advocacy. An over-reliance on Treasury and Lottery funding to support the work of SSPs meant that they were particularly vulnerable to changing government ideologies. By repositioning itself to deliver government policy objectives, PESS was able to secure significant Treasury funding for the establishment of a national youth infrastructure for PESS. However, the PESS policy area is relatively weak (Grix and Phillpots 2011, Phillpots *et al.* 2011) and reflects what Houlihan (2000) describes as a highly complex and politicized policy area that is particularly vulnerable to imposition by political decision-makers.

There has been evidence by an emerging advocacy coalition for PESS led by the YST; however, the fragility of that coalition is reflected in its powerlessness to influence the political decision to withdraw funding from SSPs in order to give schools the time and freedom to focus on providing competitive sport. Whilst in essence this might appear a reasonable decision in times of austerity, the abandonment of the PESSYP strategy and its ring-fenced funding of SSPs represents a wilful abandonment of a ground-breaking infrastructure that had the capacity to deliver the sporting legacy promises of London 2012 to all young people through schools as central hubs.

References

Altheide, D.L., 1996. *Qualitative media analysis*. London: Sage.

Bell, J., 2005. *Doing your research project*. London: OU Press.

British Olympic Association, 2004. *London Olympic bid; candidature file*. London: BOA.

Chitty, C., 2004. *Education policy in Britain*. Basingstoke: Palgrave MacMillan.

Coalter, F., 1990. The mixed economy of leisure. *In*: I.P. Henry, ed. *Management and planning in the leisure industries*. Basingstoke: MacMillan Press.

Department for Culture Media and Sport, 2000. *A sporting future for all*. London: HMSO.

Department for Culture Media and Sport, 2001. *Building on PAT 10: progress report on social inclusion*. London: HMSO.

Department for Culture Media and Sport, 2007. *Our promise for 2012: how the UK will benefit from the Olympic Games and Paralympic Games*. London: Crown Copyright.

Department for Culture Media and Sport, 2008a. *Playing to win: a new era for sport*. London: DCMS.

Department for Culture Media and Sport, 2008b. *Legacy action plans: before, during and after: making the most of the London 2012 Games*. London: DCMS.

Department for Culture Media and Sport, 2012. *Creating a sporting habit for life: a new youth sport strategy*. London: DCMS.

Department for Education and Skills, 2003. *A new specialist system: transforming secondary education*. London: DfES.

Department for Education and Skills/Department for Culture Media and Sport, 2002. *Learning through PE and sport*. Nottingham: DfES Publications.

Department of National Heritage, 1995. *Sport: raising the game*. London: DNH.

Devine, F. and Heath, S., 2002. *Sociological research methods in context*. London: Macmillan.

Eberg, J., 1997. *Waste policy and learning: policy dynamics of waste management and waste incineration in the Netherlands and Bavaria*. Delft: Uitgeverij Eburon.

Evans, D., Whelan, J., and Neal, G., 2002. *Best practice in sports colleges*. Loughborough: Youth Sports Trust.

Evans, J., 1990. Defining a subject: the rise and rise of the new PE? *British Journal of Sociology of Education*, 11 (2), 155–169.

Evans, J. and Penney, D., 1995. The politics of pedagogy: making a national curriculum for physical education. *Journal of Education Policy*, 10 (1), 27–44.

Fisher, R., 1996. Gifted children and young people in physical education and sport. *In*: N. Armstrong, ed. *New directions in PE: change and innovation*. London: Cassell Education.

Flintoff, A., 2003. The school sport co-ordinator programme: changing the role of the physical education teacher? *Sport, Education and Society*, 8 (2), 231–250.

Giddens, A., 1998. *The third way: the renewal of social democracy*. Cambridge: Polity Press.

Gove, M., 2010. *Letter to Baroness Sue Campbell* [online]. Available from: http://media.education.gov.uk/assets/files/pdf/m/michael%20goves%20letter%20to%20baroness%20sue%20campbell%20%20%2020%20october%202010.pdf [Accessed 12 November 2010].

Green, K., 2002. Physical education teachers in their configurations: a sociological analysis of every-day 'philosophies'. *Sport Education and Society*, 7 (1), 65–84.

Green, M., 2005. Integrating macro and meso-level approaches: a comparative analysis of elite sport development in Australia, Canada and the United Kingdom. *European Sport Management Quarterly*, 5 (2), 143–166.

Griffiths, M. and Armour, K., forthcoming. Physical education and youth sport in England: conceptual and practical foundations for an Olympic legacy? *International Journal of Sport Policy*.

Grin, J. and Hoppe, R., 1997. Towards a theory of the policy process: problems, promises and prospects of the ACF. *Paper presented at the ARIPS meeting*, Amsterdam.

Grix, S., 2004. *Foundations of research*. London: Palgrave.

Grix, J. and Phillpots, L., 2011. Revisiting the 'governance narrative': 'asymmetrical network governance' and the deviant case of the sports policy sector. *Public Policy and Administration*, 26 (1), 3–19.

Hart, S., 2010. *London 2012* Olympics: government accused of 'devastating' legacy with school spending cuts. *Daily Telegraph* [online], 20 Oct. Available from: http://www.telegraph.co.uk/sport/othersports/schoolsports/8076966/London-2012-Olympics-Government-accused-of-devastating-legacy-with-school-spending-cuts.html [Accessed 23 October 2011].

Heclo, H., 1974. *Modern social politics in Britain and Sweden*. New Haven, CT: Yale University Press.

Heclo, H., 1978. Issue networks and the executive establishment. *In*: A. King, ed. *The new American political system*. Washington, DC: American Enterprise.

Henry, I.P., 1993. *The politics of leisure policy*. Basingstoke: MacMillan.

Henry, I.P., 2001. *Sport in the city: the role of sport in economic and social regeneration*. London: Routledge.

Houlihan, B., 1997. *Sport, policy and politics: a comparative analysis*. London: Routledge.

Houlihan, B., 2000. Sporting excellence, schools and sports development: the politics of crowded policy spaces. *European Physical Education Review*, 6, 171–193.

Houlihan, B., 2002. *Dying to win: doping in sport and the development of anti doping policy*. Strasbourg: The Council of Europe.

Houlihan, B. and Green, M., 2006. The changing status of school sport and physical education: explaining policy change. *Sport, Education and Society*, 11 (1), 3–92.

Houlihan, B. and White, A., 2002. *The politics of sports development: development of sport or development through sport?* New York: Routledge.

Institute of Youth Sport, 2004. *School sport partnerships: annual monitoring and evaluation project report for 2004* [online]. Available from: http://www.lboro.ac.uk/departments/ssehs/research/centres-institutes/youth-sport/research/young-people-school-based/school-sport-partnership-2004.html [Accessed 12 February 2011].

Institute of Youth Sport, 2005. *School sport partnerships: annual monitoring and evaluation project report for 2005*. Loughborough: Loughborough Partnership.

Institute of Youth Sport, 2006. *School sport partnerships: annual monitoring and evaluation project report for 2006* [online]. Available from: http://www.lboro.ac.uk/departments/ssehs/research/centres-institutes/youth-sport/downloads/research-downloads/young-people-school-based-dl/school-sport-partnership-2006-dl/ssp-full-2006.pdf [Accessed 14 February 2011].

Institute of Youth Sport, 2008. *School sport partnerships: annual monitoring and evaluation project report for 2008* [online]. Available from: http://www.lboro.ac.uk/departments/ssehs/research/centres-institutes/youth-sport/research/young-people-school-based/school-sport-partnership-2008.html [Accessed 12 December 2010].

Institute of Youth Sport, 2011. *Young people, school-based and community sport* [online]. Available from: http://www.lboro.ac.uk/departments/ssehs/research/centres-institutes/youth-sport/research/index.html [Accessed 20 January 2011].

Jenkins-Smith, H.C., 1988. Analytical debates and policy learning: analysis and change in the federal bureaucracy. *Policy Sciences*, 21, 169–211.

Jenkins-Smith, H.C., 1990. *Democratic politics and policy analysis*. Pacific Grove, CA: Brooks/Cole.

John, P.J., 1998. *Analysing public policy*. London: Pinter.

Kingdon, J.W., 1984. *Agendas, alternatives and public policy*. Boston, MA: Little Brown Books.

Kirk, D., 1992. *Defining physical education: the social construction of a school subject in post war Britain*. London: Falmer Press.

Kirk, D., 1993. Curriculum work in physical education: beyond the objectives approach? *Journal of Teaching in Physical Education*, 12 (3), 244–265.

Kirk, D., 2002. Quality physical education, partnerships and multiple agendas: a response to Karel J. van Deventer. *Presentation to the Commonwealth International Sport Conference*, 19 July, Manchester.

London Organising Committee of the Olympic and Paralympic Games, 2007a. *Olympic Games concept and legacy* [online]. Available from: http://www.london2012.com/publications/theme-1-olympic-games-concept-and-legacy.ph [Accessed 16 March 2011].

London Organising Committee of the Olympic and Paralympic Games, 2007b. *Everyone's games* [online]. Available from: http://www.london2012.com/documents/locog-publications/everyones-games.pdf [Accessed 2 January 2011].

May, T., 2001. *Social research: issues methods and process*. Buckingham: Open University Press.

McDonald, I., 2002. Theorising partnerships: governance, communicative action and sport policy. *Journal of Social Policy*, 34 (4), 579–600.

Morris, E., 1998. Morris announces expansion to 500 specialist schools. Department for Education and Employment. *Press Release* (496/98), 29 October 1998.

National Audit Office, 2010. *Measuring up: how good are the government's data systems for monitoring performance against public service agreements? Review of the data systems for public service agreement 22* [online]. Available from: http://www.nao.org.uk/publications/1011/review_data_systems_for_psa_22.aspx [Accessed 28 January 2011].

Parsons, W., 1995. *Public policy: an introduction to the theory and practice of policy analysis*. Cheltenham: Edward Elgar.

Patton, M.Q., 1990. *Qualitative evaluation and research methods*. Newbury Park, CA: Sage.

Penney, D., 1994. *No change in a new era? The impact of the Education Reform Act (1988) on the provision of PE and school sport in state schools*. Thesis (PhD). University of Southampton.

Penney, D. and Evans, J., 1995. Changing structures, changing rules: the development of the 'internal market'. *School Organisation*, 15 (1), 13–21.

Penney, D. and Evans, J., 1999. *Politics policy and practice in PE*. London: E & FN Spon.

Phillpots, L., 2007. *An analysis of government policy for physical education and school sport*. Thesis (PhD). Loughborough University.

Phillpots, L., Grix, J., and Quarmby, T., 2011. Unpacking the paradox: centralised grass-roots sport policy and 'new governance': a case study of county sports partnerships in the UK. *International Review for the Sociology of Sport*, 46 (3), 265–281.

Sabatier, P.A., 1988. An advocacy coalition framework of policy change and the role of policy oriented learning therein. *Policy Sciences*, 21, 129–168.

Sabatier, P.A., 1991. Toward better theories of the policy process. *Political Science and Politics*, 24 (2), 147–156.

Sabatier, P.A., 1999. *Theories of the public policy process (theoretical lenses on public policy)*. Boulder, CO: Westview Press.

Sabatier, P.A. and Jenkins-Smith, H., eds., 1993. *Policy change and learning: an advocacy coalitions approach*. Boulder, CO: Westview Press.

Sabatier, P.A. and Jenkins-Smith, H., 1999a. *The advocacy coalition framework: an assessment*. Boulder, CO: Westview Press.

Sabatier, P.A. and Jenkins-Smith, H., 1999b. *Theories of the policy process*. Boulder, CO: Westview Press.

Schlager, E. and Blomquist, W., 1996. A comparison of three emerging theories of the policy process. *Political Research Quarterly*, 49 (3), 651–672.

Sport England, 2008. *Sport and physical activity: active England final report*. London: Sport England.

Ten-Have, P., 2004. *Understanding qualitative research and ethnomethodology*. London: Sage.

Weiss, C., 1982. Policy research in the context of diffuse decision-making. *Policy Studies Review*, 53 (6), 619–639.

Wildavsky, A., 1987. Choosing preferences by constructing institutions: a cultural theory of preference formation. *The American Political Science Review*, 81 (1), 3–22.

Woodhouse, J. and Fielden, A., 2010. *London Olympics 2010: sporting legacy, House of Commons Library* [online]. Available from: http://www.parliament.uk/briefingpapers/commons/lib/research/briefings/snha-04868.pdf [Accessed 28 August 2011].

Youth Sport Trust, 2011. *Sainsbury's UK school games* [online]. Available from: http://www.youthsporttrust.org/page/uksg-events/index.html [Accessed 22 April 2011].

Physical education and youth sport in England: conceptual and practical foundations for an Olympic legacy?

Mark Griffiths and Kathleen Armour

Department of Sport Pedagogy, School of Education, Muirhead Building, University of Birmingham, Edgbaston, Birmingham B15 2TT, UK

The concept of youth legacy, as presented in the London 2012 bid, rests on the belief that engagement in (more) sport is 'good' for children and young people. Claims are made about the range of benefits to be gained from sports participation, including physical, social and moral benefits. For example, the European Commission (2007) argues that sports participation can lead to social inclusion, social cohesion and re-engagement. One way to conceptualize legacy, therefore, is in the form of enhanced social capital for those who are inspired to 'choose sport'. Yet, analysis of existing evidence, and of social capital theory, suggests that delivering legacy for young people is likely to be far more complex than is often claimed. Indeed, the term legacy itself seems to be inappropriate because of its passive connotations of bequest from one generation to the next. This is illustrated further when the theory of change underpinning legacy activities and processes is analysed. It is suggested, therefore, that if youth legacy promises through sport are to be kept, there is a need to base programmes and activities staged in the name of Olympic legacy upon clearer conceptual and practical foundations.

Introduction

> ... delivering a mass participation legacy for sport from London 2012 is one of my three top priorities. I want to see a marked, and sustained, cultural shift toward greater participation in sport. (Robertson 2010)

The London 2012 Olympic bid was founded on promises to deliver a sustainable legacy for children and young people. Lord Coe defined the vision as one of using 'the power of the games to inspire change' and to 'inspire young people around the world to choose sport' (British Council 2008). Such views are in tune with the International Olympic Committee's concerns to see better planning for sustained impact from the Games. Evidence to date, however, suggests that legacy is an illusive outcome; much is promised before the event but quantifying legacy post-event is notoriously difficult. Gratton *et al*. (2006) commented that host cities tend to concentrate their efforts on planning to stage the mega event itself, rather than preparing for post-games legacy opportunities. Furthermore, extensive review of existing legacy research led Edcoms (2007) to conclude that analysis of past Olympic

Games offers little insight into the potential for London 2012 to meet its legacy pledges. This article critically reviews the claims made that a sustainable youth sport engagement legacy can be delivered from London 2012. Legacy claims are analysed in three ways: (1) theoretically, considering Olympic legacy as a mechanism for generating social capital for children and young people; (2) practically, analysing the assumptions underpinning the structures and processes of physical education (PE) and youth sport that have the potential to facilitate legacy aspirations; and (3) pragmatically, how the application of logic models might be used to examine the generative processes behind Olympic legacy programmes that claim to develop social capital. In doing so, we seek to identify the theory of change that appears to have underpinned assumptions made by politicians and programmers for the social legacy outcomes of London 2012.

London 2012 youth legacy ... what is it?

Much has been written and claimed about legacy from the Olympic Games. In some ways, however, legacy is a curious term in the context of the Olympics. Dictionary definitions of the term legacy include a bequest or inheritance, something handed down from the past and something that has been discontinued. The essential point seems to be that something of value is handed down from one generation to the next. In the context of London 2012, for example, the proposed education legacy is extensive in scope, seeking to secure a positive impact on young people's lifestyle choices, values and aspirations. This is to be achieved through increased participation in sport, addressing youth disaffection and orienting young people towards an understanding of their world in a global context. For instance, 'The Get Set' (2012) programme is an extensive web-led initiative at the hub of London's 2012 legacy actions. The website promotes Olympic and Paralympic values and offers a series of suggestions, resources and activities to *inspire* schools and young people of different ages. This is a dynamic website that seeks to build and sustain young people's interest in and enthusiasm for the Olympics.

The London 2012 bid is not the first to promise an enduring legacy from the Games, although it is clear that turning promises into a reality has proved challenging for previous host cities. As EdComs (2007) report: whereas the games do offer an opportunity to deliver substantial changes:

> legacy strategies will need to be *embedded in existing programmes and policy areas* to achieve success in the long term and real benefits to participation provided ... A *multi-faceted, long term approach to measuring the legacy will need to be taken* to capture soft legacy benefits and ensure the benefits bought by the Games can be isolated from other factors. (p. 9, our emphasis)

This report also notes that one of the problems with existing evidence on legacy is that whereas there is much interest (and even research) prior to the Games, once the Games are over, legacy tends to be forgotten. This explains why it is that legacy aspirations are more likely to be achieved if they are embedded within existing structures. In this regard, it could be argued that London 2012 has a unique opportunity to deliver its legacy aspirations through the UK's Physical Education and Sport Strategy for Young People (PESSYP). The strategy seeks to increase the number of young people experiencing high-quality PE and sport and involves a coordinated approach between schools, sports clubs and community groups (e.g. school sport partnerships). Critically, PESSYP is already in place in *all* schools (although this structure is likely to change before the games take place – see below), and therefore makes it possible to argue that all children and young people can be 'reached' if the existing structures are used effectively.

The UK government's target for the Sport and PE Theme legacy is set out in its Public Service Agreement (PSA). PSAs are central to government performance measurement systems and are negotiated agreements across departments, making explicit how outcomes will be met. In 2007, the UK government published its Comprehensive Spending Review that set out its priority outcomes for the period 2008–2011. Integrating the themes of sustainable legacy and quality PE experience, PSA 22 stated:

> Deliver a successful Olympic and Paralympic Games with a sustainable legacy and get more children and young people taking part in high quality PE and sport. (Government Office, PSA 22)

The PESSYP strategy was launched in the United Kingdom in 2008 and set out to create opportunities for 5 to 16-year-olds to experience 5 hours of sporting activity per week, 2 hours of quality PE and 3 h of sporting activity in school and community. Originally, PESSYP was a shared responsibility between the Department for Children, Schools and Families (DCSF) and the Department for Culture Media and Sport (DCMS) and it was clearly identified as the mechanism through which legacy could be 'delivered'. The monitoring of young people's levels of participation in sport has been underway for some time, through the research projects evaluating different strands of the Physical Education, School Sport and Club Links (PESSCL) strategy; for example, the DCMS 'Taking Part Survey' and the DCSF 'PE & Sport Survey'. However, 2012 legacy aspirations go beyond raising participation levels. Legacy also refers to a desire to embed the objectives and values of the Olympic Education Programme (OEP) in schools and colleges.

As was noted earlier, evidence from previous Olympic Games suggests it will be a major challenge to create, and provide evidence for, a sustainable legacy of increased youth participation and achievement in and through sport. This may explain why the approach to be taken in London 2012 is to promote behavioural change by ensuring that the 2012 Olympic and Paralympic Games are linked not just to achievements in sport and PE, but to addressing whole school priorities related to academic achievement, behaviour and attendance. In addition, one of the key features of the PESSYP strategy was the requirement to reach those children and young people who have benefited least from the gains made through the earlier PESSCL. This means that the 2012 legacy has an explicit focus on meeting the needs of diverse groups of children and young people who may, in the past, have been excluded in some way from sport; that is, those with no apparent interest in sport, 'looked-after' children, children and young people who experience difficulties with accessing sports and sports-related activities, pupils with a disability and young people in further education who face a distinctive set of challenges and barriers.

At the time of writing, the Youth Sport Trust (YST) in the United Kingdom is working with key partners (The London Organising Committee of the Olympic and Paralympic Games (LOCOG), the British Olympic Association, British Paralympic Association and government departments of education, sport and health) to help them develop their legacy and education programmes through the school sport partnership infrastructure. This work builds on 10 years of partnership that has been developed through the PESSCL and PESSYP strategies. However, it has been suggested by the current Secretary of State for Education (Rt. Hon. Michael Gove) that these arrangements will change – indeed will be dismantled – in the period running up to the Games. In a letter to the YST sent on 20 October 2010, government stated that:

The Coalition Government will encourage more competitive sport which should be a vibrant part of the life and ethos of all schools. We are committed to doing this through the creation of an annual Olympic-style school sport competition. The best way to create a lasting Olympic legacy in schools is to give them the freedom and incentives to organise it themselves, for themselves, rather than imposing a centralised government blueprint . . . Our approach differs fundamentally from that of the last Government. As part of this change of approach I have concluded that the existing network of school sport partnerships is neither affordable nor likely to be the best way to help schools achieve their potential in competitive sport. (p. 1)

In essence, the letter represents a political and ideological shift in thinking about the way in which PE and school sport are to be delivered in schools. The new strategy can be summarized into two clear aims:

(1) to introduce more traditional competitive sport into schools – despite clear evidence that the school sport partnerships have increased the number of children engaged in competitive sport and extended the range of sports available (Department of Education 2008, 2009) and
(2) to leave schools to decide on the amount of PE/school sport on offer – despite the success of the partnerships in increasing the amount of PE and school sport offered and the wealth of historical evidence showing that curriculum time for PE declines when schools are free to determine its allocation.

The new proposals as outlined in this letter appear to have a slightly different 'take' on Olympic legacy from that envisaged at the time of the bid; essentially the focus is much more on (traditional) competitive sport and rather less on the wider Olympic (or Olympism) aims. The proposals are being challenged but, at this stage, the outcome is uncertain.

Few would argue that Olympic legacy aspirations – such as meeting the needs of disadvantaged children and young people – are anything but laudable; they are not, however, unique. As Kohe (2010, p. 479) points out: 'Most countries have Olympic education programmes. Most assume that sport is a tool to foster social and cultural values, beliefs, morals and virtues.' Indeed, in 2004, the Athens Olympics made much of its OEP through school-based curriculum initiatives (primary and secondary schools), linking practical, theoretical and cultural activities to Olympic ideals and aspirations (Grammatikopoulos et al. 2005). Yet, taking into account the meaning of the term 'legacy' as something that is passed down to future generations, it could be argued that conceptually, the notion of legacy needs further consideration. For example, whereas it is perfectly feasible to bequeath build-ings and programmes, it seems rather more challenging to seek to bequeath intangibles such as 'motivation', 'aspiration' or broad notions of achievement. It is unclear, for example, how the process of legacy in these areas could or would happen or, indeed, how such outcomes could be measured and, importantly, attributed in some causal fashion to the Games.

Perhaps one way to conceptualize the legacy process is through the notion of helping children and young people to develop 'social capital' through their encounters with the Games and its additional programmes and activities in schools and sports clubs. Yet, there is a difficulty in considering legacy in this way because schools and sports clubs are placed in the position of being both 'cause' and 'effect' structures; that is, the structures and processes that produce social capital are also mechanisms used to measure it (Tonts 2005). Nonetheless, if schools are to be key structures through which youth legacy is to be 'delivered' it is difficult to see how this problem can be avoided. Indeed, perhaps there is a prior question to be addressed: Is the development of social capital a useful way to conceptualize Olympic legacy?

Legacy as 'social capital'

Clearly, children and young people participate in sport and physical activity for a range of reasons: because they are forced to, through compulsory programmes in school or for an array of intrinsic and extrinsic reasons. Whatever the reason, much is claimed for the benefits of engaged participation in sport and physical activity. For instance, Putnam (2000) has argued that participation in sport provides opportunities to connect individuals with each other and with other communities. In supporting this notion of 'connectedness', Bailey *et al.* (2009) noted that physical education and school sport (PESS) claims consistently to support the accumulation of personal, social and socio-moral skills which then act as forms of social capital that allow young people to engage actively in a range of social situations. Yet, despite the intuitive appeal of the proposed link between sport engagement and social benefits, it is important to point out that there remains a lack of empirical evidence to support a causal relationship. Moreover, as Kohe (2010) argues, although those in favour of the value of Olympic education in schools point to the benefits of sport, it is also important to take a critical stance towards the Olympic movement focussing on questions about 'environmental sustainability, globalisation, politics, and social justice and equality' (p. 480).

The lack of evidence about the social benefits of sport is due, in part, to a lack of large-scale and long-term evaluation programmes (Bailey 2005), and the difficulty of examining the impact of PESS programmes beyond the 'pure happenstance' of sports participation (Long *et al.* 2002, p. 3). However, despite this, long-held beliefs still persist where sports participation is seen as a form of 'social participation' and where participation, potentially, fosters the development of individual empowerment, networking opportunities, citizenship and social capital (Kay and Bradbury 2009). As a result, social capital is perceived to act as a resource for the democratic values and civic engagement of communities; hence in communities where social capital is abundant, individuals and communities learn to trust and engage with social structures. It is perhaps not surprising then that successive UK governments have promoted sport as a mechanism for addressing neighbourhood renewal and linked to issues of inequality and disaffected youth (e.g. 'Game Plan' – DCMS and Strategy Unit 2002). As Coalter (2007) has observed, there has been a marked change in UK policy documents from developing sport *in* communities to developing communities *through* sport.

In the context of engendering positive social behaviours through sport, the last 20 years has seen a growing body of literature that has used the concept of social capital to examine sports participation in terms of civic engagement, social inclusion and community revitalization (Coalter 2007). Yet despite this work, the application of social capital in such contexts has been criticized from two positions:

- first, the concept of social capital remains contested in terms of definition and scope; for instance, social capital is used to describe both the characteristics of interaction (social relations), but also the effect (e.g. trust) and
- second, much of the literature portrays social capital as a wholly positive outcome, largely ignoring the negative aspects of the theory.

Given, therefore, that London 2012 youth legacy aspirations at the point of the bid appeared to be located firmly in the territory of developing social capital in and for young people, it seems important to interrogate the concept further.

Social capital as positive engagement and empowerment

As described earlier, social capital has been used extensively in academic and policy debates as a mechanism for examining the interactions between agency and social infrastructures, and how these interactions are acted upon in the social arena (Moody and Paxton 2009). Much of this literature is grounded in the work of three writers: Bourdieu (1997), Coleman (1988) and Putnam (2000). In the context of London 2012, the work of Putnam is insightful because of his focus on the connection between 'civicness' and the role of social networks (e.g. government) in engendering, what Grix (2001) described as the 'generation of a collective good that facilitates collaborative action for all' (p. 189). Putnam (2000) defined social capital as the features of social life such as trust, networks and norms that allow individuals to actively engage with others in achieving shared objectives. As Jarvie (2006) put it, social capital is 'the elixir that thickens civil society with the potential to create strong reciprocal relationships and energetic communities' (p. 332). Informed by a structural functionalist approach, Putnam (2000) described social capital in terms of bridging or bonding relationships. 'Bridging' (inclusive) refers to the development of overlapping networks that together generate identity and reciprocity between networks. In this view, the resources available in one group are made available to other groups. 'Bonding' social capital (exclusive), on the other hand, is about closed or tightly constructed networks that reinforce an exclusive identity (e.g. private golf clubs). The negative side of such a network is that bonding forms of social capital can reinforce forms of racism, discrimination and social exclusion; what is commonly labelled, 'the dark side' of social capital (discussed later in this section).

The value of employing Putnam's (2000) network framework is that it focuses attention on the level of analysis adopted; that is, social capital has to be understood as a micro–macro concept. Research from social network theory has traditionally considered how dense networks with strong supportive ties (e.g. schools) compare with dispersed networks that bridge different social situations (e.g. business organizations and community groups) in the development of social capital (Glanville and Bienenstock 2009). However, rather than confine social capital to the context of binary network analysis (dense vs. dispersed, weak vs. strong and bonding vs. bridging), it seems sensible in the context of London 2010 legacy to consider both concurrently. This would lead to an analysis of the ways in which strong, densely connected networks (e.g. schools) engender positive social behaviours. At the same time, it is important to consider the potential of dispersed bridging networks (e.g. county sports partnerships in England) to leverage multiple networking opportunities. In the complex landscape of UK sport governance, this dual approach would seem to be essential in attempts to maximize the opportunities for sport to generate positive social outcomes for children and youth.

Whereas the legacy of mega sporting events can be seen in tangible outcomes such as physical capital (e.g. stadia) and human capital (e.g. the development of skills and abilities derived from volunteerism), social capital is a more difficult concept to capture. A useful starting point, however, is Collins' (2008) work on social exclusion, where he divides social capital into two distinct forms: personal social capital and communal capital. Personal social capital is where individuals develop confidence, knowledge, time and a network of social relationships that can support them with a shared inclination to 'take part'. Naturally, these attributes are affected by an individual's positionality in society. As a considerable body of research attests (Wilson 2002, Evans 2009), some social groups (i.e. social classes) are engaged more extensively in sport and leisure opportunities. This links to Collins' second form of capital – communal social capital – which is defined as the social glue that supports an individual's engagement in activities. Clearly, some groups in society are better endowed with communal social capital and so they can offer 'their' young people a more established network within which to generate personal social capital.

In the context of PESS in the United Kingdom, links can be made to research on the impact of physical activity programmes that aim to develop positive personal and social development of children and youth. In evaluating a number of such programmes with disaffected youth, researchers concluded that the impact of physical activity on social behaviours was situated and context specific, and that the success of transferability was determined by what might be termed as 'personalized learning' (Sandford *et al.* 2006). As they pointed out, 'sport and physical activities may well be the catalyst for change in the lives of disaffected young people, but there is no watertight guarantee that this will happen in a consistent or uniform way' (p. 266). It is an important point that is echoed in the work of Bailey *et al.* (2009) who suggested that researchers 'need to determine not only the product of participation but also the process of change' (p. 11). We address processes of change later in this article.

At the core of any understanding of social capital are three concepts: reciprocity, trust and resources. Resources may be considered as material goods, such as land, houses, club membership and money, that are embedded in specific social networks. Moving beyond critical debate that considers trust and reciprocity as either antecedents of or outcomes of social capital, Glanville and Bienenstock, (2009) define reciprocity as 'a norm that requires a return in kind of a good or service rendered' and trust as 'expectations of good will and acceptance of risk or vulnerability' (p. 1512). In practical terms, it is through the interaction of the individual with associational/civic activities that increased trust and reciprocity are developed; in other words, trust generates social participation – and participation generates trust (Foley and Edwards 1999). Yet the question remains; how are such notions of trust developed through PE, school sport and community sport for young people? In the context of a presumed 2012 youth legacy, this is an important question. Perhaps a useful way to think about social capital development in this context is as a form of, what Foley and Edwards (1999) termed, 'brokerage'. This has two distinct components: first, ensuring that individuals and groups recognize that specific resources exist (information), and second, developing the kinds of social relationships needed to seek out and access these resources. Thus, the challenge for policymakers seeking to deliver a sustained Olympic legacy is to ensure that young people not only know what is available to them, but are also empowered to actively seek participation opportunities, rather than being passive recipients of legacy opportunities. In this sense, legacy cannot be easily understood as a form of bequest to young people; instead, it has to be understood as an evolving engagement process over which they have some control. From this standpoint, legacy should be a process that enables children and young people to develop a *critical* stance towards sport and the Olympic Games, what Wright (1996) has termed critical literacy through sport.

Social capital as social exclusion

One of the critiques of the concept of social capital is, what Das (2004) has identified as, its 'overly optimistic claims' (p. 27). Three examples are illustrative. First, when structured around a 'bonding' form of networking, social capital acts to reinforce the exclusion of 'outsiders'. Second, it can be argued that research on social capital in the context of sport has been limited mainly to UK and US contexts. There is, for example, a lack of empirical research that addresses how sport develops social capital in societies dominated by poverty and a wage-labour class (Das 2004). Third, social capital can also be criticized where it is presented as a tautological relationship in which the development of social relations produces social capital (trust) in a linear fashion (Seippel 2006). Therefore, rather than viewing this relationship as largely unproblematic, the challenge is to understand the generative processes behind social interactions. In the context of sport, for example, there is ample evidence to suggest that sport has the potential to generate as many negative outcomes as positive outcomes (e.g. drugs and cheating) (Bailey *et al.* 2009). Furthermore, sport has been charged with many forms of social exclusionary practices (e.g. membership of private sports clubs). For that reason, a number of authors have argued that the development of *any* form of positive social capital through sport lacks empirical evidence (Foster *et al.* 2005, Coalter 2007). It can certainly be argued that sport is not endowed with any special or unique features that make it the kind of activity that is inherently predisposed towards the development of social capital for young people. On the other hand, it could also be argued that when it is located in a school context, for example, within a framework designed for educational purposes, sport should be well equipped to deliver positive outcomes for more children and young people.

Perhaps it is important to recall at this point that the development of social capital is best understood as engagement in communities/networks that can influence behaviour. Individuals belong to, and engage in, multiple communities (e.g. family and peer groups) and therefore the development of social capital needs to be understood within a nexus of interconnected communities. It might be pertinent to ask, therefore, how it is that PESS is designed and structured to facilitate the development of networks and communities. More broadly, what forms of social capital for children and young people are conceptualized within the concept of 'legacy' from London 2012, and how is their delivery to be facilitated?

Social capital and PESS

Despite the concerns outlined above, there is widespread support for the notion that there are, *potentially*, a wide range of benefits for young people to be gained from participation in sport (e.g. European Commission 2007). It could also be argued that because PESS takes place in schools, and is available to all, it is a socially inclusive activity ideally placed to generate social capital with and for all young people. Yet, despite the fact that PESS takes place in a school context, and is compulsory for all children in the United Kingdom from the ages of 5–16, there is some evidence to suggest that outcomes vary for different groups in society. For instance, in the 2007 Health Survey for England, Craig and Shelton (2008) found that participation in sport and exercise tended to increase as comparable household income increased. Similarly, a Sport England survey in 2002 found that young people living in the 20% of most deprived areas in England were less likely to be members of a sports club than those living in other areas (35% vs. 47%), and were less likely to take part in sport at youth clubs or other organizations (48% vs. 58%). Research also suggests that children from lower income families are also more likely to identify cost and lack of local access to facilities as barriers (Brunton *et al.* 2003). As a result of this, it has been argued that some young people experience PE differentially, according to the intersections of their social class, gender, religion, ethnicity and ability (Kirk 2005).

What can be made of such findings in the context of a youth legacy from the Olympic Games in the United Kingdom? One implication is that whereas legacy activities delivered through PESS programmes might engage those who are already engaged/interested in sport, they can do rather less for those who experience PESS as an exclusionary practice. With reference to social capital theory, this suggests that PESS has as much potential to reinforce, as to challenge, inequalities in the development of both social and other forms of capital for children and young people. The proposals put forward by the UK's new coalition government, particularly the renewed emphasis on competitive sport, may have little to offer those children and young people who are already excluded.

Measuring legacy?

Perhaps the intangible and complex nature of social capital is best illustrated when attempts are made to quantify the concept, particularly in contexts where considerable amounts of public money are committed to mega sports events, such as Fédération Internationale de Football Association (FIFA) World Cup and Summer Olympics (Preuss 2007). The difficulty lies not only in the ambiguity of the concept (what is being measured?) but also in cases where the relationship between individual behaviour and networks is the focus of measurement, whether behaviour can be quantified and what this tells us about the quality of the relationship. For instance, in a study of volunteer sports groups in Norway, Seippel (2006) initially measured social capital by quantifying individuals' membership of an organization, their membership of multiple organizations and the 'intensity' of such membership (i.e. the number of hours spent during the past month). However, the difficulty in measuring social capital in this way, as recognized by Seippel, is that research sometimes assumes that all social capital is of equal value and that all relationships provide equal access. Helpfully, Seippel (2006) goes on to suggest that future research might adopt a qualitative approach and focus on three areas: information (individuals acquire more knowledge, increasing weak ties), influence (develop individual and social skills) and identity (developing and supporting feelings of belonging and empowerment). As might be expected, Seippel (2006) suggests that connected organizations are more valuable in developing social capital than isolated organizations and, in this context, it is interesting to consider the role of school sport partnerships in expanding the network of sports experiences for young people.

A review of the wider literature suggests that the measurement of social capital can be approached in three distinct ways:

- measuring through a survey approach, using social capital as an independent variable to capture social–psychological terms such as self-confidence and identity;
- 'measuring' the development of social capital through the linkages between individuals and networks/groups, and the linkages between networks and groups; and
- social capital as a dependent variable which focuses attention on how organizations produce and shape social capital (e.g. voluntary associations, schools and youth groups).

The advantage of seeing social capital as a dependent variable is that it encourages the researcher to look at the context. Indeed, throughout this article, we have acknowledged that social capital assumes different forms because of the impact of situation and social context. As Foley and Edwards (1999) observed, the context in which social capital is embedded influences its 'use value' (p. 146).

Here again, different understandings of social capital (e.g. bridging and bonding) should be considered. What would it take, for example, to embrace a bridging understanding of social capital through sport in schools, and how might this influence the existing structures and processes? How do sports clubs and coaches conceptualize youth sport and their role in supporting young people to develop different forms of social capital? How might social capital be measured in the context of a public value vision of the Games? It could be argued that only by considering the complexity of social capital theory can we ever hope to understand fully the nature of the legacy claims being made, and the challenges inherent in addressing them. Yet for researchers and policymakers, the challenge is to understand the generative processes behind social interactions that claim to develop social capital. To some extent, this has already been acknowledged by a DCMS and Home Office Report (2006) that concluded that 'too much work using sport is still focused on output rather than outcomes' (p. 14). It is interesting to consider, therefore, the pathways to Olympic legacy that are suggested by the structures that are currently in place in England to deliver legacy (and so generate social capital), and also the ways in which those pathways would be different under the new coalition government's proposals to dismantle these structures. One way to address these issues is to examine Olympic legacy programmes through the use of logic models.

Pathways to legacy – a pragmatic approach

The development of a 'logic model' to illustrate the ways in which social programmes are intended to have an impact on participants can be a helpful process in analysing potential pathways to developing social capital in the name of legacy. Logic models (Kellogg Foundation 2004) can clarify and make explicit foundational features of a social programme, especially where aims are rather nebulous and the paths to outcomes unclear; for this reason, logic models are useful in 'telling a programs performance story' (McLaughlin & Jordan 1999, p. 71). The process of creating a logic model includes developing a basic model and then expanding the basic model to explore and explain the theory of change that describes the rationale for a specific programme. The aim of developing a basic logic model is to outline how the programme will achieve what it aims to achieve. The basic logic model involves the identification of the following aspects of the programme:

- Resources/inputs, that is, elements available to do the work
- Activities, that is, what you do with your resources
- Outputs, that is, the direct product of activities
- Short-term and long-term outcomes, that is, changes in participants' behaviour
- Impact, that is, fundamental changes (intended or otherwise) in organizations, communities, systems and so on as a result of the programme.

The first two elements of the model represent planned work (i.e. what you are planning to do), whereas the last three represent intended results (what you are expecting to happen). In attempting to construct this model the advice is to start with the outcomes. The remainder of the model begins to address how it is anticipated that these outcomes will be addressed.

Developing a logic model for Olympic legacy is complex because legacy is conceptualized as a set of programmes; nonetheless, it is an interesting process, particularly in the 'theory of change' stage where the assumptions underpinning legacy claims can be identified. A theory of change is useful, in this particular context, because it seeks to illustrate the assumptions that programmers make in linking intended outcomes with programme activities (Bailey *et al.* 2009). By evaluating a programme theory of change, it is then possible to identify fuzzy or divergent factors that might obstruct a programme potential to achieve its stated aims and objectives. For London 2012, for example, and under current arrangements where it is anticipated that legacy can be delivered through school sport partnerships, it is possible to develop the model shown in Table 1.

When considering the same logic model but in light of the UK coalition government's proposals, however, the picture could look very different. For example, the letter from the Secretary of State makes the following statement:

Table 1. Olympic legacy logic model.

Resources→	Activities→	Outputs→	Outcomes→	Impact
The Olympic and Paralympic Games	PESSYP strategy through school sport partnerships Competition managers and so on Networks of schools providing competitive sport opportunities Offering a wider range of competitive and non-competitive activities and opportunities National 'Get-Set' (2012) programme	Stronger sports-based programmes in school Primary school sports 'festivals' Targeting of excluded and low participating youth Wide range of sport and physical activity programmes available, both competitive and non-competitive Links across the curriculum to see impact on education more broadly	More children and young people engaged in sports activities Engagement in sport and physical activity by previously excluded groups Wide range of activities badged around 'Olympism' Learning and striving for personal and team success as promoted by the Olympic ideal	Greater sports participation by more people Better population health Higher educational aspiration and achievement Increased national competitive spirit and qualities of perseverance in all areas of life More social engagement leading to social inclusion Less youth disaffection Improved social capital for all groups but particularly those with comparatively low levels

Over the next year, my Department will develop a model to assist an Olympic-style approach to school sport. I firmly believe that the ideals of the Olympic and Paralympic Games can be an inspiration to all young people, not only to our most promising athletes. Indeed, they embody the ethos of achievement and self-improvement which the best schools manifest in their sports provision for all pupils. (p. 2)

If we were to reproduce the model based on this statement, it seems clear that almost all elements of Columns 2–4 would disappear. Instead, there would be an expectation more akin to that underpinning PE in the past; that is, that engagement in more competitive sport (whether children like it or not) will, in and of itself, lead to the 'Impacts' outlined in Column 5. It could be argued that not only is this ambitious, but it is also unrealistic. In other words, London 2012 may be about to lose the key differentiator it had for delivering legacy claims: an enabling structure.

In considering logic models as conceptual frameworks from which to examine approaches to change, it is interesting to further consider how the outcomes of London 2012 will increase social inclusion through increased participation in sport, particularly in terms of the wider evidence base for such a claim. For example, there is a considerable body of literature that continues to question the causal link between mega sports event and increased sports participation (Horne 2007, McCartney *et al*. 2010). Coalter (2004), for instance, observed how 'Most of the evidence ... suggests that major sporting events have no inevitably positive impacts on levels of sports participation.' (p. 11). Weed *et al*. (2008) in their systematic review of mega sports events concluded that 'The question can be asked as to whether the Olympic and Paralympic Games, with its emphasis on track and field and competitive sports, is likely to introduce people to new activities or increase levels of activity in non-Olympic activities.' (p. 14). Similarly, Collins' (2010) paper in this special issue argues that 'there is no evidence of the short lived spectacle of the Games ever sustainably promoting greater participation or health benefits' (p. 376). What the available evidence makes clear is that expecting an increase in sports participation as a direct consequence of mega sports events is problematic, and possibly naïve. If this is the case, and using logic models to highlight the critical relationship between school sport partnerships and legacy aspirations, then the potential loss of an enabling structure through which legacy can be developed, tailored for children and delivered seems even more damaging. The pathways to 2012 Olympic legacy for children and young people, until recently, appeared to be more promising than previous games in that the aspirations were supported by practical processes and structures. The new government proposals, however, appear to lead us back to the past and the chances of delivering legacy promises appear to be somewhat lower as a result.

Conclusion

In this article, we have argued for greater clarity in legacy claims, particularly those suggesting that previously excluded young people will gain social capital through enhanced participation in sport as a direct result of London 2012. This raises fundamental questions about the concept of legacy. It could be argued that legacy approaches are characterized by forms of passivity, even though activities promoted in the name of legacy are labelled as engagement and empowerment activities. At the very least, a more critical/analytical view of sport and its contribution to the development of social capital is needed.

This article has also argued that based on existing evidence, Olympic legacy aspirations should be more realistically grounded in existing sporting structures. Indeed, in pursuing an Olympic legacy that explicitly sets out to engage young people in (more) sports participation, evidence suggests that structures, such as school sports partnerships, are well placed to deliver legacy aspirations that can 'reach' all children and young people (Grix and Philpotts 2010). Yet, despite the London 2012 Olympic bid promising to deliver a sustainable 'legacy' for children and young people, confusion on how best to deliver this prevails. At the time of writing and illustrative of the emotion that sport evokes, the UK coalition government's aim to withdraw funding for school sports partnerships is now being reconsidered after considerable public opposition (Guardian Newspaper, 20 December 2010). It seems clear that such a strategy was ill-conceived in terms of an 'evidence' base, and a lack of an alternative framework for the school's sports system.

Although we have focused on the challenges of a London 2012 legacy, a number of concepts have been identified that perhaps transcend national boundaries, and as a result, invite a more critical examination when mega sports events are promoted as developing social legacy. As a result, the questions this article raises, therefore, are what types of sport activity and sporting organizational structures are most conducive to developing social capital and, most importantly, upon what assumptions are legacy claims based; in other words, what exactly is the underlying theory of change and how would this change if Olympic legacy aspirations are not grounded in existing enabling structures? Answering these questions could go some way towards developing an Olympic youth legacy through sport that has some chance of being sustained.

References

Bailey, R., 2005. Evaluating the relationship between physical education, sport and social inclusion. *Educational review*, 57 (1), 71–90.

Bailey, R., *et al.*, 2009. The educational benefits claimed for physical education and school sport: an academic review. *Research papers in education*, 24 (1), 1–27.

Bourdieu, P., 1997. The forms of capital. *In*: A.H. Halsey, H. Lauder, P. Brown, and A. Stuart Wells, eds. *Education: culture, economy, society.* Oxford: Oxford University Press, 46–58.

British Council, 2008. *International inspiration announcement* [online]. Available from: http://www.britishcouncil.org/sport-international-inspiration-seb-coe.htm [Accessed 8 November 2010].

Brunton, G., Harden, A., Rees. R., Kavanagh, J., Oliver, S. and Oakley, A., 2003. *Children and physical activity: a systematic review of barriers and facilitators.* London: University of London, EPPI Report.

Coalter, F., 2004. London 2012: a sustainable sporting legacy? *In*: A. Vigor and M. Mean, eds. *After the goldrush: a sustainable Olympics for London.* London: Ippr and Demos, 8–24.

Coalter, F., 2007. *A wider social role for sport.* London: Routledge.

Coleman, J., 1988. Social capital in the creation of human capital. *American journal of sociology*, 94, 95–120.

Collins, M., 2008. Social exclusion from sport and leisure. *In*: B. Houlihan, ed. *Sport and society.* London: Sage, 77–101.

Collins, M., 2010, From 'sport for good' to 'sport for sport's sake' – not a good move for sports development in England? *International journal of sport policy and politics*, 2 (3), 367–379.

Craig, R. and Shelton, N., eds., 2008. *Health survey for England 2007. Volume 1. Healthy lifestyles: knowledge, attitudes and behavior* [online]. Leeds: NHS Information Centre. Available from: http://www.ic.nhs.uk/pubs/hse07healthylifestyles [Accessed 24 January 2012].

Das, R.J., 2004. Social capital and poverty of the wage-labour class: problems with the social capital theory. *Transactions of the Institute of British Geographers*, 29 (2), 27–45.

DCSM-Strategy Unit, 2002. *Game plan: a strategy of delivery government's sport and physical activity objectives.* London: Cabinet Office.

Department of Culture, Media and Sport and the Home Office, 2006. *Bringing communities together through sport and culture.* London: Home Office.

Department of Education, 2008. *School sport 2007–2008* [online]. Available from: https://www.education.gov.uk/publications/standard/publicationDetail/Page1/DCSF-RW063 [Accessed 24 January 2012].

Department of Education, 2009. *Physical education and sport survey 2008–2009* [online]. Available from: https://www.education.gov.uk/publications/eOrderingDownload/DFE-RR032.pdf [Accessed 15 January 2011].

Edcoms, 2007. *London 2012 legacy research: final report*. London: DCMS.

European Commission, 2007. *White Paper on sport* [online]. Available from: http://ec.europa.eu/sport/documents/wp_on_sport_en.pdf [Accessed 24 January 2012].

Evans, J., 2009. Education and ability. *In*: R. Bailey and D. Kirk, eds. *The Routledge physical education reader*. London: Routledge, 169–182.

Foley, M.W. and Edwards, B., 1999. Is it time to disinvest in social capital? *Journal of public policy*, 19, 141–173.

Foster, C., *et al.*, 2005. *Understanding participation in sport: a systematic review*. London: Sport England.

Get Set, 2012. *The official London 2012 education programme* [online]. Available from: http://getset.london2012.com/en/home [Accessed 24 January 2012].

Glanville, J.L. and Bienenstock, E.J., 2009. A typology for understanding the connections among different forms of social capital. *American behavioural scientist*, 52 (11), 1507–1530.

Gove, M., 2010. *Refocusing sport in schools to build a lasting legacy of the 2012 games* [online]. Available from: http://www.education.gov.uk/inthenews/inthenews/a0065473/refocusing-sport-in-schools-to-build-a-lasting-legacy-of-the-2012-games [Accessed 24 January 2012].

Grammatikopoulos, V., Hassandra, M., Koustelios, A. and Theodorakis, Y., 2005. Evaluating the Olympic education program: a qualitative approach. *Studies in Educational Evaluation*, 31 (4), 347–357.

Gratton, C., Shibli, S. and Coleman, R., 2006. The economic impact of major sports events: a review of ten events in the UK. *Sociological review*, 54 (2), 41–58.

Grix, J., 2001. Social capital as a concept in the social sciences: the current state of the debate. *Democratization*, 8 (3), 189–210.

Grix, J. and Philpotts, L., 2010. Revisiting the 'governance narrative asymmetrical network governance' and the deviant case of the sports policy sector. *Public policy and administration*, 26 (1), 3–19.

Guardian Newspaper, 2010. David Cameron orders rethink over school sports cuts after outcry [online]. Available from: http://www.guardian.co.uk/education/2010/dec/01/david-cameron-school-sports-rethink?intcmp=239 [Accessed 24 January 2012].

Horne, J., 2007. *The four 'knowns' of mega sports events. Leisure studies*, 26 (2), 81–96.

Jarvie, G., 2006. *Sport, culture and society: an introduction*. London: Routledge.

Kay, T. and Bradbury, S., 2009. Youth sport volunteering: developing social capital? *Sport, education and society*, 14 (1), 121–140.

Kellogg Foundation, 2004. *Using logic models to bring together planning, evaluation & action logic model development guide* [online]. Available from: http://www.wkkf.org/knowledge-center/publications-and-resources.aspx [Accessed 2 October 2010].

Kirk, D., 2005. Physical culture, lifelong participation and empowerment: towards an educational rationale for physical education. *In*: A. Flintoff, J. Long, and K. Hylton, eds. *Youth sport, and active leisure. leisure studies*. Eastbourne: Leisure Studies Association, 3–28.

Kohe, G.Z., 2010. Disrupting the rhetoric of the rings: a critique of Olympic idealism in physical education. *Sport, education and society*, 15 (4), 479–494.

Long, J., *et al.*, 2002. *Count me in: the dimensions of social inclusion through culture, media and sport*. Leeds: Leeds Metropolitan University.

McCartney, G., Thomas, S., Thomson, H., Scott, J., Hamilton, V., Hanlon, P., Morrison, D.S. and Bond, L., 2010. The health and socioeconomic impacts of major multi-sport events: systematic review (1978–2008). *British Medical Journal*, 340. Available from: http://www.bmj.com/content/340/bmj.c2369.full [Accessed 24 January 2012].

McLaughlin, J.A. and Jordan, G.B., 1999. Logic models: a tool for telling your programs performance story. *Evaluation and program planning*, 22 (1), 65–72.

Moody, J. and Paxton, P., 2009. Building bridges linking social capital and social networks to improve theory and research. *American behavioral scientist*, 52 (11), 1491–1506.

Preuss, H., 2007. The conceptualisation and measurement of mega sport event legacies. *Journal of sport tourism*, 12 (3), 207–227.

Putnam, R.D., 2000. *Bowling alone*. New York: Touchstone.

Robertson, H., 2010. *Sport and Olympics minister sets out Olympic sports legacy plans* [online]. Available from: http://www.culture.gov.uk/news/media_releases/7152.aspx [Accessed 12 September 2010].

Sandford, R.A., Armour, K.M. and Warmington., P. C., 2006. Re-engaging disaffected youth through physical activity programmes. *British educational research journal*, 32 (2), 251–271.

Seippel, O., 2006. Sport and social capital. *Acta sociologica*, 49 (2), 169–184.

Tonts, M., 2005. Competitive sport and social capital in rural Australia. *Journal of rural studies*, 21 (2), 137–149.

Weed, M., Coren, E. and Fiore, J., 2008. *A systematic review of the evidence base for developing a physical activity, sport and health legacy from the London 2012 and Paralympic Games*. The Center for Sport, Physical Education and Activity Research (SPEAR), Canterbury Christ Church University.

Wilson, T.C., 2002. The paradox of social class and sports involvement: the roles of cultural and economic capital. *International review for the sociology of sport*, 31 (1), 5–16.

Wright, J., 1996. Mapping the discourses in physical education. *Journal of curriculum studies*, 28 (3), 331–351.

The Olympic legacy and participation in sport: an interim assessment of Sport England's Active People Survey for sports studies research

Fiona Carmichael[a], Jonathan Grix[b] and Daniel Palacios Marqués[c]

[a]Department of Management, University of Birmingham, Edgbaston, Birmingham B15 2TT, UK; [b]Department of Political Science and International Relations, University of Birmingham, Birmingham B15 2TT, UK; [c]Department of Business Administration, Technical University of Valencia, Spain

This article uses data from Sport England's Active People Survey (APS) to explore trends and demographic influences on participation in sporting and physical activities. On the basis of the analysis undertaken, this article considers the extent to which the APS data can be useful both to scholars of sport studies and to inform sport policymakers. Multivariate models are employed and a range of indicators of participation are utilized as dependent variables. These include participation in sport and exercise in general as well as participation in specific activities namely walking, cycling, swimming and athletics. The article concludes that analysis of the APS data can shed light on interesting trends and relationships that could assist an understanding of sport participation and inform policymakers.

Introduction and context

Our purpose in what follows is twofold: first, we discuss the context in which the Sport England Active People Survey (APS) has developed, including the need for quantifiable data to justify policy interventions; and second, we examine the usefulness of the APS data to sport scholars by considering whether the raw data can tell us anything of interest about sport participation in England. The first telephone interviews for APS began in 2005, the year when London was successful in its bid to host the 2012 Olympics. Aside from the star cast of ex-international athletes helping to deliver the bid, the 2012 team put forward one of the most ambitious legacy programmes ever. This included the widespread regeneration of a run-down area in East London, a commitment to providing sport facilities to the public post-Games and, crucially, a promise to increase participation in sport among the population as a result of staging the Games in London (the so-called Olympic Legacy). It is this latter legacy promise on which this article focuses. We are currently 2 years into the 5-year 'Promise 1 of Olympic Legacy Plan', the crux of which is to achieve the target of having two million more active citizens by 2012–2013 (March 2013) (National Audit Office (NAO) 2010, p. 15). The Department for Culture, Media and Sport (DCMS) is to deliver these two million extra participants via a Public Service Agreement (PSA) target with the Treasury. Sport England, an arms' length government agency charged with delivering grass-roots policy, has been given responsibility for one million of the two million more active citizens. The Legacy Plan has resulted in a major shift in sport policy post-2005, which has greatly affected the role Sport England plays in policy delivery.

Thus, in the wake of the successful Olympic bid, government sport policy shifted from a narrative focused on sport's wider benefit to society, to sport for sport's sake (DCMS 2008, Brookes and Wiggen 2009). At the same time, government drives for efficiency and accountability in the delivery of public services meant a new strategic role for Sport England to deliver on participation as part of the Olympic legacy. A Strategy Unit (formerly known as the Performance and Innovation Unit) was commissioned to advise the then Prime Minister (Tony Blair) and other government departments on an essential route map that would address the gaps and coherency in the Government's existing sport policy (DCMS/Strategy Unit 2002, p. 206). The publication of a new sport strategy *Game Plan: A Strategy for Delivering the Government's Sport and Physical Activity Objectives* (2002) sets out recommendations that focused on the development of grass-roots participation (in particular among economically disadvantaged young people, women and older people), high performance sport, mega sporting events and the delivery of organizational reform within sport. In order to address these governance issues, organizational reform and modernization became a key prerequisite of government funding for sport agencies (Grix and Phillpots 2011, DCMS/SU 2002, p. 12; on the modernization of sport in the United Kingdom, see Houlihan and Green (2009)).

In this context of modernization and reform, *Game Plan* pointed out the need for accurate and consistent data on participation rates in sport, in order for government to plan and allocate resources based on such information (DCMS/Strategy Unit 2002, p. 113). Nicholas Rowe, writing in this journal, suggested that Sport England played a major role in arguing for the need of more precise participation data to monitor public spending in sport (Rowe 2009, pp. 90–91). The result of this desire for more accurate data on sport participation has been a £5 million investment in the APS, the largest ever collection of data on participation in sport, memberships of clubs and participation in competitive sport. Several features of this survey are worth noting: first, its size. The annual sample size of 177,000 will create a very large data set from which participation rates can be tracked; also, the survey is 'evenly spread throughout a whole year' (Rowe 2009, p. 93), which helps avoid seasonal variation. In addition, Rowe also considered that this data set could effectively become a 'catalyst for transforming evidence-based sport policy' (2009, p. 89); given the paucity of accurate data on participation trends in the United Kingdom, this is to be lauded. The APS is already used, inter alia, as the key source for monitoring one of the new national indicators for Local Authorities and Local Authority partnerships, namely that for measuring adult sport and active recreation (usually abbreviated as N18; see Sport England, online, 22 June 2010).

In the 2005–2008 round of expenditure on sport activity, Sport England invested £660 million and saw overall sport participation among adults rise by 520,000. However, as the 2010 NAO report points out 'External factors, such as reactions to national sporting triumphs or the weather, may well have had an impact on participation levels ... there are inherent difficulties in demonstrating causation' (2010, p. 5). To avoid the difficulty of understanding which investment in what sport initiatives is responsible for increased participation, Sport England is relying on National Governing Bodies (NGBs) of sport to deliver its targets in the 2008–2013 funding round. Specific NGB targets are easier to monitor, which ought to make it clearer where any increases or decreases in participation lie.

Why the interest in sport participation?

It is easy to see why the government and other policy providers would be interested in accurate participation data. Participation in sport is, after all, seen as crucial to the health of the nation and the PSA target of getting one million more people doing three 30 min sessions of sport per week at a moderate level (from April 2008 to March 2011) is designed to achieve health gains among participants (NAO 2010, p. 4). The baseline for measuring Sport England's achievements and the increase in sport participation is the year 2008 in which some 16% of the population reached the '3 × 30 min' target (NAO 2010, p. 14). In a recent European Union comparison of participation in sport, the United Kingdom ranked 11th and 8th, respectively (out of 27) when comparing sport participation rates of once per week or more (participation 'with some regularity') and 5 times per week or more (participation 'regularly') (Eurobarometer 334 2010, p. 10). Interestingly, when comparing sports club membership, the United Kingdom slips to join 14th overall (with two other countries) with just 9% of those asked being members (Eurobarometer 334 2010, p. 26). This is important, because club membership usually translates into more frequent, and above all, more long-term, participation (see below).

The strongest evidence in support of getting more people to participate in sport relates to its intrinsic health benefits (Oughton and Tacon 2007). A large literature provides evidence that a lack of participation in sport and physical activity impacts negatively on health by reinforcing the occurrence of obesity and a number of chronic conditions such as cardio-vascular diseases and diabetes (Gratton and Tice 1989, Vuori and Fentem 1995, Gratton and Taylor 2005). Linked to this evidence, the European Commission (2007, p. 8) claims that the sport movement has a greater influence than any other social movement on participation in health-enhancing physical activity. While improvements in health potentially benefits the individual in terms of earnings and well-being, there are also wider economic benefits linked to productivity gains and lower costs of health care (Pratt *et al.* 2000, Wang *et al.* 2005). In the United Kingdom, these gains have been highlighted in *Game Plan* (DCMS and SU 2002), which concludes that the relation between sports participation and health is the main argument for government promotion of increased physical activity.

Participation in sport has also been claimed to enhance community cohesion through the development of social capital and social networks that support regeneration and inclusion (see Houlihan and Groeneveld 2010 for an overview). This potential for enhancing social cohesion by bonding social groups is arguably stronger in relation to participation in recreational team sports than in individual sports (Putman 2000). There may also be a role for sports volunteering in developing civic participation, and sports clubs may be able to contribute to social inclusion and development. Community cohesion is also thought to sustain social capital and Coalter (2007, p. 49) claims that it is this link that underpins a shift in policy from 'developing sport *in* communities to developing communities *through* sport'. However, he argues that the use of the concept of social capital in community-oriented initiatives (such as those of Sport England) is vague. Nevertheless, a wide range of programmes have been developed that attempt to use sport to pursue non-sport-related outcomes such as improvements in educational attainment, crime reduction and wider development aims including HIV/AIDS awareness.

Finally, many claim that participation is inextricably bound up with elite sport. There appears a tacit agreement among policymakers, politicians and sport stakeholders that the higher the participation in sport, the bigger the pool of talent from which future elite athletes will appear. The link between sport participation and elite sport is fraught with problems, not least a serious lack of evidence. Anecdotally, people often tend to cite a particular event, competition or sporting battle that inspired them to take up sport. Empirically, however, the link between success at performance sport and participation rates of the population has not been possible to prove. Rowe (2009, p. 96) argues slightly differently when he suggests that the APS data – under scrutiny here – will be able to contribute to elite sport by 'creating the right conditions that will drive talent development. . .', because the information gained will help focus strategy more sharply. This is not the same as saying that more participation will lead to better elite results, or that better elite results will lead to more participation, a virtuous cycle often underpinning politician's understanding of sport (Grix and Carmichael 2011).

The data

Given that our focus is on the 'raw' APS data, we will only comment briefly on the 'officially' published data. The latter offers sport scholars a wide range of indices with which to understand trends in sport participation, figures on people involved in competitions, club membership and so on. The data can be tracked from 2006 through to the latest at the time of writing, 2009. In a recent NAO report (2010) into Sport England's work on raising sport participation by one million more active citizens, it is perhaps surprising – in an otherwise critical text – not to find some discussion of the variables and categories used in the APS. An indicative example is that of 'athletics'. The initial results of the survey are very encouraging indeed. In the period 2008–2009, 'athletics' notched up an extremely impressive growth of some 128,000 participants. Club memberships for the same period was less impressive with the gains in people undertaking 'athletics' not translating into statistically significant numbers joining an athletics club. The link between those taking up 'athletics' as categorized by the APS and those joining athletics clubs is made difficult by virtue of the fact that they are effectively measuring different things: the definition of 'athletics' in the APS is very broad, including 'jogging' and 'road running', activities for which club membership is not essential. The increase recorded is most likely to come from those people citing 'jogging' and 'road running' as their 'athletics' activity, which in itself is a good thing; however, we need to be careful not to assume that the 0.27% increase recorded by the APS over the previous survey period (2007–2008) for athletics constitutes a boom for the no. 1 Olympic sport discipline.

The data

The data lend itself well to an examination of trends and demographic influences on participation in sporting and physical activities. At the time of writing, the raw data from the APS surveys were only available for 2 years; 2005–2006 and 2007–2008. The 2005–2006 data contain 363,724 observations, while the 2007–2008 data contain 191,325 observations. While the data from the 2008–2009 survey can be accessed in a limited way through the Sport England website, the data were not accessible through the ESRC Data Archive. They should be available at some point during 2011–2012. The 2009–2010 survey was ongoing at the time of writing.

The surveys ask about participation in sport and physical activity in general and a series of more detailed questions are repeated for all activities mentioned (271 activities, including walking and cycling, are covered in the surveys). In relation to each activity the respondent is asked about the frequency of participation in the last 4 weeks and the amount of time involved. The survey also asks whether any activity raised breathing rates and whether it made the respondent sweat or out of breath; if the respondent answers yes to these two questions, the activity is classified as moderate to vigorous. The answers to these questions are used to establish the Key Performance Indicator (KPI) of participation. This requires at least 30 min duration on three separate days each week to at least moderate intensity (interestingly, a person, say, cycling for 4 h on 2 days a week would fall outside this, but would obviously be as fit, if not fitter, than a person undertaking three sessions of 30 min at moderate intensity sport).

In relation to higher level sport participation specifically, the surveys ask a number of useful questions relating to club membership, participation in competition, tuition and coaching. Answers to these questions can be used to give a very approximate measure of participation at just below elite level. With the availability of additional years of data, it may therefore be possible to consider trends in, as well as determinants of, participation at higher levels of sport. Respondents are also asked specific questions about voluntary sports work and overall satisfaction with local provision. Both of these variables will be of interest to policymakers. Table 1 in Appendix 2 provides some detail on the participation-related variables that are available for analysis using the 2005–2006 and 2007–2008 surveys.

The survey additionally asks respondents for information on a range of demographic variables, including age, gender, ethnicity, home ownership, income, illness, disability, car ownership, employment status and occupational status (questions d1–d23). The survey also asks questions to determine the respondents' domiciliary location. The relationships between these variables and participation are interesting in their own right and their importance is well established in previous research (e.g. Collins 2003a,b, 2004, Coalter 2004, Rowe *et al.* 2004, Sport England 2004, Foster *et al.* 2005). However, since this evidence indicates that participation is dependent on a range of demographic influences, it also means that the usefulness of two-variable correlation analysis (between participation and individual variables of interest, such as, gender or class) is limited. Instead, multivariate methods are needed to control for the range of 'other' influences on participation. Failure to do so will result in omitted variable bias leading to over- or underestimation of the influence of the variable concerned (since the estimated influence of the variable will also measure indirect effects associated with excluded variables). The availability of the wide range of demographic data in the survey data means that, at least to some extent, such problems can be avoided. It also means that sampling differences between surveys can be explored.

Unfortunately, not all the data are comparable across surveys since some questions have not been repeated and some new questions have been introduced in the later surveys. For instance, only the first survey records ethnicity and only the later surveys ask whether the respondent would like to do more sport or physical activity and if so, which. The two most recent surveys additionally ask specific questions about activities relating to gardening and dancing which are treated as excluded categories in the first two surveys.

Empirical specification

The empirical analysis uses multivariate regression techniques and is conducted in two stages. In the first stage, we estimate participation equations for sport and exercise in general and participation in competition. We also estimate participation equations to determine club membership. In the second stage, we estimate participation equations for four specific activities; walking, cycling, athletics and swimming.

Appendix 1 describes the dependent and independent variables used in the analysis of the APS raw data and sets out the rationale for the estimation procedure.

Results

General participation, club membership and competition

The results of the estimation procedure are reported in Tables 4 and 5 in Appendix 2. Table 4 provides evidence on the relationship between broad indicators of participation in sports and physical activity and more qualitative indicators of activity, namely club membership, participation in competition and receipt of tuition or coaching. The figures in Columns 1–5 indicate that the odds of participating in any sports or physical activity (including or excluding walking and cycling) are *significantly higher for those respondents who were members of clubs, those who participated in competitions and those who had received coaching and training.* This is also true for participation in at least moderately intensive activities. For instance, the odds of participating in some, at least moderately intensive activities are higher by a factor of 3.59 (or 259%) for individuals who are members of a club (Column 3). The number of days in which at least moderate intensity sports and physical activity is undertaken is also higher for individuals who are members of clubs, those who participated in competitions and those who received coaching or training. This evidence can be interpreted as confirming that there is a positive link between participation in general and to at least moderate intensity and indicators of participation at just below elite level such as participation in competition, receipt of coaching and club membership.

In addition, the results show that respondents involved in volunteering were also more likely to have participated in sport themselves. Interestingly, for those who expressed satisfaction with the overall provision the odds of participating in some sports/physical activity were up to 29% higher (Column 3). Also of interest in these regressions is the sign and significance of the 2007–2008 survey year dummy variable (YEAR0708). This variable takes a significant and positive sign in estimations 1–4 in Table 4. These results suggest that after controlling for demographic influences (which will in part be due to differences in sampling) there appears to be an upward trend in general participation. However, the survey year dummy variable is not significant in estimation 5 in which the dependent variable indicates participation in at least moderate intensity activity on at least 3 days per week (MOD_3DYS). This evidence suggests that between 2005–2006 and 2007–2008 surveys data, there was no significant increase in the headline KP1 indicator for participation which requires eligible activities to be carried out on an average of at least three separate days each week. With only 2 years of data, this evidence can only be indicative. But when data from further survey years become available, it will be possible to consider such trends in a more systematic way.

The results additionally indicate that participation is in general negatively related to female gender. For example, the odds of participation in at least moderate activity are 15% lower for females (estimation 3). However, the gender gap in activity is narrower when walking and cycling are taken into account (estimation 1). Participation is also lower for those with health-limiting illnesses, but illness more generally is only negatively related to at least moderately intensive activities. In relation to tenure and relative to the reference category of owning a house through a mortgage, those renting a home are less likely to participate, but those owning their home outright are more likely to participate. Those who left full-time education below the age of 18 are also less likely to participate and in the subset of estimations (not reported) that include the educational dummy variables (available only for the 2005–2006 subsample) participation is related positively to educational attainment. Similarly for this subset of estimations, white (British or Irish) ethnicity is positively related to participation. In line with most previous research on participation in sport and exercise, participation is a decreasing function of age and an increasing function of occupational class (participation is highest for the professional classes and lowest for the unskilled).

The variables indicating employment status are relative to the reference category of full-time employment. The general pattern of odds ratios greater than 1 in estimation 1 indicates that when walking and cycling are included respondents in most other employment categories (e.g. those in part-time employment, the unemployed, students, the retired and those not working because they are looking after the home and/or children) are more likely to participate than those in full-time employment. When walking and cycling are excluded (estimation 2) or only at least moderate intensity activities are considered (estimation 3), only students and those in part-time employment are more likely to participate than the full-time employed. However, as well as students and part-time workers, the unemployed and the retired undertake at least moderate intensity activity more often than those in full time employment (estimations 4 and 5). These results suggest that people in full-time employment are deterred from participating due to time constraints. In addition, they can be taken to imply that the main activities undertaken by the unemployed and the retired are walking and/or cycling. Respondents without access to a car or van are more likely to participate when walking and cycling are included (estimation 1), but less likely to participate otherwise and they are less likely to participate in at least moderately intensive activities. This suggests, not unsurprisingly and as confirmed in Table 5 (estimations 1–4), that those without a car are more likely to walk or cycle.

Club membership and competition

The results presented in the last two columns of Table 4 (estimations 5 and 6) show that club membership and competition are positively related to each other as well as those receiving coaching and participation in sports volunteering. These results highlight the potential link between just below elite level activities (proxied by competition) and club membership and the potentially positive impact of coaching. Interestingly, the 2007–2008 survey year dummy variable is negatively related to club membership and participation in competition; the odds of club membership are 3% lower and the odds of competing are 7% lower in 2007–2008. The results also demonstrate a strong negative relationship between female gender and both club membership and, in particular, participation in competitive activities; the odds of club membership and participating in competition are 20% and 63% lower for females, respectively. These results relating to gender suggest that participation among the female population may be more tenuously related to elite performances at competition level.

Although not reported, while participation in competition declines with age, there is no significant difference between club membership for the 16–25 age group and most of the other age groups, the only exceptions being the 25–34 age group who are more likely to belong to a club and the 55–64 age group who are marginally less likely to be club members. Those with an illness are more likely to be club members, but not if their health limits their activities. In relation to employment status, retired people are more likely than either full-time workers or students to belong to a club, but full-time workers are more likely than part-time workers and those not working to be club members. Full-time workers are also more likely than any other group to be involved in competitive activities. Alongside the results in Columns 1–5 this suggests that while full-time workers are less likely to participate relative to either part-time workers or those not working, those who are active are more likely to be club members and involved in competition.

Leaving school before the age of 18 is negatively related to club membership but insignificantly related to participation in competition. Club membership increases with occupational class but those in the managerial and technical and skilled non-manual classes are the most likely to be involved in competitions (more so than professional workers). In the subset of regressions estimated for 2005–2006 only (not reported) higher educational attainment is positively related to club membership but mostly insignificantly or only weakly significantly related to competing. Perhaps more surprisingly in this subset of estimations, white (British or Irish) ethnicity is negatively related to club membership although it is positively related to participation in competition.

Walking, cycling, swimming and athletics

Table 5 reports the results of estimating participation in the four illustrative categories of walking, cycling, swimming and athletics. The results follow a similar pattern to those in Table 4 but with some notable differences. In particular female gender is positively related to walking and swimming. In addition, and as indicated in Table 4, lack of access to a car/van is positively related to participation in both walking and cycling but not the number of days walked. A further notable result is that participation in swimming is negatively related to competition and insignificantly related to coaching. The negative influence of the 2007–2008 survey year dummy in estimations 5 and 6 in Table 5 suggests that the number of people swimming has declined; the odds of participating in swimming were 6% lower in 2007–2008. Of interest is the result that the odds of participating in swimming are significantly higher for those with an illness, but having an illness that limits activity is negatively related to swimming. Although participation was found to decline with age, the odds of participating in swimming are 1.5% higher for those between 35 and 44 compared with the reference age group of 16–25 (not reported).

As indicated in Table 2, only 0.4% of the sample participates in either track or field athletics or track running. However, the results in Table 5 (estimations 7 and 8) indicate that participation in athletics has increased between the two sample periods. Club membership, competing, receipt of coaching and volunteering are all positively related to participation in athletics. Neither gender, tenure nor occupational class, impacts on the odds of participating in athletics. Not having access to a car is positively related to participation in athletics. Relative to full-time workers, part-time employment status, retirement and not-working because of home, child or caring responsibilities are negatively related to participation in athletics. Students and the unemployed are no more or less likely to participate in athletics than full-time workers. Not surprisingly, age is negatively related to participation in athletics and observations for people over 85 had to be dropped from the logistic analysis since they predicted non-participation perfectly.

Summary

The Sport England APS data are a useful resource for exploring the demographic determinants of participation in sport and physical activity. With only 2 years of raw data available to this study, the analysis reported here was, of necessity, quite limited. Nevertheless, the results presented indicate the strength of the relationship between participation and influences that are potentially responsive to policy interventions such as club membership, coaching and volunteering. In addition, the analysis reaffirms the importance of the role of demographic variables such as gender, occupational class and employment status. As additional years of data become available, the survey should also be able to facilitate invaluable investigation of trends in participation while enabling researchers to investigate and control for demographic influences.

Potentially, the data relating to participation in competitions, club membership, tuition and coaching will be useful for exploring trends in, as well as the determinants of, participation in activities at club and competition levels. Additional years of data extending beyond the 2012 Olympics may also make it possible to analyse the relationship between success in specific sports at the elite level and participation by the general public (and vice versa). To facilitate this exploration, it might also be helpful to include additional qualitative questions relating to respondents' perceptions of elite sports and elite sports men and women and how they have reacted or might react to success at the elite level. Additionally, it could be useful to know whether respondents have won any of the competitions they have participated in and at what level they were competing. However, even with the inclusion of these or similar questions, it is likely to remain difficult to establish whether there are any direct links between elite sports and participation among the wider public.

As Coalter (2007, p. 89) has rightly noted, the evaluation of sports based initiatives is far from easy given the 'problems associated with simple correlations, intervening variables and attribution. . .'. This is undoubtedly true in relation to any early evaluation of the usefulness of the APS data as undertaken here. However, we have attempted to show that even the relatively limited data gathered so far by the APS can be used to understand some relationships between important variables. One such example could be club membership and participation rates in sport: perhaps more emphasis ought to be placed on getting people into organized clubs, than on ad-hoc participation in sport and physical activity.

As the survey is continued, it is likely that the APS 'raw' data will become even more useful to scholars of sport studies seeking to understand the relationships between factors that hinder and enhance participation in sport.

References

Brookes, S. and Wiggan, J., 2009. Reflecting the public value of sport: a game of two halves? *Public management review*, 11 (4), 401–420.

Coalter, F., 2004. Future sports or future challenges to sport? *In*: Sport England, ed. *Driving up participation: the challenge for sport*. London: UK Sport 80–86.

Coalter, F., 2007. *A wider social role for sport. Who's keeping the score?* Oxford: Routledge.

Collins, M.F., 2003a. *Sport and social exclusion*. London: Routledge.

Collins, M.F., 2003b. Do we still believe in sport for all? *Recreation*, 62 (1), 32–35.

Collins, M.F., 2004. Sports participation in decline? *Recreation*, 63 (9), 26–28.

Department of Culture, Media and Sport (DCMS), 2002. *Game plan: a strategy for delivering Government's sport and physical activity objectives*. London: Cabinet Office.

Department of Culture, Media and Sport (DCMS), 2008. *Playing to win: a new era for sport*. London: DCMS.

Eurobarometer 334, 2010. *Sport and physical activity*. Brussels: European Commission.

European Commission, 2007. *White Paper on sport*. Luxembourg: European Commission.

Foster, C., *et al.*, 2005. *Understanding participation in sport: a systematic review*. London: Sport England.

Gratton, C. and Taylor, P., 2005. *The economics of sport and recreation*. London: Taylor and Francis.

Gratton, C. and Tice, A., 1989. Sports participation and health. *Leisure Studies*, 8 (1), 77–92.

Grix, J. and Carmichael, F., 2011. Why do governments invest in elite sport? A polemic. *International journal of sport policy and politics*, 4 (1), 73–90.

Grix, J. and Phillpots, L., 2011. Revisiting the 'governance narrative': 'asymmetrical network governance' and the deviant case of the sport policy sector. *Public policy and administration*, 26 (1), 3–19.

Houlihan, B. and Green, M., 2009. Modernization and sport: the reform of sport England and UK sport. *Public administration*, 87 (3), 678–698.

Houlihan, B. and Groeneveld, M., 2010. 'Social capital, governance and sport'. In: M. Groeneveld, F. Ohl, and B. Houlihan, eds. Social capital and sport governance. Routledge London, 1–20.

National Audit Office (NAO), 2010. *Increasing participation in sport*. London: The Stationary Office, House of Commons.

Oughton, C. and Tacon, R., 2007. *Sports contribuition to achieving wider social benefits* [online], Department of Culture Media and Sport Report No. DEP2008-0406. Available from: http://www.parliament.uk/deposits/depositedpapers/2008/DEP2008-0406.doc [Accessed 28 January 2012].

Pratt, M., Macera, C.A., and Wang, G., 2000. Higher direct medical costs associated with physical inactivity. *Physician and sportsmedicine*, 28 (10), 63–80.

Putman, R.D., 2000. *Bowling alone: the collapse and revival of the American community*. New York: Simon & Schuster.

Rowe, N., Adams, R., and Beasley, N., 2004. *Driving up participation in sport: the social context, trends, the prospects and the challenges. In*: Sport England, ed. *Driving up participation: the challenge for sport*. London: UK Sport, 6–13.

Rowe, N.F., 2009. The Active People Survey: a catalyst for transforming evidence-based sport policy in England. *International journal of sport policy*, 1 (1), 89–98.

Sport England, 2004. *A framework for sport in England*. London: Sport England.

Vuori, I. and Fentem, P., 1995. *Health: position paper*. Strasbourg: Council of Europe.

Wang, G., Macera, C., and Scudder-Soucie, B., 2005. A cost-benefit analysis of physical activity using bike/pedestrian trial. *Health promotion practice*, 6 (2), 174–179.

Appendix 1. Variables and estimation procedure

Dependent variables

In order to explore the determination of participation in sports and physical activity, five dependent variables measuring non-specific participation were selected (see Tables 1 and 2 in Appendix 2). SPORTEX_ALL is a dichotomous variable (i.e. a variable that only has two categories) taking the value 1 if the individual has participated in any sport or physical exercise activity, including walking and cycling in the previous 4 weeks. It takes the value 0 otherwise. SPORT_OTH is a similarly specified variable but only takes the value one if the individual participated in an activity other than walking or cycling. SPORT_MOD takes the value one if the individual participated in some activity, including walking and cycling, to at least moderate intensity (for 30 min) and takes the value 0 otherwise. 3DYS_MOD is another dichotomous variable and takes the value one if the individual participated in some moderately intensive activity for at least 3 days a week. DYS_MOD is a continuous variable indicating the number of days in the last 4 weeks the individual participated in some activity to at least moderate activity.

In order to explore the determination of participation in higher level sport, we also selected two dependent variables indicating club membership and participation in competition: CLUB and COMPETE. Both variables are dichotomous. CLUB takes the value 1 if the respondent has been a member of a club in order to participate in sport or recreational activities during the last 4 weeks. COMPETE takes the value 1 if the individual took part in organized competition in the last 12 months.

To explore participation in more depth, we selected four illustrative activities; walking, cycling, swimming (indoor and outdoor swimming and diving) and athletics (field and track athletics and track running); similar analysis could be conducted for any of the other activities recorded in the data. Walking, cycling and swimming were selected on the basis of their popularity. Athletics was selected on the basis of its potential relevance for the 2012 Olympics. Participation in walking is measured by the dependent variables WALK30 and DYS_WALK. The former takes the value 1 if the respondent has walked for at least 30 min continuously during the previous 4 weeks (0 otherwise). The latter records the number of days walked for at least 30 min during the 4-week period. The equivalent measures for cycling are CYCLE30 and DYS_CYCLE. The dependent variables measuring participation in swimming are SWIM and DYS_SWIM. The former indicates participation in indoor or outdoor swimming or diving and takes the value one or zero. DYS_SWIM records the number of days the participant took part in either swimming or diving during the 4-week period. The equivalent dependent variables indicating participation in athletics are ATHLET and DYS_ATH.

Full definitions and summary statistics for all the dependent variables used in the analysis are given in Table A2 in Appendix 2. The data indicate that 80% of the sample participated in some sports or physical activity including walking and cycling (the latter for at least 30 min). In total 78% of respondents completed at least one 30 min walk in a 4-week period and 11% completed a 30 min cycle ride. Excluding walking and cycling the participation rate falls to 45%. Only 50% of the sample population undertook some activity (excluding walking and cycling) to at least moderate intensity at least once in a 4-week period. The average number of days that respondents participated in activities to at least moderate intensity in a 4-week period is 6.4. However, only 21% of the sample undertook some moderate activity at least 3 times a week. The data can be interpreted as suggesting that 25% of the public are members of sports and fitness-related clubs and 18% receive coaching or training but only

14% participate in competitions. For comparison it is interesting to note that the Eurobarometer sport participation survey results (2010) suggest that 23% of the United Kingdom (i.e. not just England) are members of sports clubs and health or fitness clubs (Eurobarometer 334 2010, 26); 14% of the 23% were members of 'health or fitness' clubs, which may explain the discrepancy in the APS between club membership (25%) and taking part in competitions (14%). In the APS 7% of the sample were involved in sports volunteering work

Independent variables

In the estimation procedure, we explore the relationship between more recreation-based activities and higher level sport, by including COACHED and VOLUNT as independent variables. COACHED takes the value 1 if the individual received coaching or tuition during the last 12 months (and 0 otherwise). VOLUNT takes the value 1 if the individual was involved in any sport-related voluntary activity in the last 4 weeks. CLUB and COMPETE are also included in estimations where they are not dependent variables.

To control for perceptions relating to the availability of facilities, we additionally include SATIS as an independent variable. This is another dichotomous variable taking the value 1 if the individual says that they are satisfied with the sports provision in their area. The variable LIKEMORE is a related measure of satisfaction and indicates whether the individual would like to undertake more sports or recreational activity. However, it is not available from the 2005–2006 data and is therefore only included in a subset of estimations (not reported) that utilize only the data for 2007–2008 (these estimations include an indicator of actual age rather than dummy variables for age bands since actual age was not available in the 2004–2005 data).

The other independent variables in these estimations include a survey year dummy variable, YEAR0708, and a range of demographic indicators. The year dummy variable is included to control for the survey year and explore differences in participation over the 2 years of the survey. With the availability of additional years of data, this variable will become more important and will enable the investigation of trends in participation. The demographic variables are included mainly as controls in order to try and establish the sign and significance of the relationships between participation and the variables indicating club membership, participation in competition, receipt of coaching and volunteering. It is also interesting to explore whether there are differences in the influences of these variables on the alternative measures of participation. The demographic variables include indicators of age bands, age at which left full-time education, gender, occupational class, employment status, health status, and access to private transport. Unfortunately, indicators of educational attainment and ethnicity are only available for the 2005–2006 data set. These were included in a subset of estimations (not reported) utilizing the 2005–2006 data only. Indicators of income are available only for a limited set of observations. A subset of estimations was estimated for this restricted subsample but is not reported. Full definitions and summary statistics for these independent variables are provided in Table 3 in Appendix 2.

Estimation methods

For the dichotomous dependent variables, taking either the value 1 or 0 the ordinary least squares method is unlikely to be appropriate due to non-normality of the error term and the possibility that the estimated values lie outside the 0–1 range. Instead, we estimate a logit specification that is based on the normal cumulative distribution function. In Tables 4 and 5, the reported figures for the logit estimations are odds ratios; the ratio of the probability of observing a positive outcome (the dependent variable equals 1) to the probability of a negative one (the dependent variable equals 0). For a unit change in the independent variable, the reported odds ratio measures the expected factor change in the odds (holding all the other variables constant).

The dependent variables measuring the number of days of participation in at least moderate intensity sport and exercise (DYS_MOD) and the number of days of participation in walking, swimming or athletics are continuous variables with a minimum value of 0 and a maximum value of 28. Since these variables are truncated, the standard censored regression model (tobit) is utilized rather ordinary least squares. The latter could only be estimated by omitting the zero and maximum values which would lead to biased and inconsistent results. The tobit procedure overcomes these problems by using maximum likelihood methods to obtain the reported parameter estimates.

Appendix 2

Table 1. Summary of available participation measures.

Question numbers	Variable definition (all relate to previous 4 weeks unless stated)
1	At least one 5 min walk
2	At least one 30 min walk
5	Number of days walked for health/recreation
6	At least one 30 min cycle ride
7	Number of days cycled for at least 30 min
9	Any other sporting or recreational physical activity
10a001 to 10a271	Undertook a specified activity for example, indoor/outdoor swimming/diving (10a3–4); field/track athletics/track running (10a70–71); cycling (10a008); walking (10a146)
11_001–11_271	Number of days participated in specified activity
12_001–12_271	Usual amount of time participated in specified activity
13_001–13_271	Effort usually enough to raise breathing rate when undertaking specified activity
14_001–14_271	Effort usually enough to make sweat or out of breath when undertaking specified activity
15 (15_all)	How many days participated in any activity to at least moderate level (activities that raised breathing rate and some activities considered automatically of moderate intensity) for at least 30 min (includes walking and cycling)
15 and 15_all_KPI	At least 3 days a week × 30 min at least moderate participation (includes walking and cycling)
16 and KPI3	Member of club so that can participate in sports or recreational physical activities
16b1–16b5	Type of club: Health and Fitness; social; sports; other; other
16a1–16a271	Undertook a specified activity as member of a sports club for example, swimming (16a1–4); Tennis (16a65); Athletics (16a70–71); Running (16a74–76)
17 and KPI4	Received tuition or coaching (in specified activity in last 12 months; 1–271)
17a1–17a271	Received tuition or coaching in specified activity in last 12 months; 1–271
18 and KPI5	Took part in any organized competition in last 12 months
18a1–18a271	Took part in any organized competition in last 12 months in specified activity: 1–271
19	Participated in voluntary sports work
20 and 20_all_KPI	Participated in voluntary sports work for at least 1 h a week to support sport
21_ spss and KPI6)	Overall satisfaction with sports provided in area
22	Would you like to do more sport/recreational physical activity
23	Which sport/recreational physical activity would you most like to do or do more often?

Table 2. Participation variables: definitions, number of observations and means.

Variable	Observations	Mean	Max	Min
SPORTEX_ALL; participated in any sport/physical activity (includes walking/cycling for ≥30 min) in last 4 weeks (constructed from questions 2, 6 and 9)	554,076	0.8	1	0
SPORT_XWC; participated in any sport/physical activity excluding walking/cycling in last 4 weeks	551,391	0.45	1	0
SPORT_MOD; participated in any activity to at least moderate intensity in last 4 weeks	549,676	0.5	1	0
DYS_MOD; no. of days participated in at least moderate activity in 4 weeks	549,676	5.69	28	0
3DYS_MOD; participated in at least moderate activity for at least 3 days a week (in last 4 weeks)	549,676	0.21	1	0
CLUB; member of club to participate in sports/physical activity	554,966	0.25	1	0
COMPETE; took part in organized competition in last year	554,911	0.14	1	0
WALK30; walked for ≥30 min in last 4 weeks	548,462	0.71	1	0
DYS_WALK; no. of days walked for ≥30 min in last 4 weeks	544,848	5.38	28	1
CYCLE30; cycled for ≥30 min in last 4 weeks	554,960	0.11	1	0
DYS_CYCLE; no. of days cycled for ≥30 min in last 4 weeks	554,685	0.72	28	0
SWIM; participated in indoor/outdoor swimming/diving in last 4 weeks	555,049	0.13	1	0
DYS_SWIM; no. of days swam/dived in last 4 weeks	555,045	0.82	28	0
ATHLET; participated in field/track athletics or track running	555,049	0.004	1	0
DYS_ATH; no. of days participated in field/track athletics or track running	555,017	0.03	28	0
COACHED; received coaching/tuition in last year	554,850	0.18	1	0
VOLUNT; participated in sports volunteering in last 4 wks	551,539	0.07	1	0
SATIS; satisfied with sports provision (answered yes to question 21_spss)	479,762	0.69	1	0
LIKEMORE; would like to do more sports/recreational activity (answered yes question 22)	98,230	0.52	1	0

Table 3. Demographic variables: definitions, number of observations and means (medians).

Variable	Definition	Observations	Mean
YEAR0708	Dummy variable equals 1 if observation is from the 2007–2008 data set 0 otherwise	555,049	0.345
FEMALE	Female respondent (0 otherwise)	555,049	0.587
AGE	Age (2007–2008 onwards only)	555,049	50.34
AGEBAND1–8	Dummy variables indicating age bands (16–25; 25–34; 35–44; 45–54; 55–64; 65–74; 75–84; 85+; youngest age band, AGEBAND1, is control)	555,049	3.97 (median = 45–54; mode = 55–64)
WHITE_br_ir	Respondents ethnic group is white British or Irish (2005–2006 only)	3,637,245	0.905
LEFTED_LS18	Left full-time education at age under 18	528,049	0.559
RENT	Dummy variable indicating tenure; Rents home	541,507	0.221
OWN_HOUSE	Dummy variable indicating tenure; Owns own home outright	541,507	0.363
MORTGAGE	Dummy variable indicating tenure; Owns own home with mortgage (modal and reference category)	541,507	0.405
NOCAR	No access to car or van in household	549,711	0.178
ILLNESS	Has a long-standing illness/disability/infirmity	548,612	0.242
HLTH_LIMITS	Illness limits activities	548,612	0.168
FULLTIME	Dummy variable indicating works full time (modal category and control)	546,753	0.422
PARTTIME	Dummy variable indicating works part time	546,753	0.155
UNEMP	Dummy variable indicating unemployed	546,753	0.043
RETIRED	Dummy variable indicating retired	546,753	0.261
STUDENT	Dummy variable indicating student	546,753	0.038
NOTWRK_L	Dummy variable indicating not working looking after house/child	555,049	0.05
NOTWRK_C	Dummy variable indicating; not working looking after long term sick or disabled other	555,049	0.025
EMP_OTH	Dummy variable indicating employment status is 'other'	555,049	0.006
INCOME1–11 (limited availability in all years)	Dummy variables indicating annual household income band (highest income band ≥£5200 is INCOME11 is modal and reference category in subset of regressions)	272,589	5.92 (median = band 6; £26,000–31,199)
SOCSTAT1–6	Dummy variable indicates SEG occupation class; 1 is professional etc; 2 is managerial or technical; 3 is skilled non-manual; 4 is skilled manual; 5 is partly skilled; 6 is unskilled (control)	555,049	(median is class 3; mode is class 2)
EDUC1–10 (2005–2006 only)	Dummy variables indicating level of educational attainment (EDUC1 is higher education, degree or equiv; EDUC2 is other higher level below degree; EDUC3 is A level equiv; EDUC4 is trade apprenticeships; EDUC5 is gcse/o a*-c 5 or more; EDUC6 is gcse/o less than 5 a*-c; EDUC7 is other quals; EDUC8 is no qualifications; EDUC9 is not yet finished school; EDUC10 is never went to school (control is EDUC8)	363,724	3.76 (median level is EDUC3; mode is EDUC1)

Table 4. Participation in all activities, club membership and competition.

Independent	Dependent variable (estimation procedure)						
	1. SPORTEX_ALL (logit)	2. SPORT_OTH (logit)	3. SPORT_MOD (logit)	4. DYS_MOD (tobit)	5. 3DYS_MOD (logit)	6. CLUB (logit)	7. COMPETE (logit)
YEAR0708	1.09*** (0.01)	1.07*** (0.01)	1.07*** (0.01)	0.15*** (0.04)	1.01 (0.1)	0.97*** (0.01)	0.93*** (0.1)
CLUB	2.93*** (0.04)	5.89*** (0.06)	3.59*** (0.03)	6.62*** (0.05)	2.52*** (0.2)		4.53*** (0.05)
COMPETE	2.04*** (0.04)	2.4*** (0.03)	1.62*** (0.02)	2.95*** (0.06)	1.52*** (0.2)	4.54*** (0.05)	–
COACHED	1.86*** (0.03)	2.24*** (0.02)	2.06*** (0.02)	3.86*** (0.05)	1.69*** (0.2)	3.95*** (0.04)	1.85*** (0.02)
VOLUNT	1.24*** (0.03)	1.07*** (0.21)	1.27*** (0.02)	1.76*** (0.08)	1.27*** (0.1)	1.98*** (0.03)	2.99*** (0.04)
SATIS	1.23*** (0.01)	1.37*** (0.01)	1.29*** (0.01)	1.17*** (0.5)	1.22*** (0.1)	1.46*** (0.01)	1.06*** (0.01)
FEMALE	0.98** (0.01)	0.94*** (0.01)	0.85*** (0.01)	−0.53*** (0.05)	0.97*** (0.1)	0.8*** (0.01)	0.37*** (0.01)
LEFTED_LS18	0.75 (0.01)	0.81*** (0.01)	0.73*** (0.01)	−1.64*** (0.05)	0.83*** (0.1)	0.83*** (0.01)	0.99 (0.01)
OWN_HOUSE	1.19*** (0.02)	1.03*** (0.01)	1.09*** (0.01)	1.04*** (0.06)	1.18*** (0.1)	1.1*** (0.01)	1.05*** (0.01)
RENT	0.89*** (0.02)	0.88*** (0.01)	0.81*** (0.01)	−0.87*** (0.06)	0.93 (0.1)	0.79*** (0.01)	0.88*** (0.01)
ILLNESS	0.98 (0.02)	0.98 (0.01)	0.91*** (0.01)	−0.29*** (0.08)	0.98*** (0.2)	1.03*** (0.02)	0.92*** (0.02)
HLTH LIMITS	0.4*** (0.01)	0.65*** (0.01)	0.54*** (0.01)	−4.39*** (0.1)	0.57*** (0.1)	0.74*** (0.01)	0.73*** (0.02)
NOCAR	1.12*** (0.01)	0.76*** (0.01)	0.80*** (0.01)	−1.28*** (0.07)	0.89*** (0.1)	0.75*** (0.01)	0.67*** (0.01)
PTTIME	1.23*** (0.02)	1.06*** (0.01)	1.07*** (0.01)	0.48*** (0.06)	1.04*** (0.1)	0.91*** (0.01)	0.91*** (0.01)
UNEMP	1.21*** (0.04)	1.04 (0.03)	1.0 (0.03)	0.79*** (0.15)	1.11*** (0.3)	0.78*** (0.02)	0.84*** (0.03)
RETIRED	1.11*** (0.02)	1.01 (0.01)	0.96*** (0.01)	0.39*** (0.09)	1.17*** (0.2)	1.18*** (0.02)	0.97 (0.02)
STUDENT	1.51*** (0.18)	1.23 *** (0.1)	1.28*** (0.1)	1.53*** (0.44)	1.25*** (0.09)	1.05 (0.09)	0.72 (0.08)
NOTWRK_L	1.16*** (0.03)	0.91*** (0.02)	0.88*** (0.01)	−0.26*** (0.1)	1.0 (0.2)	0.81*** (0.02)	0.66*** (0.02)
NOTWRK_C	0.53*** (0.01)	0.7*** (0.02)	0.59*** (0.02)	−3.2*** (0.18)	0.74*** (0.3)	0.81*** (0.03)	0.51*** (0.03)
EMP_OTH	1.01 (0.06)	0.9*** (0.04)	0.91*** (0.04)	−0.22 (0.28)	1.02 (0.5)	0.9** (0.05)	0.82*** (0.06)
AGEBAND2–8	Included	Included	Included	Included	Included	Included	Included
SOCSTAT1–5	Included	Included	Included	Included	Included	Included	Included
No. of obs.	415,972	414,012	412,945	412,945	412,945	416,566	416,566
LL ratio χ²	50,283***	123,440***	104,209.4***	96,447.27***	49,022.35***	82,169.42***	70,563.32***
Pseudo R²	0.135	0.213	0.1829	0.0464	0.111	0.1681	0.2

Notes: Reported figures are odds ratios for logit estimations and coefficients for tobit estimations (constant included in tobit estimation); standard errors in parentheses.
*** and ** Indicate statistically significant at 1% and 5% levels, respectively.

Table 5. Participation in walking, cycling, swimming and athletics.

Independent	Dependent variable (estimation procedure)							
	1. WALK30 (logit)	2. DYS_WALK (tobit)	3. CYCLE30 (logit)	4. DYS_CYCLE (tobit)	5. SWIM (logit)	6. DYS_SWIM (tobit)	7. ATHLET (logit)	8. DYS_ATH (tobit)
YEAR0708	1.05*** (0.01)	0.39*** (0.05)	1.05*** (0.01)	0.24*** (0.08)	0.94*** (0.01)	-0.35*** (0.05)	1.17*** (0.06)	1.26*** (0.44)
CLUB	1.12*** (0.01)	0.49*** (0.05)	1.21*** (0.01)	1.36*** (0.09)	1.96*** (0.02)	4.1*** (0.06)	2.18*** (0.13)	6.1*** (0.49)
COMPETE	1.17*** (0.01)	1.15*** (0.07)	1.28*** (0.02)	1.99*** (0.1)	0.75 *** (0.01)	-1.62*** (0.07)	2.14*** (0.08)	6.14*** (0.51)
COACHED	1.26*** (0.01)	1.3*** (0.06)	1.23*** (0.02)	1.39*** (0.09)	1.01 (0.01)	0.15** (0.06)	1.84*** (0.12)	3.41*** (0.47)
VOLUNT	1.26*** (0.02)	1.54*** (0.08)	1.42*** (0.01)	2.52*** (0.12)	1.13*** (0.02)	0.62*** (0.08)	1.19*** (0.07)	5.33*** (0.56)
SATIS	1.08*** (0.01)	0.53*** (0.05)	1.05*** (0.01)	0.28*** (0.08)	1.28*** (0.01)	1.3*** (0.05)	0.94 (0.06)	1.29*** (0.47)
FEMALE	1.14*** (0.01)	1.3*** (0.05)	0.5*** (0.01)	-5.27*** (0.08)	1.90*** (0.02)	3.33*** (0.06)	0.79*** (0.05)	-0.68 (0.47)
LEFTED_LS18	0.79** (0.01)	-0.95*** (0.05)	0.83*** (0.02)	-1.16*** (0.08)	0.77*** (0.01)	-1.32*** (0.08)	0.77*** (0.01)	-2.08*** (0.47)
OWN_HOUSE	1.21*** (0.01)	1.09*** (0.06)	1.07*** (0.01)	0.76*** (0.1)	1.04*** (0.01)	0.35*** (0.7)	1.09 (0.08)	0.4 (0.58)
RENT_	0.96 (0.01)	-0.59*** (0.06)	0.86*** (0.01)	-0.75*** (0.1)	0.89*** (0.01)	-0.58*** (0.7)	0.99 (0.07)	0.75*** (0.1)
ILLNESS	0.98* (0.01)	0.32*** (0.08)	0.87*** (0.02)	-0.91*** (0.15)	1.09*** (0.02)	0.52*** (0.09)	0.77** (0.1)	0.09 (0.58)
HLTH_LIMITS	0.48*** (0.01)	-3.92*** (0.1)	0.69*** (0.02)	-2.55*** (0.19)	0.82*** (0.02)	-1.1*** (0.11)	0.61** (0.12)	-2.38** (1.0)
NOCAR	1.23*** (0.01)	-1.7*** (0.07)	1.12*** (0.02)	1.92*** (0.12)	0.74*** (0.01)	-1.65*** (0.08)	0.74*** (0.01)	-3.74*** (1.42)
PTTIME	1.28*** (0.02)	1.27*** (0.06)	1.24*** (0.02)	1.16*** (0.01)	1.25*** (0.02)	1.01*** (0.07)	0.76*** (0.06)	-2.46** (0.63)
UNEMP	1.32*** (0.04)	1.6*** (0.16)	1.12*** (0.04)	0.62*** (0.24)	1.08** (0.03)	0.32* (0.17)	0.91 (0.15)	-0.57 (1.35)
RETIRED	1.22*** (0.02)	2.96*** (0.09)	0.92*** (0.03)	-0.78*** (0.17)	1.14*** (0.02)	0.69*** (0.1)	0.37*** (0.08)	-13.18*** (1.27)
STUDENT	1.55*** (0.14)	1.88*** (0.47)	1.48*** (0.14)	2.03*** (0.69)	1.18* (0.01)	0.73 (0.48)	1.29 (0.5)	2.93 (3.19)
NOTWRK_L	1.36*** (0.03)	1.71*** (0.1)	0.95*** (0.03)	-0.9*** (0.18)	1.2*** (0.02)	0.87*** (0.11)	0.6*** (0.09)	-3.93*** (1.11)
NOTWRK_C	0.6*** (0.1)	-0.92*** (0.17)	0.58*** (0.03)	-3.94*** (0.34)	0.86*** (0.03)	-0.77*** (0.19)	0.3*** (0.15)	-8.09** (3.44)
EMP_OTH	1.18*** (0.06)	1.89*** (0.28)	1.01 (0.07)	-0.12 (0.48)	1.11* (0.06)	0.56* (0.03)	0.69 (0.28)	-4.67 (3.29)
AGEBAND2–8	Included	Included	Included	Included	Included	Included	Included	Included
SOCSTAT1–5	Included	Included	Included	Included	Included	Included	Included	Included
No. of observations	413,103	413,103	416,529	416,368	416,566	416,563	412,867	416,540
LL ratio χ^2	22,451***	14.558.75***	21,115.52***	20,879.2***	22,946.74***	22,301.84***	2177.01***	2128.06***
Pseudo R^2	0.0468	0.007	0.0717	0.0367	0.0622	0.03	0.1064	0.0723

Notes: Reported figures are odds ratios for logit estimations and coefficients for tobit estimations (constant included in tobit estimation); standard errors in parentheses; ***, ** and *Indicate statistically significant at 1%, 5% and 10% levels, respectively.

Can viewing London 2012 influence sport participation? – a viewpoint based on relevant theory

Ian David Boardley

School of Education, University of Birmingham, Birmingham, B15 2TT, UK

Sport England has been given the responsibility of delivering a mass participation legacy for sport from the London 2012 games. Delivering such a legacy will require a change in motivation for sport participation in the general public; one way this could be influenced is through a demonstration effect stimulated by media coverage of the 2012 games. This article has two purposes: first, to introduce to sport-policy scholars aspects of theories relevant to sport participation; second, to use this material to discuss the potential impact of viewing the 2012 games on viewers' sport motivation, and therefore stimulate debate around this topic. The outcome of this theoretical investigation suggests there is some potential for at least a short-term positive effect of viewing the 2012 games on sport motivation.

Introduction

The research process often begins with a problem that is subsequently addressed via appropriate methodology and subsequent data analysis. However, conclusions drawn from such an approach to the investigation of changes in sport participation as a result of the 2012 games would come too late to inform policy decisions affecting the London Games. An alternative approach is to use existing theory to investigate the potential impact of future events on sport participation. This article does this by introducing and applying relevant theory to the issue of whether the 2012 games is likely to influence the sport motivation of the general public. The aim of this article is not to make categorical statements regarding the influence that viewing the 2012 games will definitely have, but to stimulate debate around this subject and discuss policy decisions that may be informed by the issues raised.

Increased mass participation in sport leads to an increase in the health of the nation. This is the assumption that appears to be driving considerable government interest in promoting sport participation in the United Kingdom. Both the National Audit Office (2010) and the government's *Game Plan* sports strategy (Department for Culture, Media and Sport (DCMS)/Strategy Unit 2002) explicitly link mass sport participation and the overall health of the nation. Tied in with this belief is the government's interest in using the 2012 games as a vehicle to stimulate increased participation in sport in the United Kingdom.

Hugh Robertson, the current UK Government Minister for Sport and the Olympics, has stated that delivering a mass participation legacy for sport from the 2012 games is one of his three top priorities (Robertson 2010). Robertson (2010) defined a mass participation legacy for sport as '. . . a marked, and sustained, cultural shift toward greater participation in sport' and has informed Sport England that along with supporting sports governing bodies through the Whole Sport Plans, delivering a mass participation sports legacy from London 2012 is one of its two clear priorities.

The DCMS has a considerable task if it is to achieve the targets set for increased sport participation in the United Kingdom. The specific target set was to have 2 million more active citizens by 2012–2013 (National Audit Office 2010). Although Robertson (2010) asserted that Sport England would focus primarily on improving facility provision and delivering sport at a community level in order to deliver this sports legacy, it is likely the DCMS is also relying on the 2012 games facilitating an increase in sport participation via more direct means. A more direct impact could derive from what has been termed a demonstration effect. Demonstration effects are processes by which people are inspired to participate in sport through observation of elite sport, sports people or sports events (Hindson *et al.* 1994, Hogan and Norton 2000). Although it is difficult to verify whether such effects exist, the intuitive appeal of demonstration effects has led to their widespread acceptance (Stewart *et al.* 2005).

The assumed existence of demonstration effects appears to underpin government and governing-body policy regarding the funding of elite sport. For example, UK Sport suggests that satisfying the UK's craving for international sporting success will hopefully lead to a more inspired, active and healthy nation (UK Sport 2008). Similarly, Sportscotland (2003) justifies funding of elite athletes on the grounds that high-performance athletes encourage people to take part in sport. Accordingly, Grix and Carmichael (2012) describe a virtuous cycle in which investment in elite sport is thought to promote mass sport participation, which, in theory, then provides a greater 'pool' from which elite champions of the future can be drawn therefore feeding growth in elite sport. The previous government's belief in the former part of this cycle is highlighted by their belief that governments should invest in high-performance sport because it acts 'as a driver for grassroots participation, whereby sporting heroes inspire participation' (DCMS/ Strategy Unit 2002, p. 117).

If the 2012 games were able to create a demonstration effect, this could have a huge impact on mass participation in sport in the United Kingdom. It is likely that over the course of the 2012 games many millions of currently inactive UK citizens are going to view Olympic sport, largely through media outlets such as television and the Internet. However, in order to capitalize on the potential for a demonstration effect resulting from the 2012 games, Sport England needs to consider ways in which they can maximize the likelihood of a demonstration effect occurring. By doing so they could increase their chances of delivering a sports legacy through London 2012.

Initiation of sport participation is influenced considerably by motivation (Weiss and Amorose 2008). Thus, if demonstration effects occur, it is reasonable to expect that changes in sport motivation are implicated in explaining their impact. Thus, through the application of relevant theories/models it may be possible to consider the possibility of a demonstration effect resulting from the 2012 games. Such an exercise also permits the postulation of possible changes to policy that could increase the likelihood of a demonstration effect resulting from the 2012 games. The purpose of the following section is to introduce pertinent aspects of relevant theories and then discuss the likelihood of a demonstration effect being influenced by these factors. In addition, it is hoped that sport-policy scholars may make use of theories such as these to inform their own empirical analyses.

Pertinent themes

There are numerous theories and models that have been utilized to attempt to explain and promote participation in physical activity. Some of the more popular theories applied to this context are Bandura's (1997) self-efficacy theory, Deci and Ryan's self-determination theory (Deci and Ryan 1985, Ryan and Deci 2000), Ajzen and Madden's (1986) theory of planned behaviour and Prochaska *et al.*'s (1992) transtheoretical model. All are grounded in a positivist epistemology – as is the vast majority of sport psychology research – that proposes causal relationships that involve testable processes involving directly perceivable variables. As such, they lend themselves to an analysis of the likelihood of the 2012 games influencing motivation for sport participation.

Although there are undoubtedly other theories/models with relevance to this subject, the theories/models chosen are considered to be particular relevant to the current debate. By introducing key aspects of these theories/models to sport-policy scholars, it is hoped a thought-provoking debate surrounding the potential for a demonstration effect resulting from the 2012 games will be initiated. Investigation of the previously mentioned theories/models reveals three themes that have particular relevance to the present debate: confidence/competence; attitudes and norms; and stage of participation. The following sections will debate the potential for a demonstration effect in light of theoretical predictions based around these themes.

Confidence/competence

One theme consistently linked with participation in sport relates to participants' confidence/competence. Self-efficacy theory (Bandura 1997), self-determination theory (Deci and Ryan 1985, Ryan and Deci 2000), the theory of planned behaviour (Ajzen and Madden 1986) and the transtheoretical model (Prochaska *et al.* 1992) all acknowledge the importance of related constructs. Thus, the present section will first outline why these theories/models propose confidence/competence to be important, before debating whether the 2012 games is likely to have any impact in this area.

One theory that places particular emphasis on confidence is self-efficacy theory (Bandura 1997) as it centres on a situation-specific form of confidence termed self-efficacy. Self-efficacy is defined as 'beliefs in one's capabilities to organize and execute the courses of action required to produce given attainments' (Bandura 1997, p. 3) and therefore relates to confidence in one's abilities to perform specific behaviours. Self-efficacy beliefs are thought to impact upon important factors such as choice of activity and effort expended during an activity (Bandura 1982, 1991). Self-efficacy beliefs in sport are apparent in behavioural (e.g. ability to run 100 m in under 11 seconds), cognitive (e.g. tactical decisions) and emotional (e.g. dealing with anxiety) forms (Maddux and Lewis 1995). Bandura (1997) proposes that when people anticipate desirable outcomes as a result of successful performance in an activity, engagement in that activity will largely be determined by their efficacy beliefs specific to the activity. Consistent with this proposition, physical activity self-efficacy (i.e. a person's confidence in his/her ability to be physically active on a regular basis) is a consistent predictor of physical activity behaviour in empirical research (see Trost *et al.* 2002). Thus, high sport-related efficacy beliefs are likely to be an important prerequisite for regular engagement in sport.

A model of behaviour change that also considers the importance of self-efficacy beliefs is the transtheoretical model (Prochaska *et al.* 1992). Originally applied to cessation of negative health behaviours such as smoking, this model has since been applied to exercise behaviour (e.g. Marcus *et al.* 1992). Importantly, the model considers peoples' current intentions towards and/or engagement with physical activity, categorizing people into one of five stages based upon these characteristics. The stages range from precontemplation (i.e. not currently participating in physical activity or intending to in the next 6 months) to the target stage of maintenance (i.e. exercising regularly for more than 6 months). Importantly, this model highlights the importance of peoples' readiness for behaviour change, and research has consistently reported a positive relationship between readiness for adoption of physical activity and self-efficacy (e.g. Marcus and Owen 1992, Marcus *et al.* 1994). Thus, it is possible that increases in self-efficacy may facilitate peoples' transition through the various stages described in the transtheoretical model and therefore towards long-term engagement in physical activity.

Another theory that shares common ground with self-efficacy theory is the theory of planned behaviour (Ajzen and Madden 1986). This theory proposes that intentions are extremely influential in determining motivated behaviour and that perceived behavioural control influences behaviour change both through changes in intention as well as through a direct effect on behaviour (Ajzen and Madden 1986). Perceived behavioural control reflects the perception that one has the ability to carry out a particular behaviour and it therefore has conceptual similarities with self-efficacy (Ajzen 1991).

Other theories also implicate efficacy-related constructs when explaining motivated behaviour. One such theory is self-determination theory (Deci and Ryan 1985, Ryan and Deci 2000). Deci and Ryan highlight how people need to consider their actions and involvement with their social milieu as effectual (White 1959, Deci 1975, Harter 1978) and propose competence to be one of three (alongside autonomy and relatedness) basic psychological needs considered central to optimal motivation in any context. The importance of competence to optimal motivation for exercise has been supported in research adopting this theory (see Hagger and Chatzisarantis 2008).

As constructs relevant to confidence and competence appear to be key elements of motivation in undertaking physical activity, it is important that the current debate considers whether there is likely to be any effect of the 2012 games on viewers' perceptions of sport confidence/competence. One theory that suggests efficacy beliefs can be promoted through observation of others is self-efficacy theory (Bandura 1997). Vicarious experiences (i.e. observational learning, modelling) influence efficacy beliefs when people observe others' performances and subsequently form expectancies regarding their own behaviour and its consequences. Thus, observation of successful performances (e.g. feats of endurance and power) and desirable outcomes (e.g. enjoyment, social recognition) during the 2012 games has the potential to positively influence the efficacy beliefs and outcome expectancies of those viewing the 2012 games. However, an important caveat to this is that the influence of vicarious experiences is subject to perceived similarity between the observed and the observer (Bandura 1997). Thus, any positive impact of vicarious experiences on viewers' efficacy beliefs during the 2012 games is likely to be restricted to the small number of people watching the games who perceive themselves as having similar abilities to the competing athletes. This is likely to apply only to certain infrequent and lapsed sport participants rather than those with no history of sport involvement.

For those with no history of sport involvement, viewing the 2012 games could actually have the opposite effect by negatively impacting their efficacy beliefs. This is because people viewing the 2012 games who draw comparisons between their own abilities and those of the elite-level athletes competing may actually lower their perceived competence judgements as a result (see Weed *et al.* 2009). Further, if viewing the 2012 games strengthens the belief that positive outcomes from sport are only experienced when performing at an elite level, then watching the 2012 games could potentially demotivate people who believe they do not have the necessary skills and competence to benefit from sport involvement (see Hindson *et al.* 1994). Although people may enjoy marvelling at the incredible performances of elite athletes, it is possible that viewing such performances may actually decrease the perception that interactions with the sport environment would be effectual for those with little past history of sport participation. Further, for those who have previously had unsuccessful interactions with sport, their sport confidence is likely to already be diminished as actual experiences are the most powerful antecedent of self-efficacy beliefs (Bandura 1997).

In summary, relevant theory highlights the importance of confidence/competence in supporting motivation for sport participation. Thus, increases in confidence and/or perceived competence in physical activity contexts would be one possible mechanism for a demonstration effect to occur as a result of the 2012 games. However, in contrast to the desired impact, viewing the 2012 games may actually decrease such perceptions for the majority of viewers if coverage centres purely on elite sport. Thus, it is important that sport-policy scholars debate ways in which such a trend could be prevented or reversed.

Attitudes and norms

As well as ascribing a key role for perceived behavioural control when describing factors involved in engendering behaviour change, the theory of planned behaviour (Ajzen and Madden 1986) also includes other variables with relevance to the current debate. In addition to the influence of perceived behavioural control, this theory also proposes that behavioural intentions are impacted by attitudes towards the behaviour and social norms. Attitudes towards the behaviour are the degree to which a person appraises or evaluates the target behaviour favourably or unfavourably (Ajzen 1991) whereas subjective norms refer to the perceived social pressure to perform/not perform the behaviour (Ajzen 1991).

Application of the theory of planned behaviour to sport suggests that intention to participate results from the combination of an individual's attitudes towards sport, his/her perceptions of subjective norms regarding sport participation as well as his/her perceived behavioural control regarding sport. Notably, a meta-analysis of theory of planned behaviour research in the physical activity domain supported the importance of attitudes, subjective norms and perceived behavioural control in explaining engagement in physical activity (Hagger *et al.* 2002). Further, the analyses of Hagger *et al.* (2002) demonstrated attitudes and perceived behavioural control to be more effective predictors of intention than subjective norms.

Attitudes towards a particular behaviour reflect a personal disposition towards engaging in that behaviour and represent one's assessment of his/her beliefs regarding the effectiveness of the behaviour in question in producing outcomes as well as an evaluation of these outcomes (Hagger *et al.* 2002). An individual's behavioural beliefs are thought to influence his/her attitudes towards a behaviour (Ajzen 1991). Thus, when debating whether viewing the 2012 games could influence one's attitudes towards sport, it is important to consider the possible effect of viewing the 2012 games on peoples' behavioural beliefs regarding sport.

Although it is possible to hold many beliefs about a particular behaviour, one can only attend to relatively few at any given time. It is therefore the salient beliefs at any instance that are most likely to impact upon behavioural attitudes (Ajzen 1991). One way viewing the 2012 games could therefore impact attitudes towards sport would be by making positive beliefs relating to sport more salient in those viewing the 2012 games. Some viewers may already hold positive beliefs about sport (e.g. participation leads to improved health), but not currently attend to these beliefs. In such people it is possible that viewing the 2012 games may increase the possibility of such beliefs becoming salient by reminding them of the reasons they originally formed these beliefs.

Beliefs are generally formed through the association of a behaviour with certain attributes (Ajzen 1991). Therefore, viewing the 2012 games could also potentially impact behavioural attitudes by forming new associations between sport and particular attributes and by supporting positive evaluations of such associations. This may be particularly productive for those viewers with little previous experience of sport. For example, viewing the 2012 games could form associations between sport participation and attributes such as improved mood, better health and greater self-esteem. Such belief formation in those with little familiarity with sport could improve the attitudes of such people, therefore potentially leading to increased intention to exercise. In summary, there are two viable pathways through which viewing the 2012 games may positively influence the attitudes of spectators and therefore promote intentions towards engaging in sport.

In a similar way to which behavioural beliefs are thought to underpin development of attitudes towards a behaviour, normative beliefs are considered to underlie the formation of subjective norms (Ajzen 1991). These beliefs represent the likelihood that significant others (e.g. friend, parent, partner or sibling) approve or disapprove of engagement in a particular behaviour. The effect of each normative belief on perceived subjective norms is then determined by the individual's motivation to comply with the referent significant other. One way in which viewing the 2012 games could positively impact subjective norms is by increasing the perception of approval of physical activity in referent groups/individuals. This appears possible given that people viewing the 2012 games are likely to be doing so with friends and family who hold positive attitudes towards sport and therefore may encourage participation. It is also possible that viewing the 2012 games could potentially increase an individual's motivation to comply with referents perceived to encourage engagement in sport given that viewing the 2012 games is likely to result in positive behavioural belief formation as previously discussed. Thus, viewing London 2012 may positively influence intentions to take part in sport through a positive impact on subjective norms towards sport.

Overall, application of the theory of planned behaviour suggests viewing the 2012 games may potentially increase intentions towards sport participation. However, it is important to recognize that although increases in intentions would be a desirable outcome, any change in actual behaviour would be subject to requisite levels of perceived behavioural control (Ajzen 1991). As described earlier, there would appear to be less potential for increases in perceived behavioural control as a result of viewing the games. It is therefore important to consider whether it is possible to increase perceptions of viewers' behavioural control towards sport in order to complement a possible positive impact on intention. This key issue is addressed later in the discussion.

Stage of participation

As described earlier, people can be categorized into different stages of behaviour adoption based upon the five stages outlined in the transtheoretical model (see Marcus *et al.* 1992, Prochaska *et al.* 1992). The five stages outlined in the transtheoretical model are precontemplation (defined earlier), contemplation (i.e. not currently exercising but intend to do so in the next 6 months), preparation (i.e. infrequent exercisers; not exercising for 20 minutes at least three times a week), action (i.e. exercising regularly but have done so for less than 6 months) and maintenance (defined earlier). Progression through the stages reflects an increase in physical activity adoption. Thus, it is important to consider whether viewing the

2012 games may increase the likelihood of stage progression in viewers not currently in the action or maintenance stages of the model.

With adults' physical activity levels in England below the minimum recommendation for the majority of the population (e.g. 61% of men, 71% of women in 2008; NHS Information Centre 2010), it would appear that a significant proportion of the UK population is in the early stages of exercise adoption (i.e. precontemplation to preparation). Thus, it is especially important to consider the likelihood of viewing the 2012 games impacting stage progression in this region of the model. For example, such a transition would be observed if people not currently considering engaging in regular exercise (i.e. precontemplation) were encouraged to at least start to think about participating in sport during the next 6 months (i.e. contemplation).

A key aspect of the transtheoretical model is that it proposes specific processes of change aimed at facilitating stage transition. These processes were identified by Prochaska *et al.* (1992) as potent predictors of stage transition and their applicability to the physical activity context has largely been supported (see Marshall and Biddle 2001, Spencer *et al.* 2006). One process – consciousness raising – has particular relevance to the current debate, as it involves increasing awareness of a behaviour through information gathering, education and personal feedback (Prochaska *et al.* 1992). Becoming more knowledgeable about the benefits of the target behaviour and how to engage in it is thought to increase peoples' likelihood of adopting the behaviour or at least to consider doing so. As viewing the 2012 games should increase knowledge of the benefits of sport participation for those in the initial stages of the model, it is possible that viewing the 2012 games could facilitate early stage transition through consciousness raising. Any such effect could be particularly important as consciousness raising is considered to be a potent change process during early stage transitions in the physical activity context (Reed 1999).

Another key component of the transtheoretical model is decisional balance (Prochaska *et al.* 1992). Decisional balance reflects an individual's assessment of the perceived advantages (e.g. increased health) and disadvantages (e.g. time investment) of behaviour change. Importantly, as perceived advantages increase in number and perceived disadvantages decrease, the likelihood of behaviour adoption increases. With a predominant focus on the positive outcomes of sport involvement likely during the Olympics, it is possible that watching the 2012 games could have a positive impact on decisional balance by increasing viewers' perceptions of the advantages of an active lifestyle. Importantly, Marshall and Biddle (2001) demonstrated that transition from precontemplation to contemplation was accompanied by a significant and robust increase in the perceived benefits of adoption of physical activity. Further, the effect of an increase in perceived benefits was twice that for decreases in perceived disadvantages, which suggests increased perceptions of the benefits of behaviour change may be particularly beneficial in facilitating change between these two stages. Thus, it is possible that viewing the 2012 games could result in stage progression for viewers in the initial stages of the model at the time of the Olympics. Such an outcome would be consistent with the London 2012 legacy plan commitment to target the least active.

Transitions from precontemplation to contemplation would not be reflected in assessments of sport participation levels made following the games as neither stage is associated with actual behaviour. However, such stage transitions would at least increase the number of people considering participation. In addition, progression to contemplation may also inhibit reversion back to precontemplation as stage progression is thought to follow a spiral pattern whereby regression back to precontemplation is unlikely (see Prochaska *et al.* 1992). Thus, it is possible that people who do transit to the contemplation stage as a result of seeing the 2012 games may be unlikely to revert back to a state whereby they have no intention to exercise in the future (see also Weed *et al.* 2009).

Overall, with respect to stage of participation, it would appear that there is some potential that watching the 2012 games will have a positive impact on stage of participation. In particular, an effect may be seen on viewers not contemplating participation in sport prior to watching the games. The means through which this could occur is by providing information on different sports and how to participate in them (i.e. consciousness raising) and by highlighting the positive benefits of sport participation (i.e. positive decisional balance). However, it is important to bear in mind that increases in self-efficacy may also be necessary for continued stage progression (see Marcus and Owen 1992, Marcus *et al.* 1994, Marshall and Biddle 2001). Thus, stage transitions may largely be limited to the early stages of the model unless any changes in intentions to take part in sport are accompanied by increases in self-efficacy. Given the repeated importance placed on self-efficacy and related beliefs throughout this investigation, this is one of the main foci in the subsequent section.

Discussion

Thus far, consideration of relevant theory has suggested that viewing the 2012 games may have a positive impact on intention to participate in sport through changes in attitudes, perceived subjective norms and encouraging readiness for participation. However, it is important to recognize that changes in intentions do not necessarily lead to behaviour change and that increases in sport competence beliefs may also be needed to facilitate such changes. Significantly, research has shown that past games have not generated any enduring increase in sport participation (Coalter 2004, Girginov and Hills 2008), although London is the first Olympics to *explicitly* promise a legacy in mass sport participation.

It is possible the manner in which the games are presented by the media may impact the likelihood of a demonstration effect given the majority of people will view the 2012 games on television and through the Internet. Many of the reasons why it has been argued that viewing the 2012 games is unlikely to have a desirable impact on sport competence beliefs is due to an anticipated focus of Olympic media coverage being, by its very nature, on elite sport. For example, self-efficacy theory suggests that lack of similarity in competitive level between those watching and the elite athletes taking part will negate the potential positive impact of vicarious experiences on the self-efficacy beliefs of most viewers. In fact, it has been suggested that the differences in ability between these two groups may in fact lead to a decrease in viewers' perceived competence (see Weed *et al.* 2009). Thus, a sole focus of media coverage during the 2012 games on elite-level competition may have a detrimental impact on many viewers' sport confidence/competence beliefs.

Previous television coverage of the Olympics has tended to focus almost entirely on elite competition even though other models of coverage have proved successful when applied to other events. An example of television coverage of sport that balances elite and non-elite competition that has proved popular is the presentation of the London Marathon. When presenting the London Marathon on television, the British Broadcasting Corporation (BBC) incorporate coverage of competition at all levels, from the World's elite to fun runners in fancy dress. This style of coverage presents sport as a much more inclusive context, one that is available and rewarding to all. The motivational effects of such coverage are reflected in the fact that the online ballot for the London Marathon has closed within 2 weeks of opening for the 2010, 2011 and 2012 races upon reaching its limit of 120,000 entries for the 40,000 places available.

There are, however, distinct differences between the Olympics and events such as the London Marathon. Specifically, the London Marathon and similar events inherently incorporate both elite and non-elite competition. In contrast, the Olympics by definition incorporate elite athletes only. Thus, in order to facilitate the presentation of both elite and non-elite sport as part of television/Internet broadcasts, outlets such as the BBC would have to look beyond the sport occurring during the 2012 games themselves. It has been suggested that leveraging the main event through the provision of supplemental activities that establish a link between elite events and community participation in physical activity should increase the likelihood of a mass sport legacy resulting from the 2012 games (Weed *et al.* 2009). It is likely that including coverage of such supplemental activities during media broadcasts would increase awareness of such events and therefore increase their potential for facilitating a sport legacy resulting from the games. The difficulty is, of course, that the government does not own – and therefore cannot directly impact – a state's media outlets.

One London 2012 initiative that will provide many examples of sport at all levels of competition is the Inspire Programme. This initiative recognizes projects and events in many areas, including sports that encourage accessibility, participation, inspiration and stimulation. As such, sport events with the Inspire Mark would be ideal examples of inclusive sport activities that could be detailed during television coverage of the 2012 games. In an ideal world, such non-elite activities would receive a wider coverage, as the likelihood of a positive sport legacy resulting from the games may be enhanced by such coverage. For example, seeing success and positive outcomes for non-elite sport participants could bolster the self-efficacy beliefs and outcome expectancies of viewers via vicarious experiences (Bandura 1997). Further, respected media figures describing how non-elite participants can experience success and positive outcomes in sport could also increase self-efficacy and contribute to positive outcome expectancies through verbal persuasion (i.e. when respected and trusted others express faith in one's abilities or expound the positive outcomes that may result from successful completion of a task; Bandura 1997). Similarities could be drawn here for both possible mechanisms with the way in which coverage of the London Marathon appears to have fuelled a running revolution among previously inactive viewers.

Such an approach to television/Internet coverage could also increase the potential for a positive impact of viewing the 2012 games on intentions to participate in sport. The theory of planned behaviour (Ajzen and Madden 1986) suggests that more positive behavioural attitudes and perceived subjective norms towards a specific behaviour positively impact one's intentions to engage in that behaviour. It has already been argued that viewing the 2012 games may aid formation of positive behavioural and normative beliefs regarding sport participation as well as increasing the salience of such beliefs. However, the increased media coverage of non-elite sports may increase the likelihood of this occurring by making it easier for many viewers to relate to television/Internet coverage of the 2012 games.

A particular media focus on sport-based projects that promote community cohesion and inclusion may have a particular impact on feelings of relatedness (i.e. a sense of belongingness with and connectedness to those around us; Baumeister and Leary 1995, Ryan 1995) in those who constitute such communities. As one of the three psychological needs identified in self-determination theory (Deci and Ryan 1985, Ryan and Deci 2000), such increases in relatedness should help community members feel as though they would belong to such projects and therefore motivate participation. Such initiatives are aligned with a shift in government policy towards developing communities through sport (see Coalter 2007). Further gains in satisfaction of the need for relatedness could also be achieved by portraying elite athletes as role models within the local communities where they live (see Weed *et al.* 2009).

It has been suggested presently that there is some potential – especially in the short term – for a positive impact on motivation for sport participation through changes in intention to participate in sport. Further, the chances of these outcomes occurring are likely to be increased if television/Internet coverage focuses on both elite and non-elite sport. Such a change may also create possible increases in sport confidence/competence beliefs. However, in isolation viewing the 2012 games is still unlikely to contribute to a lasting sporting legacy. Continued improvements in attitudes and confidence/competence are likely to be contingent on any subsequent engagement in sport occurring in an environment in which participants feel comfortable and confident (Hagger *et al.* 2002). This is clearly an issue that needs to be addressed by sport providers who are encouraged to base their practice around the main tenets of the theories drawn upon in the current investigation.

In summing up this section, it is suggested that an increase in coverage of non-elite sport on television/Internet during the 2012 games may increase the potential for a demonstration effect resulting from London 2012. However, such an effect is only likely to be reflected in long-term increases in sport participation if people inspired to participate in sport by the 2012 games enter into sport environments that then promote optimal motivation.

Concluding remarks

In order to achieve their objective of increasing the number of active citizens by 1 million by 2012/2013, Sport England and the DCMS may need a major contribution from a demonstration effect. This article utilized relevant theory to investigate the likelihood of such an effect resulting from the 2012 games. Application of such theory suggested that positive outcomes resulting from spectators' engagement with the 2012 games may be limited if attention is not given to the coverage of non-elite sport. Also of concern is a possible negative impact on sport competence beliefs if viewers compare their own abilities with those of the elite athletes they watch. Such predictions are supported by existing post-games evaluations which although limited in number and rigour suggest that major sporting events such as the 2000 Sydney Olympics (Veal 2003) and the 2002 Manchester Commonwealth Games (MORI 2004) had no positive impact on post-games sport participation.

One could argue that it should not be that surprising that viewing elite sport is unlikely to result in increased mass sport participation. Clearly such a link is intuitively appealing, but there is no reason that such a link should automatically exist. Comparing sport to other contexts highlights this point. For example, one may be mesmerized by the performance of a virtuoso pianist or delight in exquisite food created by a Michelin-starred chef, but this does not necessarily result in the desire to learn the piano or become a chef. In order for such experiences to motivate engagement with an activity, it is likely that a proactive approach highlighting the benefits for the viewer and not just the viewed is required. In sport, such an approach may bridge the gap between elite and mass sport participation and increase the chances of London 2012 delivering a sporting legacy.

Some have suggested that specifically targeting current-but-infrequent and lapsed sports participants would increase the potential for a demonstration effect resulting from the 2012 games (see Weed *et al.* 2009). However, it could be argued that targeting such groups to boost participation following the 2012 games would merely create a 'weak' sporting legacy that consisted only of people who were already aware of and in some cases already experiencing some of the myriad benefits sport participation can bring. A stronger legacy – and surely the one Lord Coe was alluding to when bidding for the 2012 games in Singapore in 2005 – would be an increase in participation in those not currently involved in and with little previous experience of sport. Thus, as well as targeting current or lapsed sport participants, Sport England needs to consider ways in which they can motivate participation in those who have little experience of sport, particularly in the young. This would be more consistent with key DCMS briefs such as 'engaging', 'encouraging' and 'inspiring' youngsters to take up sport (HM Treasury 2007, p. 14).

References

Ajzen, I., 1991. The theory of planned behaviour. *Organizational behavior and human decision processes*, 50, 179–211.

Ajzen, I. and Madden, T.J., 1986. Prediction of goal-directed behavior: attitudes, intentions, and perceived behavioral control. *Journal of experimental social psychology*, 22, 453–474.

Bandura, A., 1982. Self-efficacy mechanism in human agency. *American psychologist*, 37, 122–147.

Bandura, A., 1991. Social cognitive theory of self-regulation. *Organizational behavior and human decision processes*, 50, 248–287.

Bandura, A., 1997. *Self-efficacy: the exercise of control*. New York: W.H. Freeman.

Baumeister, R. and Leary, M.R., 1995. The need to belong: desire for interpersonal attachments as a fundamental human motive. *Psychological bulletin*, 117, 497–529.

Coalter, F., 2004. Stuck in the blocks? A sustainable sporting legacy. *In*: A. Vigor, M. Mean, and C. Tims, eds. *After the gold rush: a sustainable Olympics for London*. London: IPPR/Demos, 91–108.

Coalter, F., 2007. *A wider social role for sport: who's keeping the score?* London: Routledge.

DCMS/Strategy Unit, 2002. *Game plan: a strategy for delivering government's sport and physical activity objectives*. London: DCMS/Strategy Unit.

Deci, E.L., 1975. *Intrinsic motivation*. New York: Plenum Press.

Deci, E.L. and Ryan, R.M., 1985. *Intrinsic motivation and self determination in human behavior*. New York: Plenum Press.

Girginov, V. and Hills, L., 2008. A sustainable sports legacy: creating a link between the London Olympics and sports participation. *International journal of the history of sport*, 25, 2091–2116.

Grix, J. and Carmichael, F., 2012. Why do governments invest in elite sport? A polemic. *International journal of sport policy and politics*, 4, 73–90.

Hagger, M.S. and Chatzisarantis, N.L.D., 2008. Self-determination theory and the psychology of exercise. *International review of sport and exercise psychology*, 1, 79–103.

Hagger, M.S., Chatzisarantis, N.L.D., and Biddle, S.J.H., 2002. A meta-analytic review of the theories of reasoned action and planned behavior in physical activity: predictive validity and the contribution of additional variables. *Journal of sport & exercise psychology*, 24, 3–32.

Harter, S., 1978. Effectance motivation reconsidered. *Human development*, 21, 34–64.

Hindson, A., Gidlow, B., and Peebles, C., 1994. The trickle down effect of top level sport: myth or reality? A case-study of the Olympics. *Australian journal of leisure and recreation*, 4, 16–24.

HM Treasury, 2007. *PSA delivery agreement 22: deliver a successful Olympic Games and Paralympic Games with a sustainable legacy and get more children and young people taking part in high quality PE and sport*. London: Stationary Office.

Hogan, K. and Norton, K., 2000. The 'price' of Olympic gold. *Journal of science and motivation in sport*, 3, 203–218.

Maddux, J.E. and Lewis, J., 1995. Self-efficacy and adjustment. *In*: J.E. Maddux, ed. *Self-efficacy, adaptation, and adjustment*. New York: Plenum Press, 37–68.

Marcus, B.H., *et al.*, 1992. The stages and processes of exercise adoption and maintenance in a worksite sample. *Health psychology*, 11, 386–395.

Marcus, B.H., *et al.*, 1994. Self-efficacy, decision making and stages of change: an integrative model of physical exercise. *Journal of applied social psychology*, 24, 489–508.

Marcus, B.H. and Owen, N., 1992. Motivational readiness, self-efficacy and decision-making for exercise. *Journal of applied social psychology*, 22, 3–16.

Marshall, S.J. and Biddle, S.J.H., 2001. The transtheoretical model of behaviour change: a meta-analysis of applications to physical activity and exercise. *Annals of behavioural medicine*, 23, 229–246.

MORI, 2004. *The sports development impact of the Commonwealth Games 2002: final report*. Research conducted for UK Sport in Greater Manchester, Blackburn, Congleton and Liverpool.

National Audit Office, 2010. *Increasing participation in sport*. London: Stationary Office.

NHS Information Centre, 2010. *Statistics on obesity, physical activity and diet: England, 2010* [online]. Leeds, The Health and Social Care Information Centre. Available from: http://www.ic.nhs.uk/webfiles/publications/opad10/Statistics_on_ Obesity_Physical_Activity_and_Diet_England_2010. pdf [Accessed 3 February 2012].

Prochaska, J.O., DiClemente, C.C., and Norcross, J.C., 1992. In search of how people change. *American psychologist*, 47, 1102–1114.

Reed, G.R., 1999. Adherence to exercise and the transtheoretical model of behavior change. *In*: S.J. Bull, ed. *Adherence issues in sport and exercise*. Chichester: Wiley, 19–45.

Robertson, H., 2010. *Sport and Olympics minister sets out Olympic sports legacy plans* [online]. London, Department for Culture, Media, and Sport. Available from: http://www.culture.gov.uk/news/media_releases/7152.aspx [Accessed 21 July 2010].

Ryan, R.M., 1995. Psychological need and the facilitation of integrative processes. *Journal of personality*, 63, 397–427.

Ryan, R.M. and Deci, E.L., 2000. Self-determination theory and the facilitation of intrinsic motivation, social development and well-being. *American psychologist*, 55, 68–78.

Spencer, L., *et al.*, 2006. Applying the transtheoretical model to exercise: a systematic and comprehensive review of the literature. *Health promotion practice*, 7, 428–443.

Sportscotland, 2003. *Shaping Scotland's future. Sport 21 2003–2007. The national strategy for sport*. Edinburgh: Sportscotland.

Stewart, B., *et al.*, 2005. *Australian sport: better by design? The evolution of Australian sport policy*. London: Routledge.

Trost, S.G., *et al.*, 2002. Correlates of adults' participation in physical activity: review and update. *Medicine and science in sports & exercise*, 34, 1996–2001.

UK Sport, 2008. *Press release, 29.12.08 'Cycling leaps in popularity as survey shows public pride in British sporting success'* [online]. Available from: http://www.uksport.gov.uk/news/sporting_preferences_dec_08/ [Accessed 3 December 2010].

Veal, A.J., 2003. Tracking change: leisure participation and policy in Australia, 1985–2002. *Annals of leisure research*, 6, 245–277.

Weed, M., Coren, E., and Fiore, J., 2009. *A systematic review of the evidence base for developing a physical activity and health legacy from the London 2012 Olympic and Paralympic games*. A report commissioned by Physical Activity Network West Midlands on behalf of Regional Physical Activity Teams in the West Midlands, the East Midlands, the East of England, London and the South East.

Weiss, M. and Amorose, A.J., 2008. Motivational orientations and sport behavior. *In*: T.S. Horn, ed. *Advances in sport psychology*. Champaign, IL: Human Kinetics, 115–155.

White, R.W., 1959. Motivation reconsidered: the concept of competence. *Psychological review*, 66, 297–330.

London 2012 Olympic legacy: a big sporting society?

Cathy Devine

University of Cumbria, Sport and Physical Activity, Bowerham Road, Lancaster LA1 3JD, UK

The Olympic Charter (International Olympic Committee [IOC], 2010. Olympic charter. Lausanne: IOC. Available from:http://www.olympic.org/Documents/Olympic%20Charter/ Charter_en_2010.pdf [Accessed 13 July 2011]) asserts that 'the practice of sport is a human right' and outlines role 12 of the IOC as being 'to encourage and support the development of sport for all'. This signals an aspiration to the right to sport for all. Notwithstanding this, the UK Conservative/Liberal Democrat coalition government has consolidated and extended a shift in UK sport policy from 'sport for social good' to 'competitive sport for sport's sake'. In December 2010, the government published 'Plans for the Legacy from the 2012 Olympic and Paralympic Games'. The first of the four areas of focus is to harness 'the United Kingdom's passion for sport to increase grass-roots participation, particularly by young people' and encourage 'the whole population to be more physically active'. This appears to relate to sport for some, and physical activity for others. Nevertheless, the coalition has signalled a belief in 'big society' and democratic not bureaucratic accountability.

This article proposes a theoretical framework of a 'big sporting society' comprising three generations of sporting rights. This enables an evaluation of emergent sport policy in relation to the London 2012 Olympic Games legacy and the Olympic Charter. It is argued that the realization of the 2012 legacy relating to the IOC's aspiration to sport as a human right for all, and consequent democratic sporting accountability, necessitates a 'sport for all' rather than 'competitive sport for sport's sake' policy direction, and the development of all three generations of sporting rights, resulting in a 'big sporting society'.

Introduction

This article aims to trace and critique shifts in the stated purpose of sport policy following the awarding of the 2012 Olympic Games to London and to introduce the concept of a 'big sporting society'. This will be theorized within a conceptual framework of three generations of human rights, involving comprehensive sporting rights and resulting in big sporting democracy. The framework will then be used to evaluate the impact of emergent coalition sport policy on the London 2012 legacy, as that legacy pertains to sport as a human right for all.

UK sport policy has come full circle since 1995 when the Conservative policy document, *Sport: raising the game* (Department of National Heritage [DNH] 1995), was published. This strategy emphasized competitive team games and volunteering, and ignored the major contribution of local authorities to the national sporting infrastructure. When New Labour came to power in 1997, sport (and physical activity) policy departed radically from the traditional conservative rhetoric of 'sport for sport's sake' and adopted an evidence-based instrumental view of 'sport for social good'. This is outlined in a range of policy documentation including *England, the Sporting Nation* (English Sports Council [ESC] 1997); *Sport England (SE) Lottery Fund Strategy 1999–2009*, (Sport England [SE] 1999a); *The Value of Sport* (SE 1999b); and *Game Plan* (Department for Culture Media and Sport [DCMS] 2002).

However, in 2005 the successful UK bid to host the 2012 Olympic Games in London had a powerful impact on UK sport policy. By 2008, coincidentally or otherwise, the New Labour government had abandoned the 'sport for social good' project and promoted a resurgence of a 'sport for sport's sake' policy stance, but with no definition of sport offered, and minimal justification of its value outlined. Thus, the European Sports Charter's definition of sport as 'all forms of physical activity which, through casual or organized participation, aim at expressing or improving physical fitness and mental well-being, forming social relationships or obtaining results in competition at all levels' (Council of Europe [COE] 1992, 2001), which is also the definition adopted by the European Commission (EC) White Paper on Sport (European Commission [EC] 2007), was abandoned, and 'sport' and 'physical activity' were redefined as ontologically different.

This shift was exemplified by the Sport England Strategy 2008–2011 which stated that 'with the Olympics and Paralympics due to come to London and the UK a little over four years from now, it is an appropriate time to take a clear look at the sport development system'. The document legitimized the shift in policy direction by claiming 'an unprecedented level of consensus' from 'over 100 stakeholders from across the sport sector'. It argued that 'the driving force behind the strategy and investment is to address the needs of sports participants across the country' which 'provides a clear distinction with the physical activity agenda being driven by a number of departments, including the Department of Health (DH) and Department of Transport'. The Strategy also flagged up 'a shift in emphasis and role for National Governing Bodies' which were awarded 'greater autonomy over the investment of public funds within their sport' via 'Whole-Sport Plans' (SE 2008). The document also demonstrated the full-scale adoption of 'governmentalization', 'modernization', governance by new public management and new managerialism (Green 2009, Grix 2009, Houlihan 2009, Lindsey 2009) which can be considered as bureaucratic executive democracy.

The New Labour plans for the London 2012 legacy were based on five 'promises'; the first of which related to sport and was 'to make the UK a world-leading sporting nation'. This included 'offering all 5 to 16 year-olds in England five hours of high-quality sport a week and all 16 to 19 year-olds three hours a week by 2012', and 'getting people more active' by helping 'at least two million more people in England be more active by 2012' (DCMS 2007, 2008).

This government regarded local authorities as a 'key delivery partner' (SE 2008) and considered that 'many of the (legacy) benefits will come from enhancing existing programmes, and within existing Departmental budgets'. It was also clear that direct legacy funding for the Legacy Trust UK, at £40 million 'from existing sources' and not just for sport projects, was relatively small scale; that the Inspire programme was a branding rather than funding project; and that most of the legacy funding would be provided via the sporting infrastructure already in existence. This acknowledged that local government spending on sport in the United Kingdom (including school sport but excluding DH spending on physical activity) was estimated at around £1.8 billion per annum, of the estimated total government expenditure on sport of £2.2 billion in 1999/2000. This included exchequer and lottery funding in addition to local government funding but excluded the £9.4 billion committed to the 2012 Olympics (Bell 2009). The Local Government Association (LGA 2010a) agreed, claiming that 'councils spend five times as much on sport as the government does'. Thus the local authority financial contribution to sport continues to far outstrip that from both national government and the lottery. The LGA (2010b) claims that 'the government's own research shows that if councils and their partners meet their ... targets they will have increased participation in sport by 950,000 and increased the numbers of the physically active by 350,000 – putting us well on the way to achieving government's flagship sports legacy target of 2 million people more active by 2012/13'.

The Conservative/Liberal Democrat coalition government, which came to power in May 2010, has protected the funding for the London 2012 Olympic Games and consolidated and extended a 'competitive sport for sports sake' policy direction. This carries an implicit justification of competitive sport as an obvious good, as outlined by the Culture Secretary who stated in June 2010 that 'for this government, competitive sport really matters ... in its own right' and that 'competition addresses a basic human desire to stretch ourselves to the limit of our potential' (Hunt 2010a). Nevertheless, the Minister for Sport and the Olympics has stated that 'I want to see London 2012 leave a lasting legacy of mass participation in sport. It is my vision that the Games will inspire a whole new generation of young people to take up sport and keep it up for life' but that 'we have taken an important step forward by announcing plans to set up an Olympic and Paralympic-style sports competition for UK-wide schools. Through this annual event, every child in every school in the country will have the chance to take part in competitive sport' (Robertson 2010). This then emphasizes that for the coalition, sport, the Olympic legacy, and even mass participation in sport relate primarily to competitive sport for sport's sake.

This echoes pre-election statements made in both the Conservative Sport Manifesto, which stated, 'we will ... raise the profile of competitive sport in schools' and 'encourage a culture of school sport competition by setting up and publishing competitive school sport league tables' (Conservative Party 2009a) and Extending Opportunities: A Conservative Policy Paper on Sport, which advocated placing 'competition at the forefront of school policy' (Conservative Party 2009b). Thus, initial coalition priorities involved the announce-ment of a nationwide Olympic and Paralympic style competition open to every child in the country (Hunt 2010a), but the withdrawal of free swimming for the under 16s and over 60s (Hunt 2010b). Furthermore, that the government 'will not continue to provide ring-fenced funding for school sport partnerships' (SSPs) and 'is lifting, immediately, the many require-ments of the previous Government's PE and Sport Strategy, so giving schools the clarity and freedom to concentrate on competitive school sport' (Gove 2010). However, following widely reported criticism from, amongst others, high-profile elite sportspeople, and lobby-ing from the Youth Sports Trust, the government backed down slightly and agreed to 'pay £47m to keep the SSPs going until summer 2011' and to find 'a further £65m ... (to) guarantee that all schools can release one PE teacher for one day a week from 2011 to 2013, to promote pupils' participation in a range of PE and sporting activities' (Campbell 2010, Department for Education [DfE] 2010c).

It appears therefore that although both the Conservative Sports Manifesto and the Conservative Policy Paper on Sport advocate the importance of 'grass-roots sport', they are clear, unlike their New Labour predecessors, that this should be primarily provided via increased lottery funding, 'the new concentration on leveraging money from the private sector', and the London 2012 Olympics legacy. In addition, they emphasize that 'volunteers are key to the delivery of sport'. The Department for Culture Media and Sport Structural Reform Plan outlines five departmental priorities, three of which (1, 2 and 5) relate to the Conservative vision of a sporting infrastructure as follows:

(1) 2012 Olympics and Paralympics (including delivery of 'a genuine and lasting legacy throughout the country')

(2) Boost the Big Society (including increased lottery money for sport and ensuring 'only voluntary and community sector projects are funded and to prevent the funding of politicised projects')

(5) Encourage Competitive Sport in Schools (including directing 'the Sport Lottery Distributor to take responsibility for the community sports legacy following London 2012')

(DCMS 2010a)

These appear, in relation to 'grass-roots sport', to collapse primarily into one overarching priority, that is to use lottery money to promote competitive sport in schools as part of the London 2012 Olympic Games legacy. There is no mention of local government funding of grass-roots sport, mass participation or sport for all. This was confirmed in December 2010 with the publication of the coalition government's 'Plans for the legacy from the 2012 Olympic and Paralympic Games', which outlines the first of the four areas of focus as 'harnessing the United Kingdom's passion for sport to increase grass roots participation, particularly by young people' and encouraging 'the whole population to be more physically active' (DCMS 2010c).This appears to relate to sport for some, and physical activity for others. The document also advocates 'bringing back a culture of competitive sport in schools' and claims that 'levels of competitive sport are not as high as they should be'. There is no mention of the previous government's 'promise' to get two million more active people by 2012. However, a House of Commons Briefing paper (Woodhouse 2010) steers firmly away from this promise and concludes by citing a 2007 report which concluded that 'no host country has yet been able to demonstrate a direct benefit from the Olympic Games in the form of a lasting increase in participation' (DCMS 2007).[1]

In a similar vein, the Secretary of State for Education (2010 cited DfE 2010a) has announced 'I want competitive sport to be at the centre of a truly rounded education that all schools offer' and that 'the Government is clear that at the heart of our ambition is a traditional belief that competitive sport, when taught well, brings out the best in everyone, be they the Olympian of tomorrow or the child who wants to keep fit and have fun learning new sports and games'. Furthermore, the Schools White Paper went on to outline government plans to revise the PE curriculum, stating 'we will provide new support to encourage a much wider take up of competitive team sports. With only one child in five regularly taking part in competitive activities against another school, we need a new approach to help entrench the character-building qualities of team sport' (DfE 2010b).

The policy direction away from the local government provision is coherent with the Emergency Budget announcement (HM Treasury 2010a) which has been hailed as the biggest attack on the welfare state since its inception, fiscally regressive (Browne 2010), and a 'change in the way our country is run ... from big government to big society' (Cameron 2010a). However, the huge cuts in public spending signposted in this Budget and elaborated in the Spending Review in October 2010 (HM Treasury 2010b), and the further deregulation of schools and the lottery, are likely to impact significantly on the sporting infrastructure, and return sport to the realm of the exclusive, private and voluntary, rather than public sectors. Furthermore, the biggest problem facing national governing bodies of sport is getting new and replacement volunteers (Taylor 2002) and many, especially small, informal sports clubs either do not understand the devolved remit for extending participation or do not wish to do this (Harris *et al.* 2009). This will consequently impact on the advances in sporting equality, and hence mass participation and sport for all, made since the Wolfenden Report (Central Council for Physical Recreation [CCPR] 1960), and the realization of the Olympic Charter's claim that the practice of sport is a human right. This will be via significantly reduced state funding for sport for social good (equality, social inclusion as opposed to social control) and diminished public space and access entitlements. Residual state funding, and lottery funding, is being refocused in two ways: (1) via a strengthened emphasis on youth (despite the fact that the greatest health and cost benefits to the national health service come from the over 40s [Collins 2010]), competition, talent identification and elitism on the one hand and (2) via an individual responsibility to be active in order to reduce health spending and obesity as outlined in 'Healthy Lives Healthy People' (Department of Health [DH] 2010), on the other. Thus sport, and sport policy, has been redefined initially by New Labour and now by the coalition, in a shift from sport for social good to competitive sport for sport's sake.

The purpose of sport policy

Given this context, it is timely to revisit the purpose of sport policy and critique the narrative which offers for UK sport policy only a binary opposition between 'sport for social good' and 'sport for sport's sake'. This opposition was critically highlighted in New Labour's Game Plan policy document which elucidated that 'sport for good' refers 'to the use of sport to achieve greater social objectives; and sport for sport' refers 'to participation in sport as an end in itself'. Furthermore, it stated that 'We consider these definitions are unhelpful and have chosen not to use them' (DCMS 2002).

'(Competitive) sport for sport's sake'

The 'sport for sport's sake' policy purpose rests on the implicit assumption that sport can be considered to have an interest of its own, internal goods and intrinsic value. This begs a number of questions, in particular, what do we mean by sport, and can such a thing as sport to be considered to have an interest independent or otherwise of the interests of people? Furthermore, if we argue that sport (however we define it) has goods of its own, what are these and should we value them?

Defining sport has been attempted across a range of academic disciplines and policy communities. For example, within the philosophy of sport, in contrast to the Council of Europe definition, the favoured position is that 'roughly speaking, sport is a rule governed activity that is about excellence, an understanding of how to play the game, and, in competitive sports, winning' (Abad 2010). Strangely, there is often little reference within the philosophy of sport, to physicality or movement. However, in contrast, Kretchmar (1994) has used the term sport more 'broadly and generically to refer to many movement activities', that is 'human movement with a focus on five of its intentional or purposeful forms: sport, dance, exercise, games, and play'. This approach illustrates the way in which sport has been used as both an overarching and a partial category, and this dual (at least) meaning is evident also throughout the sport policy literature.

As to whether sport can be considered to have an interest *for its own sake*, a standard argument from the wider literature would be that 'individual living things, as teleological centres of life' have a good of their own while other things do not' (Sandler 2007 cited McShane 2008). The 'sport for sport's sake' claim, therefore, might be considered rather strange given that only living creatures, or sentient beings, or even just persons, might be considered to have interests, rights or sakes, not cultural practices such as sport. However, Foot argues that natural goodness is 'attributable only to living things themselves and to their parts, characteristics, *and operations*' (Foot 2001 cited Thompson 2008). Given that sport is a cultural practice, it could therefore be considered to have an interest contingent on the interests of people. In this vein, the sport philosophy literature draws extensively on MacIntyre's conception of practices (MacIntyre 1984, p. 187) to argue 'sports are practices and ... practices are the sort of things that can have interests. Respect for the game will thus entail respect for the interests of the game (or sport) as a practice' (Butcher and Schneider 2001). However, as McFee elucidates, this means 'the practice operates normatively over my choices and the standard thereby created "partially defines" the practice'. Furthermore, he asks 'to what degree does this account evade the charges of relativism: that is, does it render practices immune to criticism?' (McFee 2004). McFee then uses Loland's conception of the internal goods of sport as 'goods that can only be realized inside the very practice of a shared, just ethos of the sport in question' (Loland 2002 cited McFee 2004) to point out that 'if this is right, we can criticise the practice if the ethos is not *shared*, not *just*, and so on' (McFee 2004).

An over interpretation of 'sport for sport's sake' then, runs the risk of presenting sport uncritically as autotelic and elevating it to the status of an ideal or embodied subject in its own right with people as subordinate objects of instrumental value to service the interests or 'sake' of sport, given, as Butcher and Schneider argue, 'a practice takes on a life of its own' (2001, p. 46). Thus, without a justification of the internal goods of sport or the value of sport, philosophically and/or empirically, the sport for sport's sake approach, evident within current sport and physical education policy documentation, runs the risk of crediting sport with an idealistic, unassailable, independent, natural and static existence; an obvious good, independent of time and space; what Coalter has called mythopoeic (Coalter 2007). This notion of sport is in danger of harking back to a narrative of empire, heritage, nostalgia and tradition, becoming effectively an evangelical mantra.

However, as has been extensively argued, sport is a cultural practice which has a constructed, contested, historical and dynamic existence. The relevant literature in this area is vast and includes the fields of critical, cultural and feminist theory. For example, the Frankfurt School, and Adorno's critical theory, argued for a materialist rather than idealist 'art for art's sake' notion of art, music and culture (Adorno 2002), recognizing the socially embedded nature of cultural practices which include sport. This approach was evident in New Labour's Game Plan strategy which adopted Patriksson's (1995 cited DCMS 2002) view that 'the futility of arguing whether sport is good or bad has been observed by several authors. Sport, like most activities, is not a priori good or bad, but has the potential of producing both positive and negative outcomes ... Questions like "What conditions are necessary for sport to have beneficial outcomes?" must be asked more often'. In this tradition, Pringle argues that 'play games and sport are not intrinsically good but are typically understood by critical sport scholars as social constructions that are constituted by, and constitutive of, broader social practices and the workings of power' and that 'numerous critical sport scholars have long recognised that sport practices are not fundamentally meritocratic or democratizing' (Pringle 2010).

Nevertheless, if we want to argue that sport (however we define it) has internal goods and intrinsic value, the nature of these goods and this value need to be (and have been) explored and crucially *should be explicit within sport policy documentation.* Admirably, the philosophy of sport literature has recognized this, but here, the intrinsic value of sport is often linked to moral development (encapsulated in the two metaphors of fair play and a level playing field) and the place of competition in achieving moral development (see e.g. McFee 2004). However, this is a claim that is difficult to support empirically, and it is not clear in any case that this good would be exclusive to sport. The literature relating to alternative conceptions of the intrinsic value of sport is also substantial and relates to movement/physical literacy (Whitehead 2010), movement intelligence (Gardner 1985), well-being, happiness (Layard 2005), joy, deep play (Kretchmar 2005), flow (Csikszentmihalyi 1975), human capabilities (Sen 2009) and real hedonism. For example, Inglis (1998) considers that 'the metaphysical point of sport is that it presages and embodies the active, expressive, and beautiful life of men and women contained within a benign and munificent nature'. Butcher and Schneider (2001) contend that 'for many, perhaps most, participants in sport, its activities are intrinsically rewarding. They bring a feeling of pleasure and provide experiences that are enjoyable and worthwhile'. Kretchmar (2008, p. 153) argues that 'the lusory attitude suggests that we are not only a problem-solving species but, even more fundamentally, that we are meaning seeking creatures'. Furthermore, Pringle (2010) usefully reviews the literature relating to the intrinsic value of movement pleasure, albeit within physical education.

At best, therefore, 'sport for sport's sake' claims to speak of the intrinsic value of 'sport', but why then define this narrowly as *competitive* sport given that the nature of sport's intrinsic goods are contested? Eichberg's 'philosophy of moving people' attempts to outline a philosophy of 'sport for all' which he terms 'the other sport' and claims that 'the philosophy of sport has … kept a strange distance from … complex empirical reality' and has 'remained to a large extent captured by the ideas of competitive elite sport'. He argues that 'the turn from sport for the few to body cultural practice of the popular masses can thus help the philosophy of sport to overcome its traditionally narrow focus on the mythology of achievement and the normative moral philosophy of fairness'. Thus, sport can be considered to be an essentially contested concept, a discourse, 'requiring dialectical methods of analysis' (Eichberg 2009). He also argues for a more bottom-up and plural definition of sport and sees 'popular sport' as 'where people meet in festival dance and play' and as 'basically relational sport, the sport of togetherness', inductively, empirically, plural (Eichberg 2009).

Turning to the empirical evidence, it has been extensively documented that women and girls are significantly less interested than men and boys in competitive team games (Mulvihill *et al.* 2000) and yet Sport England's nine targeted sports to prevent 'drop-off' (badminton, basketball, football, gymnastics, hockey, netball, rugby league, rugby union and tennis) include seven competitive team games (SE 2010a). Furthermore, it is of interest and concern that Sport England's Active People Survey 4 for 2009/2010 reported that while the number of male sports participants has increased (not significantly) to 4.176 million (still only 20.3%), there has been a statistically significant decline in participation among females from 2.787 million (13.1%) to 2.761 million (12.8%) (SE 2010a). This indicates that sport participation may increase (even though still a minority interest) but become less representative and inclusive. It appears, therefore, that defining sport as 'competitive sport for sport's sake' arguably this time around as a direct result of being awarded the London 2012 Olympic Games, may act to normalize and legitimize a partial movement culture, that of many boys and men, whilst positioning that of many women and girls as 'other' or primarily concerned with physical activity for health purposes.

Furthermore, at worst, the dual rhetoric of 'sport for sport's sake' and 'competitive sport' have ideological work to do, so that competitive sport is conflated with and legitimated by movement culture and traditional team games or Olympic sports with broader sport, in a ideological project of regressive public policy to normalize the notion of a 'big (pseudo) meritocratic (unequal) society' and a redistribution of common sporting wealth from females (and the poor) to males (and the rich). This traditional conservative policy approach is likely to result in increased sporting inequality with a (reduced) safety net provision for women (and the very poor), rather than develop towards the 2012 legacy aspiration to sport as a human right for all.

Sport for social good

Sport for social good, which was the policy purpose of early New Labour in relation to an overarching social inclusion agenda, has been thoroughly reviewed elsewhere in the sport policy literature (see Collins and Kay 2003, Coalter 2007, Collins 2010). Here, interestingly, 'sport for social good', at best, would also be defined in relation to the intrinsic value of sport, as sport for well-being, happiness, joy, deep play or real hedonism, crucially, *for all*, with echoes of the iconic 'Sport for All' campaigns of the1970s and the national demonstration projects of the 1980s. Thus, early New Labour sport policy documentation including Game Plan outlined a range of 'possible beneficial outcomes from sport and physical activity' which included not only 'personal satisfaction and better social life' but also the extrinsic goods of 'improved health; improved educational outcomes; crime reduction; social inclusion; and enhancing the environment'. Game Plan also makes explicit the fact that 'the health benefits of physical activity are the most strongly supported by the evidence' (DCMS 2002, p. 44), and of course sport narrowly defined does not hold a privileged position in relation to broader movement culture or sport for all, in relation to this good.

However, sport for social good as a policy justification in these new public management times, with an emphasis on centralized technocratic executive governance rather than devolved bottom-up representative government (Grix 2009, Green 2009), runs the risk of descending into a reductionist instrumentalism, survivalism, rationalism and healthism within a hegemonic audit culture. This was exemplified by the outgoing Chief Medical Officer's suggestion (Donaldson 2010), that all children should be fitness tested in schools to help combat the 'obesity crisis' (incidentally, referred to in jest as the 'big society' by Boris Johnson, Mayor of London [2010 cited Freedland 2010]). Once again, this argument runs the risk of over-interpretation, where people are subordinated objects used instrumentally for the greater good of the subject; this time society, policy or government.

Sport for peoples' sakes/sport for all

Sport, or movement culture, which can be considered to be essentially contested concepts, should not be reduced to partial competitive sport, logically is not autotelic: that is, cannot be an end 'in its own right' or 'for its own sake' *independent of human interests* and nor should it be reduced to merely an instrument for social good. If it has value at all, it is far more important than either of these purposes to embodied persons, or what MacIntyre (1999) called 'dependent rational animals'. It is part of where we have come from, who we are and how we become. Consequently, a third alternative, a critical synthesis, is to focus on sport for peoples' (individuals, communities and societies) sakes or sport for well-being, joy or happiness, that is sport for all. This necessitates government by discussion, public reason (Sen 2009); participatory (meaning not just internal stakeholders), as opposed to bureaucratic, executive or market, democracy, (Devine 2009); and practical reason (MacIntyre 1999). To this end, sport policy would be concerned with Eichberg's bottom-up, plural, inductive, definition of sport for all (Eichberg 2009), with the differential value of a range of movement/sport forms for developing human movement capabilities and flourishing, and with practical reason regarding the recognition and distribution of the individual, shared and common goods (MacIntyre 1999) which constitute movement and sport.

This view of sport policy is consistent with Coalter's claim that 'cultural shifts and increased pressure on time has led to a shift away from traditional, Olympic-type, sports to forms of activity which are flexible, individualistic and non-competitive (e.g. aerobic, hi-tech fitness, cycling, walking)' (Coalter 1999). Evidence for this is provided by the LGA which calculates that in 2008, 7.92 million people were members of sports clubs and 10 million people played informal sport in council owned and community facilities (LGA 2010a). Furthermore, the Active People Survey 4 reports that 'since 2007/08, participation in athletics (including running and jogging) has grown by 263,400 to 1.876 million adults (4.5%)' and 'cycling has grown from 1.767 million adults (4.3%) in 2007/8 to 1.866 million adults (4.4%) in 2009/10, an increase of 99,200 participants'. This contrasts with a statistically significant decline in participation in the following sports: swimming, football, golf, tennis, bowls, rugby union, cricket, basketball, snowsport, hockey, weightlifting, sailing, rugby league, gymnastics, rowing, volleyball, rounders and fencing (SE 2010a).

However, the value of movement in the current political and policy climate appears to be a hegemonic project around competition, talent spotting, elitism, masculinity and sport, on the one hand, and healthism, fitness and femininity, on the other. This has echoes of sport for the haves, leaders, subjects, men, and fitness or exercise for the have-nots, followers, objects, women. Of course, it could be argued that sport and movement are ontologically different. Nevertheless, either sport is broadly and inclusively defined as in the Council of Europe definition (COE 1992/2001), in which case it could be considered to be of fundamental value to human becoming, a human right as claimed by the IOC, or it is narrowly defined, and it becomes much harder to argue for its universal value: for its own sake, for social good or for peoples' sakes.

Sport for peoples' sakes: big society and citizenship rights

This article will now focus on the London 2012 Olympic legacy in relation to sport as a human right and sport for all, that is the right to sport for all, by drawing on the resurgence of interest in citizenship and civil society both under New Labour (active citizenship) from 1997 to 2010 and under the coalition government (big society) which came to power in 2010. To this end, the concept of a 'big sporting society' will be situated within a discourse of citizenship rights, freedoms and entitlements, responsibilities and duties, and 'big democracy'. This enables an evaluation of the emergent coalition London 2012 legacy UK sports system regarding its 'fitness for purpose', with the purpose being the right to sport for all. Civil and political rights (e.g. freedom to move, ownership of sporting land/property and sport democracy), social economic and cultural rights (e.g. movement and sporting equalities) and collective rights (e.g. environmental, land, water, natural resources, development, movement) will be considered.

Human and citizenship rights

Citizenship rights were famously outlined by Marshall as an evolving process with three tiers of rights: civil, political and social (Marshall 1950). A division into three generations following 'liberte, egalite, fraternite' was initially proposed by Karel Vasak in 1977 at the International Institute of Human Rights in Strasbourg (Wellman 2000). Rights are now often conceptualized in these three generations (Gomes et al. 2002) as outlined in Table 1. First-generation rights, for example, those outlined in the International Covenant on Civil and Political Rights (ICCPR) (United Nations [UN] 1966a) and the European Convention on Human Rights (ECHR) (COE 1950), are civil and political rights. They are centred around personal liberty and

Table 1.   Three generations of human rights with selected articles: (UNDHR, ICCPR, ICESCR).

First generation (ICCPR): held by individuals		Second generation (ICESCR): held by individuals		Third generation: held by communities or whole states
Civil and political (liberty) right to (article):		Social, economic and cultural (equality) right to (article):		Collective (fraternity) right to:
1	Self determination. Freely own, trade and dispose of natural wealth and resources	2	Same rights without discrimination	Environment
3	Equality between men and women	3	Equality between men and women	Land
6	Life and survival	6	Work, feely chosen	Water
7	Freedom from inhuman or degrading treatment	7	Just conditions of work, fair wages, equal pay for equal work, safe and healthy working conditions, rest and leisure	Group
8	Freedom from slavery and servitude	8	Form and join trade unions and to strike	Development
9	Freedom from arbitrary arrest	9	Social security	Natural resources
12	Liberty and freedom of movement*	10	Family. Children protected from economic exploitation	Cultural heritage
14	Equality before the law, presumed innocent until proven guilty, fair and public hearing	11	Adequate standard of living	Intergenerational sustainability
17	Privacy	12	Highest attainable standard of physical and mental health	Movement?
18	Freedom of thought	13	Education. Compulsory & free primary education	
21	Peaceful assembly*	15	Take part in cultural life	
22	Freedom of association			
25	Participate in conduct of public affairs, vote, be elected			

Note: *Shall not be subject to any restrictions except those which are provided by law, are necessary to protect national security, public order, public health or morals or the rights and freedoms of others.
Source: Adapted from the UN (1948, 1966a, 1966b).

protecting individuals from undue interference or violation by the state and are sometimes seen as negative rights. The International Covenant on Economic, Social and Cultural Rights (ICESCR) (UN 1966b) and European Social Charter (ESC) (COE 1961/1999) outline a range of second-generation rights, sometimes viewed as positive rights, concerned with entitlement from the state. These are socio-economic and cultural rights locating individuals within a social structure and relating to a more equal distribution of socio-economic and cultural goods services and opportunities.

The third-generation rights are collective rights, sometimes called group or solidarity rights, and they can be considered emerging rights. They locate individuals and communities within a physical structure and protect and entitle *peoples* from the state or states. Thus they can only be held in common by communities rather than exercised individually. Examples include the right to a healthy environment, land, water, natural resources, *development* (interestingly for sport development) and ownership of the common heritage of humankind (Jones 2005). We can also draw on MacIntyre's (1999) conception of the difference between shared goods which might relate to second-generation, and common goods which might relate to third-generation, rights. Interestingly, article 1 of both the ICCPR and the ICESCR outlines the right of peoples to self-determination, and Jones (2005) points out that 'the use of the term peoples' signals that the right is ascribed to each people as a group rather than to individuals'. Thus this is a high-profile example of a third-generation right which must be held in common.

It is now widely argued that civil and political rights, and social economic and cultural rights, are indivisible. In the words of the ICCPR, 'the ideal of free human beings enjoying civil and political freedom ... can only be achieved if conditions are achieved whereby everyone may enjoy his civil and political rights as well as his economic, social and cultural rights'.

Big society small state

Drawing on the above discussion, 'big sporting democracy', it could be argued, is dependent on three generations of sporting rights and freedoms. Consequently, a 'big sporting society' based on 'big sporting democracy' and 'big sporting citizenship' needs to address all three generations. However, the governments' conception of freedom or fairness appears to relate only to the first-generation civil rights, at the expense of second- and third-generation rights. Thus the coalition's 'big society' is a long way from US President Lyndon Johnson's notion of a 'great society', the basis of which was massive public expenditure, and which was encapsulated thus: 'the challenge of the next half century is whether we have the wisdom to use that wealth to enrich and elevate our national life, and to advance the quality of our (American) civilization' (Johnson 1964).

The Conservative Manifesto 2010 states that 'to protect our freedoms from State encroachment and encourage greater social responsibility, we will replace the Human Rights Act with a UK Bill of Rights' (Conservative Party 2010). However, the government has retreated from this renunciation of the first- and second-generation rights enshrined in the Human Rights Act and instead, announced in the Queens Speech on 25 May 2010, a Freedom (Great Repeal) Bill (Prime Minister's Office 2010). This is designed to 'roll back the State, reducing the weight of government imposition on citizens that has increased in recent years through legislation and centralised programmes'. Proposed benefits include 'restoring freedoms and civil liberties' and 'providing for greater accountability of the State to citizens'.[2]

Whilst refocusing on repealing violations of civil rights by the state is important and arguably overdue, if the resultant legislation prioritizes first-generation rights over, or at the expense of, second- and third-generation rights, as signalled by the big society, small state rhetoric, the consequences, unintended or otherwise, are likely to be freedoms for some rather than all, with the focus on limited and partial social provision in civil society and the voluntary sector. Weir (2006), even argues that social, economic and cultural rights, rather than just civil liberties should be embedded in the UK's legal system in the form of a Bill of Rights, precisely because of the erosion of the welfare state which was the traditional vehicle for delivering equality.

Devolving social, cultural, and therefore sporting, provision solely or primarily to civil society and the voluntary sector, crucially *in a context of a maintained or increasing inequality*, is likely to result in the take up of opportunities primarily by those with the power and resources to do so, with a continued and extended disenfranchisement of the under-represented, who may not even be considered as stakeholders. If we choose to learn historical lessons, it is clear that local communities (including sporting communities) and the decision makers in them may be parochial, exclusive, undemocratic and privileged (MacIntyre 1999). Thus, a commitment to the end of bureaucratic accountability may not rule out new managerialism and may translate as deregulation, regressive fiscal policy and a retreat from second generation, never mind third-generation freedoms. The resultant so-called democratic accountability (Cameron 2010a), it could be argued, relates to small or thin democracy and is merely rhetoric for the deregulated freedom of the market with opportunities to 'choose' and 'compete' distributed across an axis of differential power and resources.

Thus, although the language of the 'big society' may be that of the community and the citizen, the likely result within one of the most unequal 'developed' or rich societies, will be a hierarchical relationship of 'citizens', minimally defined, as individuals and consumers. Furthermore, the extent to which new public management rather than the public sector is dismantled, remains to be seen. Arguably, real democratic accountability relies on big democracy (three generations of rights), bottom-up democratic planning and the regulation of the market.

The seminal work of Wilkinson and Pickett (2009) draws attention to the statistically significant correlations between the degree of income inequality in rich countries and a range of economic, social and cultural indicators that relate to second-generation rights and can be considered to be necessary conditions of a 'big society'. Thus, they show that 'across whole populations, rates of mental illness are five times higher in the most unequal compared to the least unequal societies' and that 'in more unequal societies people are five times as likely to be imprisoned, six times as likely to be clinically obese, and murder rates may be many times higher'. This shows that what is important is not just reducing poverty via a safety net provision for the 'socially excluded' because 'the effects of inequality are not confined just to the least well-off: instead they affect the vast majority of the population'. Thus it is inequality rather than poverty or exclusion that needs to be addressed by a 'big society'. Wilkinson and Pickett show that the United States and United Kingdom, two of the most unequal rich countries, consistently fare worst on a range of social and cultural indicators, as demonstrated in Figure 1 in relation to obesity in women. The Scandinavian countries and Japan, the most equal rich countries, consistently fare best. Despite the methodological criticisms that have been made, the overall picture remains unassailable. Any attempt to create a 'big sporting society', it appears, needs to adopt what Wilkinson and Pickett call 'evidence-based politics'. Arguably, a revival or development of an inclusive representative civil society, or sport for all and mass participation, requires a context of relative equality, rather than relative inequality, in order to thrive. Furthermore, universal benefits, goods and stakeholding (not limited to stakeholders internal to competitive sport) appear to be necessary components of a fully realized sporting citizenship.

Big sporting society: three generations of rights

Sport and human rights: a three-generation rights model

The right to sport, as asserted by the Olympic Charter, and the guidelines for sport for member states within Europe and the European Union, which are set out by the European Sports Charter (COE 1992/2001) and the European Commission White Paper on Sport (EC 2007), respectively, are not enshrined in law either nationally or internationally. However, there is an array of rights instruments that can be related to sport, that are enshrined in law. An emerging body of work in sport and human rights (e.g. Kidd and Donnelly 2000, Brackenridge 2004, Donnelly and Petherick 2004, David 2005, Giulianotti and McArdle 2006) has primarily,

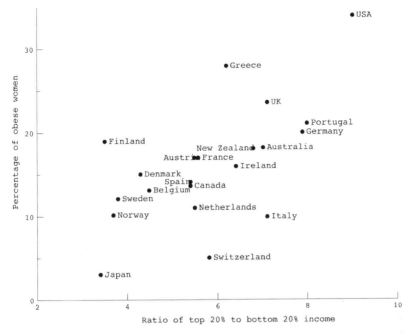

Figure 1. Evidence-based politics? Obesity-income inequality.
Source: Pickett *et al*. (2005).

although not exclusively (see Simpson 2005, Donnelly 2008, Coalter 2010), focused on sporting violations of negative freedoms and protection issues. These are violations within sport of first-generation rights, but generally not articles 13 and 12 of the UDHR and ICCPR, respectively, relating to the freedom to move. Kidd and Donnelly's work, however, outlines a range of issues as detailed in Figure 2, across the rights generations.

A big sporting society can be conceptualized as necessitating a sporting infrastructure which addresses 'big sporting democracy' by encompassing all three generations of rights as outlined in Table 2. This enables a mapping exercise in relation to emerging sport policy and the London 2012 legacy and an evaluation of the emergent government big society/small state policy direction in relation to 'big sporting society', 'big sporting democracy' and the right to sport for all.

> - Shrinking of the public sphere
> - Widening inequality of condition
> - Rights of the child in sport
> - Trafficking and sale of young athletes
> - Rights of refugees to sport
> - Reflecting millennium development goals (e.g. reducing world poverty and hunger, achieving universal primary education, empowering women and achieving gender equality)
> - Sport-based approaches to internationalism

Figure 2. Universal declaration of human rights and sport.
Source: Kidd and Donnelly (2000).

Table 2.   London 2012 Olympic Legacy: Big Sporting Society?

Civil and political rights (sport for some): protection from state: individual goods	Economic, social and cultural rights (sport for all): entitlement from state: shared goods	Collective rights (movement for all): common goods: movement rights
£50m to sport from deregulated lottery[1]	LA's: 25% + cuts to £1bn sport spend[2]	Defra plans to sell off nature reserves, rivers, forests[3]
Olympic Games (4 weeks): £9.375bn[4]	DCMS: 25% + cuts to £2bn total spend[5]	LA's cut budgets for public rights of way and open spaces[6]
'Competitive sport for sports sake'[7]	Schools: 11% cuts to £55bn sports facilities programme[8]	Extension of CROW 2000 Act?
'Light touch regulation at the heart of sport policy'[9]	Free swimming for under-16s and over 60s: £40m cuts[10]	Urban 'Right to Roam'?
Structural Reform Plan 15.7.10: lottery delivers community sport legacy[11]	Swimming pool refurbishment: £25m cuts[12]	Extension of Marine and Coastal Access Act 2009?
Nationwide Olympic and Paralympic style competition for schools[13]	Top tax rate of 50%	Commodification of movement/ sport/ physical space[14]
'Volunteers are crucial'[15]	£235m Playbuilder Scheme to create 3 500 playgrounds frozen[16]	Historical, for example, mass trespass: Kinder Scout (1932)
'The private sector has a key role to play in developing sport'[17]	Office for Civil Society cuts of £11m	Ramblers: urban path policies, claim the coast[18]
Curriculum review to embed competitive sport[19]	NCVO warns many charities will fold	BMC: access and conservation trust, make the most of the coast campaign[20]
Individual responsibility to exercise[21]	Charity Commission loses 60 jobs + 5% funding cuts	CTC: right to ride, right to ride to school[22]
	Premier League CEO'S: £1M + Footballers: up to £10m pa	BCU's rivers access campaign[23]
	Public health remit moves to LA's	Lidos/outdoor pools/wild swimming

Notes: [1] DCMS 2010b; [2] BBC 2010; [3] Jowit et al. 2010; [4] Bell 2009; [5] BBC 2010; [6] Ashbrook 2010; [7] Hunt 2010a; [8] Curtis 2010; [9] Conservative Party 2009a; [10] Hunt 2010b; [11] DCMS 2010a; [12] Conn 2010; [13] Hunt 2010a; [14] Judt 2010; [15] Conservative Party 2009a; [16] Vasagar 2010; [17] Conservative Party 2009a; [18] Ramblers 2010; [19] Department for Education 2010b; [20] British Mountaineering Council 2010; [21] DH 2010; [22] Cycle Touring Club 2010; [23] British Canoe Union 2010. LA, Local authority; NCVO, National Council for Voluntary Organization; BMC, British Mountaineering Council, CTC, Cycle Touring Club; BCU, British Canoe Union.

Interestingly, the three generation rights model for sport is coherent with Eichberg's project to develop 'a philosophy of sport for all' based around the 'demos' of democracy, and incorporating 'libertie, egalitie, and fraternite' (Eichberg 2009). As Eichberg points out 'commercial sport is a sport for those who can pay, and in this respect, a 'sport for not-all'. Whereas, sport for all, when adopted by civil society, involves 'other perspectives on sport for all than the strategies of governments or ministries'. Furthermore, in many cases civil society, social movements and sport for all involve 'the principle of voluntary cooperation in more or less communitarian and non-competitive sports' (Eichberg 2009). Drawing on Eichberg's argument, it is not therefore clear that civil society would accept a top-down, imposed definition of 'competitive sport for sport's sake'. Defining sport in this way is not coherent with bottom-up provision of sport in civil society: that is, the right to sport for all.

First-generation sporting rights

First-generation rights require protection for individuals from sporting violations of all articles comprising the legally binding ICCPR (and, in Europe, the ECHR). This involves some difficult issues for sport. For example, article 25 addresses the right to participate in the conduct of public affairs, vote and be elected. However, the government intends 'light touch regulation at the heart of sport policy' (Conservative Party 2009a); that funding for sport will come from £50m to sport from a deregulated lottery (DCMS 2010b); that the (fiscally regressive) lottery is to deliver the community school legacy; and that 'the private sector has a key role to play in developing sport' (Conservative Party 2009a). Given that lottery funding is not government funding, and will be minimally regulated anyway, this may mean that sport is taken out of what constitutes 'public affairs' and is not considered to be subject to the representative democracy outlined in article 25. Furthermore, the government's *very definition* of sport appears to be the partial 'competitive sport for sport's sake' which encapsulates the sporting practices of a relatively small demographic. If article 25 relates only to sport policy community stakeholders defined this narrowly, the majority of the population, disproportionately women, will be further disenfranchized in relation to sport. This will work against the 2012 legacy aspiration of the right to sport for all.

First-generation sporting rights also include protection from violations of an individual's freedom to move. However, this is subject to the caveat that it should not contravene other first-generation rights, and crucial here is the right to property. The balance between these two rights plays out differently in different 'developed' or rich countries, for example, the United Kingdom and Finland, and is dependent on the extent to which second-generation rights are addressed. Consequently, second-generation rights are crucial as they relate to how economic, social and cultural sporting resources, such as facilities, clubs, land and water, are shared. First-generation sporting rights without second-generation rights may result in sport *management* of sport for not-all (those already playing, paddling, climbing and so on) and a stratified or terraced, as opposed to a level, playing field. This is a merit and desert conception of fairness, in an unequal sporting society, arising from a position of fairness as 'equal treatment' or even some conceptions of 'equal opportunity'. Furthermore, it could be argued that in order to exercise the first-generation right to move, we need a third-generation 'freedom to move', a right held in common in relation to access to land and water, and urban and rural physical space.

Second-generation sporting rights

Second-generation rights, as outlined in the legally binding ICESCR (and in Europe, the ESC), require sport 'to take steps to the maximum of its available resources to achieve progressively the full realization of the rights in this treaty' (UN 1966b). Notwithstanding Girginov and Hills's assertion that 'sustainable (sport) development has ... been a much contested concept because it directly engages with justice and equality' (Girginov and Hills 2009), in this case it can be argued that for sport this means sport *development* to work towards, not away from, the right to 'sport for all'. This is a needs and equality conception of fairness and justice, working towards a more 'equal outcome'. Once again, a 'big sporting society' will find some, if not all, of these rights challenging. For example, working towards article 3, equality between men and women would be much easier to address with a broad, inclusive definition of sport. Similarly, working towards article 7 (relating to just conditions of work, fair wages, equal pay for equal work, safe and healthy working conditions, rest and leisure), and towards article 8 (the right to form and join trade unions and to strike) are immensely challenging for sport.

Particularly of concern in relation to second-generation sporting rights is the policy direction 'from big government to big society' (Cameron 2010a), together with the policy choices relating to the reduction of the public financial deficit. Second-generation sporting rights are particularly vulnerable to public sector spending cuts because the provision of sport is non-statutory and sporting equalities are addressed primarily in the public sector, via, for example, sport development, as opposed to management, initiatives. In the first months in power, the coalition announced: the cancellation of free swimming for under 16s and over 60s resulting in a saving of £40m (Hunt 2010b); the cancellation of the £55bn school building programme, of which it is estimated, 11% was to have been set aside for new sports facilities; £25m cuts to the swimming pool refurbishment programme; a freeze on the £235m Playbuilder Scheme to create 3500 playgrounds (Curtis 2010, Conn 2010, Vasagar 2010); and the phased ending the £162 million PE and Sports Strategy of the previous administration (Gove 2010, Campbell 2010). Furthermore, the 'average real terms budget cuts of 25% over four years – except for health and international aid' (BBC 2010) apply to the £1.8bn sport spend of local authorities, and the total DCMS spend, and are of a different order to the relatively small increase in funding to sport from the deregulated lottery.

The cancellation of the free swimming initiative is an interesting indicator of the new policy direction. The previous New Labour administration argued that 'swimming is the country's most popular sporting activity. The Government's free swimming initiative is an important part of our plans to secure a long-term legacy from London hosting the 2012 Olympic and Paralympic Games – and to get two million people more active and more healthy' (DCMS Archive). However, the current government declared in July 2010 that 'funding for free swims under the free swimming programme will end this summer, in the light of new research which shows that the scheme has not delivered value for money. Figures published today show that the majority of those participating in the scheme would have gone swimming anyway, even if they had to pay, and that the scheme has not significantly increased physical activity' (SE 2010b). However, The Evaluation of the Impact of Free Swimming Year 1 report documents that 'For those aged 60 and over, we estimate that there have been around 1.5 million net additional swims over the first year of the FSP by about 23,000 net additional swimmers. For those aged 16 and under, there have been around 5.5 million net additional swims and just under 115,000 net additional swimmers' (PricewaterhouseCoopers 2010). This could be considered a startling success and raises the issue of the place of universal benefits, the strengths of which relate to an inclusive vision of citizenship and big society. Conversely, the weaknesses of such benefits are that they can appear unfair particularly in societies with steep socio-economic gradients.

The wisdom of monetarists is disputed by Keynesians such as Lord Skidelsky, who asserts 'I must remain sceptical about the newly fashionable doctrine of expansionary fiscal contraction, as it is known; the idea that if you contract the budget deficit, the economy will expand' (Skidelsky 2010). Even amongst those who support contraction, the mandate for the scale and speed of the cuts is questioned, but given this policy decision, there is no reason why sport should be protected. However, given that rights structure relations of equality 'not only between citizens and state but also between citizens' (Nedelsky 2008), the 'we are all in this together' (Cameron 2010b) philosophy is dependent on conditions of relative equality. Consequently, second-generation rights should be protected even in times of austerity. In terms of sport, this might mean that local authority sport and physical activity *development* teams should be protected and prioritized over the *management* of local authority sporting facilities which in any case disproportionally service the needs of the already included

(Collins and Kay 2003). However, a more equal society and universal benefits could be argued to be preferable in relation to a cohesive big sporting society, big sporting democracy and the right to sport for all.

Third-generation sporting rights

Finally, although third-generation rights are less well established than first and second, and are not systematically incorporated in a legally binding instrument, it can be argued that the right to move (a first-generation right) is dependent on a third-generation freedom to move. Thus, a 'big sporting society' needs a third-generation 'right to move' which is a right held in common in relation to access to land and water, and urban and rural physical space. This would involve not just some delimited socially controlled 'level playing fields', but much greater access to physical space: urban and rural, water and land.

However, for a 'developed' or rich country, the United Kingdom has relatively modest third-generation movement rights as compared with, for example, the Scandinavian countries, which have an extensive 'right to roam' known as 'everyman's right' (The Finnish Ministry of the Environment 2007). Furthermore, The Open Spaces Society claims that 'local authorities are cutting budgets for public rights of way and open spaces, which they see as expendable' (Ashbrook 2010), and it has been reported that the Department for Environment Food and Rural Affairs (DEFRA) is considering 'plans to sell off nature reserves, rivers, forests' with the 'fears (that) huge cuts to (the) environment department risk (an) "austerity countryside" "and that the" "crown jewels" of Britain's landscape could be sold off' (Jowit et al. 2010, Vidal et al. 2010).[3] Also, there has been steady privatization of urban public space so that significant chunks are, in fact, privately owned. As Judt details "Stratford City", in east London, covering 170 acres, "Cabot Circus" in Bristol, "Highcross" in Leicester, "Liverpool One" (which spans 34 streets and is owned by Grosvenor, the Duke of Westminster's property company) are all privately-owned and privately-controlled spaces at the heart of what were once public municipalities'. Furthermore, 'they reserve the right to impose a range of restrictions (such as) no skateboarding, no rollerblading' (Judt 2010). There is much talk of rising obesity levels, a sedentary population and 'factory farmed' as opposed to 'free range' children. However, the usual culprits are considered to be 'stranger danger' which has not increased since 1985 (Home Office 2002), and traffic, which has. There has been much less discussion of the commodification of movement, sport and physical space; and the resultant limited access or freedom to move in both rural and urban space enjoyed by the UK population relative to other 'developed' countries.

Conclusion: London 2012 Olympic legacy – a right to sport for all?

Although the IOC outlines the right to sport . . . for all, and the government has a legacy aim of 'harnessing the United Kingdom's passion for sport to increase grass roots participation, particularly by young people' and encouraging 'the whole population to be more physically active', current sport policy is in danger of working away from these objectives. Thus the hegemonic definition of sport as competitive sport for sport's sake excludes a richer, fuller, inductive and inclusive right to sport for all.

The government's emergent sport policy appears, at best, to address only first-generation rights, that is individual rights for some, given the competitive sport for sport's sake parameter and internal stakeholders, and the actual and proposed regression in second- and third-generation rights. It advocates sport for some, the already privileged and/or male, sport for not-all. Thus sport policy becomes about sport (*new, or new public*) *management* or sport development *for some*, rather than 'sport for all' or sport *development* for all, which is about extending the sporting franchize beyond the players and stakeholders already within the boundaries of sporting communities, defined by the current government as competitive sport for sport's sake. As Bourdieu (1978) has pointed out 'the field of sporting practice is the site of struggles in which what is at stake, inter alia, is the monopolistic capacity to impose the legitimate definition of sporting practice'.

Participatory democracy (Devine 2009) or democracy via public discussion (Sen 2009) necessitates bottom-up big democracy and democratic planning rather than New Labours new managerialism or 'executive democracy' (Devine 2009). The coalition's project to dismantle bureaucratic democracy does not appear to involve the corollary of extending big democracy, but rather, consists of increased deregulation and a neoliberal agenda with the ideological project of protecting and extending (sporting) privilege.

Consequently, the London 2012 Olympic legacy is likely to be an individual *entitlement* to sport for the haves and an individual *duty* to exercise with diminished *entitlement* to physical space for the have-nots. It can be encapsulated as

(1) driving & legitimising a shift in the purpose of sport policy from sport for social good to competitive sport for sports sake,
(2) driving & legitimising a bifurcation between 'sport' narrowly defined and 'physical activity' as exercise for health,
(3) defining stake holders as internal to narrowly defined competitive sport and thus disenfranchising further under-represented groups, notably women,
(4) retreating from second generation never mind third generation rights to sport for all and
(5) shifting the responsibility for the sporting infrastructure from local government to the voluntary & private sectors, with a resultant decreased investment in both hard and soft sporting infrastructure.

Finally, it would be useful to develop further the concepts of 'big sporting democracy' and a 'big sporting society'. This could be done by developing a democratic audit or assessment tool addressing all three generations of human rights in relation to the sporting landscape. Democratic Audit, an independent research organization, now hosted by the University of Liverpool, has developed an assessment methodology 'based on the two basic principles of representative democracy – *popular control and political equality*' and states that 'a democratic audit is a comprehensive and systematic assessment of a country's political life in order to answer the question: how democratic is it and how well are human rights protected?' (Democratic Audit 2010). An assessment tool relating to the sport policy community and sporting institutions would be a useful way of extending a democratic audit around three generations of movement rights to evaluate further whether or not emerging UK sport policy is 'fit for purpose' in relation to a London 2012 Olympic legacy aspiration of the right to sport for all.

Acknowledgement

I would like to thank Susanne Gibson, Carol Osborne, Ann Long, Pat Devine and two anonymous reviewers for their input at various stages during the development of this article.

Notes

1. Since this article was written, the Culture Secretary Jeremy Hunt 'confirmed the second target (to get a million more people doing physical activity) had been quietly dropped shortly after the

coalition government came to power. The first target (to inspire a million more people to play sport) . . . nominally remains in place for now but it is understood that it too will shortly be dropped in favour of a "more meaningful" national measure' (Gibson 2011).

2. This bill is now progressing through the House of Commons renamed the Protection of Freedoms Bill and is widely considered to be much less ambitious than originally intended.

3. On 27 January 2011, the government launched a 3-month consultation on 'plans to sell off public forests in the biggest change in land ownership for more than 80 years. The forests sell-off could raise £150–250m over 10 years' (Vidal *et al.* 2010). However, a huge campaign ensued and the government backed down very publically when Caroline Spelman, the Environment Secretary said, on 17 February 2011, 'I am sorry, we got this one wrong' (Watt 2011). The Guardian also reported that 'A YouGov poll found that 84% of people agreed the woods and forests should be kept in public ownership for future generations, while only 2% disagreed (Carrington, 2011).'

References

Abad, D., 2010. Sportsmanship. *Sport, ethics and philosophy*, 4 (1), 27–42.

Adorno, T., 2002. *Essays on music*. London: University of California Press.

Ashbrook, K., 2010. *Letter to the guardian*. General Secretary, The Open Spaces Society. 17 August 2010.

BBC, 2010. *Budget key points: at a glance*. Available from: http://www.bbc.co.uk/news/10374475 [Accessed 6 October 2010].

Bell, B., 2009. *Sport studies*. Exeter: Learning Matters.

Bourdieu, P., 1978. Sport and social class. *Social science information*, 17, 819–840.

Brackenridge, C., 2004. Women and children first? Child abuse and child protection in sport. *Sport in society*, 7 (3), 322–337.

British Canoe Union (BCU), 2010. Available from: http://www.ctc.org.uk/DesktopDefault.aspx? TabID=4517 [Accessed 5 October 2010].

British Mountaineering Council, 2010. *Access and conservation*. Available from: http://www.thebmc. co.uk/Category.aspx?category=1 [Accessed 5 October 2010].

Browne, J., 2010. Distributional analysis of tax and benefit changes. Presentation: *IFS 2010 Spending Review Briefing*. London: Institute for Fiscal Studies, 21 October. Available from: http://www.ifs. org.uk/publications/5313 [Accessed 14 July 2011].

Butcher, R. and Schneider, A., 2001. Fair play as respect for the game. *In*: W.J. Morgan, K.V. Meier and A.J. Schneider eds. *Ethics in sport*. Champaign: Human Kinetics, 21–48.

Cameron, D., 2010a. *We will make government accountable to the people*. Conservatives.com, 8 July. Available from: http://www.conservatives.com/News/Speeches/2010/07/David_Cameron_We_ will_make_government_accountable_to_the_people.aspx [Accessed 14 July 2010].

Cameron, D., 2010b. *Together in the national interest. Speech to the conservative party conference*. 6 October. Available from: http://www.conservatives.com/News/Speeches/2010/10/David_ Cameron_Together_in_the_National_Interest.aspx [Accessed 14 July 2011].

Campbell, D., 2010. *U-turn as Michael Gove agrees to continue funding school sport system*. Guardian.co.uk, 20 December. Available from: http://www.guardian.co.uk/politics/2010/dec/20/ u-turn-michael-gove-school-sport-partnership [Accessed 13 July 2011].

Carrington, D., 2011. Huge majority oppose England forest sell off, poll finds. *The Guardian* [online], 22 Jan. Available from: http://www.guardian.co.uk/environment/2011/jan/22/poll-england-forest-sell-off [Accessed 25 January 2012].

Central Council for Physical Recreation (CCPR), 1960. *Sport and the community: the report of the Wolfenden committee on sport 1960*. London: CCPR.

Coalter, F. 1999. Sport and recreation in the UK: flow with the flow or buck the trends? *Managing leisure*, 4 (1), 24–39.

Coalter, F., 2007. *A wider role for sport: who's keeping the score?* London: Routledge.

Coalter, F., 2010. The politics of sport-for-development: limited focus programmes and broad gauge problems? *International review for the sociology of sport*, 45 (3), 295.

Collins, M., 2010. From 'sport for good' to 'sport for sport's sake' – not a good move for sports development in England? *International journal of sport policy and politics*, 2 (3), 367–379.

Collins, M. and Kay, T., 2003. *Sport and social exclusion*. London: Routledge.

Conn, D., 2010. The coalition's deep cuts to sport will leave Britain playing catch up for years. *The Guardian*, 14 July, p. 6.

Conservative Party, 2009a. *Conservative sport manifesto*. London: Conservative Party. Available from: http://www.conservatives.com/~/media/Files/Downloadable%20Files/sports-manifesto. ashx?dl=true [Accessed 29 June 2010].

Conservative Party, 2009b. *Extending opportunities: a conservative policy paper on sport*. London: Conservative Party.

Conservative Party, 2010. *The conservative manifesto 2010*. London: Conservative Party. Available from: http://media.conservatives.s3.amazonaws.com/manifesto/cpmanifesto2010_lowres.pdf [Accessed 4 October 2010].

Council of Europe (COE), 1950. *European convention on human rights*. Strasbourg: COE.

Council of Europe, 1961 (revised 1999). *European social charter*. Strasbourg: COE.

Council of Europe, 1992 (revised 2001). *European sports charter*. Strasbourg: COE. Available from: http://www.coe.int/t/dg4/sport/sportineurope/charter_en.asp [Accessed 6 January 2011].

Csikszentmihalyi, M., 1975. *Beyond boredom and anxiety*. San Francisco: Jossey-Bass.

Curtis, P., 2010. School building programme scrapped in latest round of cuts. *The Guardian*, 6 July, p. 10.

Cycle Touring Club, 2010. *Campaigns and policy*. Available from: http://www.ctc.org.uk/Desktop Default.aspx?TabID=4517 [Accessed 5 October 2010].

David, P., 2005. Human rights in youth sport. Oxford: Routledge.

DCMS, 2007. *Our promise for 2012: how the UK will benefit from the Olympic and Paralympic Games*. London: DCMS.

DCMS, 2008. *Before, during and after: making the most of the London 2012 games*. London: DCMS. Available from: http://webarchive.nationalarchives.gov.uk/+/http://www.culture.gov.uk/ images/publications/2012LegacyActionPlan.pdf [Accessed 13 July 2011].

DCMS Archive. *Free swimming programme*. DCMS Snapshot 12 May 2010. Available from: http:// webarchive.nationalarchives.gov.uk/+/http://www.culture.gov.uk/what_we_do/sport/5809.aspx [Accessed 15 July 2011].

DCMS, 2010a. *Department for culture media and sport structural reform plan*. 15 July 2010. Available from: http://www.culture.gov.uk/publications/7246.aspx [Accessed June 2010].

DCMS, 2010b. *Olympic sports legacy plans, wider changes*. 10 June 2010. Available from: http:// www.culture.gov.uk/news/news_stories/7153.aspx [Accessed 16 June 2010].

DCMS, 2010c. *Plans for the legacy from the 2012 Olympic and Paralympic Games*. London: DCMS. Available from: http://www.culture.gov.uk/images/publications/201210_Legacy_Publication.pdf [Accessed 15 July 2011].

Democratic Audit, 2010. *About us*. Available from: http://www.democraticaudit.com/index.php [Accessed 4 October 2010].

Department for Culture, Media and Sport (DCMS), 2002. *Game Plan, a strategy for delivering Government's sport and physical activity objectives*. London: DCMS and the Strategy Unit.

Department for Education (DfE), 2010a. *Gove: 'I want competitive sport to be at the centre of a truly rounded education'*. London: DfE. Available from: http://www.education.gov.uk/inthenews/ inthenews/a0071188/gove-i-want-competitive-sport-to-be-at-the-centre-of-a-truly-rounded-education [Accessed 13 July 2011].

DfE, 2010b. *The importance of teaching – the schools white paper 2010*. London: DfE. Available from: https://www.education.gov.uk/publications/eOrderingDownload/CM-7980.pdf [Accessed 13 July 2011].

DfE, 2010c. *A new approach for school sports – decentralising power, incentivising competition, trusting teachers*. 20 December 2010. Available from: http://www.education.gov.uk/inthenews/ inthenews/a0071098/a-new-approach-for-school-sports-decentralising-power-incentivising-competition-trusting-teachers [Accessed 12 July 2011].

Department of Health (DH), 2010. *Healthy lives, healthy people: our strategy for public health in England*. London: The Stationary Office. Available from: http://www.dh.gov.uk/prod_consum_dh/ groups/dh_digitalassets/documents/digitalasset/dh_127424.pdf [Accessed 13 July 2011].

Department of National Heritage (DNH), 1995. *Sport: raising the game*. London: DNH.

Devine, P., 2009. Social ownership and democratic planning. *In*: P. Devine, A. Pearman and D. Purdy, eds. *Feelbad Britain. How to make it better*. London: Lawrence and Wishart, 117–129.

Donaldson, L. (2010). *2009 Annual report of the chief medical officer*. London: DH. Available from: http://www.dh.gov.uk/prod_consum_dh/groups/dh_digitalassets/@dh/@en/@ps/documents/ digitalasset/dh_114012.pdf [Accessed 13 July 2011].

Donnelly, P., 2008. Sport and human rights. *Sport in society*, 11 (4), 381–394.

Donnelly, P. and Petherick, L., 2004. Workers' playtime? Child labour at the extremes of the sporting spectrum. *Sport in society*, 7 (3), 301–321.

Eichberg, H., 2009. Bodily democracy: towards a philosophy of sport for all. *Sport, ethics and philosophy*, 3 (3), 441–461.

English Sports Council (ESC), 1997. *England, the sporting nation*. London: ESC.

European Commission [EC], 2007. *White paper on sport*. Brussels: European Commission. Available from: http://ec.europa.eu/sport/white-paper/whitepaper8_en.htm#1 [Accessed 6 January 2011].

Freedland, J., 2010. There's a good idea in Cameron's 'big society' screaming to get out. *The guardian*, 20 July, p. 27.

Gardner, H., 1985. *Frames of mind: the theory of multiple intelligences*. New York: Basic Books.

Gibson, O., 2011. Jeremy Hunt admits London 2012 legacy targets will be scrapped. *The Guardian* [online], 29 March, p. 1. Available from: http://www.guardian.co.uk/sport/2011/mar/28/jeremy-hunt-london-2012-legacy [Accessed 25 January 2012].

Girginov, V. and Hills, L., 2009. The political process of constructing a sustainable London Olympics sports development legacy. *International journal of sport policy*, 1 (2), 161–181.

Giulianotti, R. and McArdle, D., 2006. *Sport, civil liberties and human rights*. London and New York: Routledge.

Gomes, R. *et al.*, 2002. *A manual on human rights education with young people*. Budapest: Council of Europe.

Gove, M., 2010. *Refocusing sport in schools to build a lasting legacy*. Department for Education. Available from: http://www.education.gov.uk/inthenews/inthenews/a0065473/refocusing-sport-in-schools-to-build-a-lasting-legacy-of-the-2012-games [Accessed 6 January 2011].

Green, M., 2009. Podium or participation? Analysing policy priorities under changing modes of sport governance in the United Kingdom. *International journal of sport policy*, 1 (2), 121–144.

Grix, J., 2009. The impact of UK sport policy on the governance of athletics. *International journal of sport policy*, 1 (1), 31–49.

Harris, S., Mori, K., and Collins, M., 2009. Great expectations: voluntary sports clubs and their role in delivering the national policy of English sport. *Voluntas*, 20 (4), 404–423.

HM Treasury, 2010a. *Budget 2010*. London: The Stationary Office. Available from: http://cdn.hm-treasury.gov.uk/junebudget_complete.pdf [Accessed 13 July 2011].

HM Treasury, 2010b. *Spending review 2010*. London: The Stationary Office. Available from: http://cdn.hm-treasury.gov.uk/sr2010_completereport.pdf [Accessed 13 July 2011].

Home Office, 2002. *Crime in England and Wales*. Statistical Bulletin 07/02, 2001/2002.

Houlihan, B., 2009. Mechanisms of international influence on domestic elite sport policy. *International journal of sport policy*, 1 (1), 51–69.

Hunt, J., 2010a. *Sports keynote speech*. Department for Culture Media and Sport, 28 June. Available from: http://www.culture.gov.uk/news/ministers_speeches/7207.aspx [Accessed 29 June 2010].

Hunt, J., 2010b. *DCMS savings announced*. DCMS news release, 17 June. Available from: http://www.culture.gov.uk/news/media_releases/7191.aspx [Accessed 4 October 2010].

Inglis, F., 1998. The state of play: sport, capital and happiness. *In*: L. Allison, ed. *Taking sport seriously*. Aachen: Meyer & Meyer, 155–172.

International Olympic Committee (IOC), 2010. *Olympic charter*. Lausanne: IOC. Available from: http://www.olympic.org/Documents/Olympic%20Charter/Charter_en_2010.pdf [Accessed 13 July 2011].

Johnson, L. 1964. *Remarks at the University of Michigan*. 22 May 1964. Available from: http://www.lbjlib.utexas.edu/johnson/archives.hom/speeches.hom/640522.asp [Accessed 7 January 2011].

Jones, P., 2005. Group rights. *The essentials of human rights*. London: Hodder Arnold.

Jowit, J., Carrell, S., and Vidal, J., 2010. Plans to sell off nature reserves risks 'austerity countryside'. *The guardian*, 14 August, p. 1. Available from: http://www.guardian.co.uk/politics/2010/aug/13/plan-sell-nature-reserves-austerity-countryside [Accessed 13 July 2011].

Judt, T., 2010. *Ill fares the land*. London: Allen Lane.

Kidd, B. and Donnelly, P., 2000. Human rights in sport. *International review for the sociology of sport*, 35 (2), 131–148.

Kretchmar, R.S., 1994. *Practical philosophy of sport*. Champaign: Human Kinetics.

Kretchmar, R.S., 2005. *Practical philosophy of sport and physical activity*. Champaign: Human Kinetics.

Kretchmar, R.S., 2008. Gaming up life: considerations for game expansions. *Journal of the philosophy of sport*, 35, 142–155.

Layard, R., 2005. *Happiness: lessons from a new science*. London: Allen Lane.

Lindsey, I., 2009. Collaboration in local sport services in England: issues emerging from case studies of two local authority areas. *International journal of sport policy*, 1 (1), 71–88.

Local Government Association (LGA), 2010a. *Putting the people back into participation: consultation draft*. London: LGA.

Local Government Association (LGA), 2010b. *Written evidence from the Local Government Association*. London: UK Parliament. Available from: http://www.publications.parliament.uk/pa/cm200910/cmselect/cmcumeds/memo/olympics/ucm2302.htm [Accessed 13 July 2011].

MacIntyre, A., 1984. *After virtue*. Notre Dame: University of Notre Dame.

MacIntyre, A., 1999. *Dependent rational animals*. London: Duckworth.

Marshall, T.H., 1950. *Citizenship and social class*. Cambridge: Cambridge University Press.

McFee, G., 2004. *Sport, rules and values*. London: Routledge.

McShane, K., 2008. Virtue and respect for nature: Ronald Sandler's. *Character and environment, ethics, place and environment*, 11 (2), 213–218.

Mulvihill, C. *et al.*, 2000. Views of young people towards physical activity: determinants and barriers to involvement. *Health education*, 100 (5), 190–199.

Nedelsky, J., 2008. Reconceiving rights and constitutionalism. *Journal of human rights*, 7, 139–173.

Pickett, K. *et al.*, 2005. Wider income gaps, wider waistbands? An ecological study of obesity income inequality. *Journal of epidemiology and community health*, 59 (8), 670–674.

PricewaterhouseCoopers, 2010. *Evaluation of the impact of free swimming*. London: PricewaterhouseCoopers LLC. Available from: http://www.culture.gov.uk/images/publications/FSP-exec-summary-June2010.pdf [Accessed 13 July 2011].

Prime Minister's Office, 2010. *Freedom (Great Repeal) Bill. HM Government* [online]. Available from: http://www.number10.gov.uk/news/queens-speech-freedom-great-repeal-bill/ [Accessed: 25 January 2012].

Pringle, R., 2010. Finding pleasure in physical education: a critical examination of the educative value of positive movement affects. *Quest*, 62, 119–134.

Ramblers, 2010. *Campaigns and policy*. Available from: http://www.ramblers.org.uk/Campaigns+Policy/Campaigns+Policy [Accessed 5 October 2010].

Robertson, H., 2010. *London 2012 Olympic and Paralympic Games quarterly report*. July 2010. Available from: http://webcache.googleusercontent.com/search?q=cache:5xmpc9IreZEJ:www.culture.gov.uk/images/publications/DCMS_GOE_QR_July_2010.rtf+I+want+to+see+London+2012+leave+a+lasting+legacy+of+mass+participation+in+sport.+It+is+my+vision&cd=3&hl=en&ct=clnk&gl=uk [Accessed 6 January 2011].

Sen, A., 2009. *The idea of justice*. London: Allen Lane.

Simpson, B., 2005. Cities as playgrounds: active leisure for children as a human right. *In*: Caudwell, J. and Bramham, P. eds. *Sport, active leisure and youth culture* (LSA Publication No. 86, Brighton), 3–23.

Skidelsky, R., 2010. *Speech to the house of lords*. 1 November 2010. Available from: http://blogs.ft.com/economistsforum/2010/11/lord-skidelskys-speech-on-the-uks-spending-review/ [Accessed 6 January 2010].

Sport England (SE), 1999a. *Sport England lottery fund strategy 1999–2009*. London: Sport England.

Sport England, 1999b. *The value of sport*. London: Sport England.

Sport England, 2008. *Sport England strategy 2008–2011*. London: Sport England.

Sport England, 2010a. *Active people survey 4*. London: Sport England. Available from: http://www.sportengland.org/research/active_people_survey/active_people_survey_4.aspx [Accessed 13 July 2011].

Sport England, 2010b. *DCMS savings announced*. London: Sport England. Available from: http://www.sportengland.org/media_centre/press_releases/dcms_savings_announced.aspx [Accessed 13 July 2011].

Taylor, P., 2002. Driving up participation: sport and volunteering. *In*: Sport England, ed. *Driving up participation: the challenge for sport*. London: Sport England.

The Finnish Ministry of the Environment, 2007. *Everyman's right in Finland*. Helsinki: The Finnish Ministry of the Environment. Available from: http://www.ymparisto.fi/download.asp?contentid=25603&lan=en [Accessed 28 September 2010].

Thompson, A., 2008. Natural goodness and abandoning the economy of value: Ron Sandler's character and environment. *Ethics, place and environment*, 11 (2), 218–226.

United Nations, (UN) 1948. *Universal declaration of human rights*. [online] Available from: http://www.un.org/en/documents/udhr/index.shtml [Accessed 25 January 2012].

United Nations, 1966a. *International covenant on civil and political rights*. [online] Available from: http://treaties.un.org/doc/Publication/UNTS/Volume%20999/volume-999-I-14668-English.pdf [Accessed 25 January 2012].

United Nations, 1966b. *International covenant on economic, social and cultural rights*. [online] Available from: http://www2.ohchr.org/english/law/cescr.htm [Accessed 25 January 2012].

Vasagar, J., 2010. Plans for hundreds of new playgrounds shelved. *guardian.co.uk*, 11 August.

Vasak, K., 1977. Human rights: a thirty-year struggle: the sustained efforts to give force of law to the universal declaration of human rights. *UNESCO courier*, 30, 11.

Vidal, J., Carrell, S., and Jowit, J., 2010. 'Crown jewels' of Britain's landscape could be sold off. *The guardian*, 14 August, p. 6. Available from: http://www.guardian.co.uk/environment/2010/aug/13/crown-jewels-britains-landscape-sold [Accessed 13 July 2011].

Watt, N., 2011. Forest sell-off abandoned: I'm sorry, I got it wrong, says Caroline Spelman. *The Guardian* [online], 17 Feb. Available from: http://www.guardian.co.uk/environment/2011/feb/17/forest-sell-off-abandoned-sorry-caroline-spelman [Accessed 25 January 2012].

Weir, S., 2006. *Unequal Britain, human rights as a route to social justice*. London: Politico's.

Wellman, C., 2000. Solidarity, the individual and human rights. *Human rights quarterly*, 22 (3), 639–657.

Whitehead, M., 2010. *Physical literacy*. London: Routledge.

Wilkinson, R. and Pickett, K., 2009. *The spirit level, why more equal societies almost always do better*. London: Allen Lane.

Woodhouse, J., 2010. *London Olympics 2012: sporting legacy*. London: House of Commons Library (Standard Note SN/HA/4868).

The Olympic Movement and Islamic culture: conflict or compromise for Muslim women?

Tansin Benn and Symeon Dagkas

School of Education, Muirhead Tower Room 546, University of Birmingham, Edgbaston, Birmingham B15 2TT, UK

This discursive article critiques the interface of religious and secular values through analysis of Islamic culture and the Olympic Movement. Recent resurgence in religious interest gives importance to this topic. The authors address the paradox between Olympic ideals for inclusion and sport policies that exclude, in this case, particularly Muslim women. For example, the Olympic Charter commits to universal human rights to participate in sport and be free from discrimination on the grounds of gender and religion; and yet Olympic sport dress code regulations can deny Muslim women's religious requirements of modesty in covering the body. Diverse effects of conflicts between religious and secular values are illustrated through sociological studies into the lives of Muslim sports women and recent events in sport. Different paths to influencing policy-makers to become more inclusive of Muslim women in sport are examined. Recommendations propose using the global power and reach of the Olympic Movement in order to move towards negotiated compromise and greater flexibility for more inclusive sport policy and practice.

Introduction

With the 2012 London Olympics on the horizon, this is an opportune time to reflect on complex, sensitive and controversial issues concerning athlete participation. This article takes a critical stance in examining the interface of the Olympic Movement (Western and secular) and Islamic culture in relation to experiences of Muslim sports women. Focus is on the apparent paradox between Olympic ideals for inclusion and policies and practices that exclude. The Olympic Charter commits to universal human rights to *participate in sport* and to *be free from discrimination* on the grounds of *gender* and *religion*. Conflict or compromise for Muslim women is questioned because, for example, some Olympic sports' dress code policies, such as the International Volleyball Association's beach volleyball regulations, require much of the body to be uncovered in public competition environments. This is anathema to those Muslim women wishing to adhere to religious requirements for body modesty. Such policies are tantamount to excluding Muslim athletes and exacerbating the wider prejudice and discrimination that Muslim sports women can face. Drawing on socio-logical research, including life history accounts of Muslim sports women, as well as pertinent sports events, the purpose of this article is to argue for a change in sport policy and practice to foster the wider inclusion agenda of Muslim women in the sporting arena.

The position of Muslim women in sport is contested. Some Western feminists have regarded Muslim women as oppressed and have embarked on campaigns, including the 'Atlanta+' lobbyists who fought against the fact that 35 men-only teams from Islamic countries had attended the Barcelona Olympics (Hargreaves 1994, 2000, Benn and Ahmad 2006). Although the participation of Muslim women in the Olympic Games has improved (Pfister 2000, 2003, 2010), with only Saudi Arabia, Qatar and Kuwait sending men-only teams to the 2008 Beijing Olympics, representation is still minimal and in a limited number of sports. The reality is complex with multiple reasons contributing to the marginalization of Muslim sports women. Some have faced political, cultural and religious resistance to participation, with negative sanctions such as exile, and vilification by male Islamist clerics, as recently experienced by the Indian tennis star Sania Mirza who was criticized for wearing short tennis skirts (Hargreaves 1994, 2000, Benn *et al.* 2011a). Other barriers to participation lie in sport policies and practice. While the position of Muslim men and sport also raises important issues and contradictions, they have not suffered the same discrimination or high media profile as Muslim sports women; therefore, this article takes a feminist perspective and focuses on women.

The discursive approach (offering a pathway of discussion to conclusions through reasoned argument) explores issues through analysis of Islamic and Olympic cultures where secular and religious values meet. Secular is used here to refer to the doctrine that rejects religious considerations. Recent revivalist attention to the significance of faith and embodied behaviour will provide an underpinning rationale for the ensuing discussion. Diverse ways in which embodied religious and sporting identities are managed by Muslim sports women are then shared, alongside recent examples of excluding and including actions by sports federation. Two current but opposing pathways being used to gain greater inclusion of Muslim women are explored and discussed, illustrating the contested nature of the field. Emergent recommendations are offered to the Olympic Movement and sporting stake-holders to move towards greater flexibility in inclusive policy and practice that 'Accepts and Respects' the diverse voices and choices of Muslim women.

Revivalist interest in religion and bodily practices

Shilling's (2008, pp. 144–161) ideas on *Believing* identify renewed global interest in spirituality, religion and religiosity as part of the new world order struggle in the twenty-first century. Citing Ruel's (1982) work on belief and Asad's (1993) work on Christianity, Shilling argues that belief and religion were historically more closely associated with bodily techniques, dispositions and practices. These activities were pursued because they developed humility, virtue and collectivity. Shilling argues that in the Western development of a technological culture, belief has become a private, mental and psychological activity:

> This characterisation not only obfuscates the great variety of forms belief has taken in the West itself, but misrepresents the very different internal and external environments of religious practice in other regions. It can also lead us to overlook important cultural changes occurring presently in Europe and the United States. (Shilling 2008, p. 144)

The way in which Western societies have embraced technological culture has desensitized and disconnected people, leading to the need and space for revivalist movements and new forms of spirituality. Esposito and Mogahed (2007) discuss the recent revival and growth of

Islam; Muslims' shared expressions of religious practice expressed through bodily techniques of fasting, prayer and dress; and the sense of embodiment of religiously motivated dispositions leading to a sense of fulfilment, completion and peace. Reactions to atrocities such as 9/11 in 2001 and incidents such as Western interventions in Iraq and Afghanistan, both fuel Islamophobia among non-Muslims, in the United Kingdom (Richardson 2004), Europe (Allen and Nielsen 2002, Fekete 2008) and beyond (Esposito and Mogahed 2007), *and* reciprocally, increase Muslim people's sense of belonging to a global community. The sports world is not immune. Hargreaves (2000, p. 68) suggests: 'There is a progressive sense of global Islam in the international Muslim women's sport movement, which grows in strength and effectiveness'. The importance of dialogue and negotiation of religion and religious needs is, therefore, crucial to any aspiration of inclusive sport or sport for development and peace. Islam gives a particular set of values, bodily techniques and purpose to life, rooted in Divine belief, which cannot be ignored:

> Instead of dismissing the importance of religious cultures, then, it may make more sense to see their continuation and resurgence in terms of their concern to nurture types of lived experience that invest individuals with a sense of meaning. For all their differences they are associated with embracing forms of belief that transcend the individualised, psychologised version accepted as the norm within technological culture. (Shilling 2008, p. 161)

The notion of 'embodied faith' (Benn 2009, Benn *et al.* 2011b) helps to further understanding of ways in which religious bodily practices, such as faith-based dress codes and gendered behaviour, become central to identity. This develops from Garrett's (2004) work on bodies as '... both inscribed with and vehicles of culture' in a world where '... the concept of *embodiment* of a physical identity acknowledges the material, physical, biological (*and the authors would add spiritual*) as well as the social whole of the "lived body"' (Garrett 2004, p. 141). The contested nature of the private/public faces of religious identity is significant and helps to explain different manifestations of religion. For some Muslim women:

> Faith is embodied in the sense that presentation of the body, appearance, physicality, social interaction and behaviour are integral to religious identity, to lived reality of the daily embodiment of religious belief. *Embodied faith* reflects outward manifestations inseparably connected to internalised belief. The concept gives meaning to the interconnectedness of faith, body and identity. (Benn 2009)

The notion of *embodied faith* brings sensitivity to an understanding of difference in the ways in which Muslim women adhere to their faith, and the preferences of some to participate covered, and/or in sex-segregated environments. Ways in which the structures and policies of modern sport interface with such Islamic body practices affect the lives of Muslim sports women will be addressed in the remainder of this article.

Islamic and Olympic Movement cultures

The Olympic Movement was founded on the ideology of Olympism, a universal, secular social philosophy; a quasi-religious set of values based on the role of sport in international understanding, education, peace and development (Segrave and Chu 1988, Powell 1994, Muller 2000, Girginov and Parry 2005). For example, Damkjaer (2004, p. 213) suggests that Olympism is '... couched in a quasi-religious language, equal to other secular ideologies'. The first Modern Olympics in 1896 was underpinned by universal philosophical ideals and ethical principles central to Olympism, combining culture, education and sport with core elements of tolerance, generosity, solidarity, friendship, non-discrimination and respect for others (Parry 2007, p. 193). The ideals of Olympism are manifested every quadrennial in the most iconic global sporting event, the Olympic Games.

Today, there are many critiques of the Olympic Movement, for example, Bale and Christensen (2004), Damkjaer (2004) and Wamsley (2004) who identify a paradox in the movement: 'The basic contradiction is that the games, in their contemporary incarnation, are the antithesis of the very Olympic ideals they ostensibly cherish' (Wamsley 2004, p. 234). Most of the criticisms relate to the linking of Olympism with the spectacle of the Olympic Games and elite level sport, with its history of politicization, commercialization, cheating and inequalities; for instance, founded as a male-only event in 1896.

Issues of gender equality have been fought from the Universal/Western standpoint, for example, of working for equality of the sexes in different events and the equalizing of numbers of participants from both sexes. Much success has been gained, including in crossing gender hegemonic boundaries, for example, women's boxing will appear in the 2012 Olympics. Critics suggest the improvement of gender inclusion in sport has also led to increased exploitation of women athletes' bodies (Brackenridge 2001). This trend can only negatively influence the gender equality debate in Islamic cultures where protection and privacy of women's bodies are important. Promotion of gender equity in sport leadership, for example, at National Olympic Committee level, has been much less successful than at athlete level but, in recent years, three Muslim women have served at the highest International Olympic Committee (IOC) administrative levels (Pfister 2010).

Islamic culture and Olympic sport have discrete corpuses of values, beliefs and behaviours regarding bodily discipline. For athletes, the devotion to bodily discipline, physical strength and power is predominantly connected to winning, or improving personal performance. For believers nothing can surpass devotion to Allah. Bodily practices involve pursuit of religious adherence, for example, fasting during Ramadan, adoption of modest clothing (for men and women) and committing to ablutions and prayer rituals 5 times a day. Both cultures share commitment to the maintenance of physical well-being and a holistic sense of self.

There is no intention to homogenize Muslim people. Islam is the second largest global religion with 1.3 billion followers, one-fifth of the world's population, located across the world (Esposito and Mogahed 2007). Islamic culture is a way of life encompassing the everyday commitment to being Muslim and following guidance in the Holy texts of the Qu'ran and Hadiths. These texts shape life meaning, values, beliefs, behaviours and social interaction. Muslim people live in different political, linguistic, economic and socio-cultural situations, some in Islamic countries, under Shariah Law, such as Iran and Oman; others as part of the majority population in secular countries such as Turkey; while others live as minority groups, often as part of the increasing global Diaspora, in non-Muslim Western countries, for example, across Europe. Each situation can bring different opportunities and barriers to many aspects of life, including sporting participation. Recognizing such diversity helps to explain differences in Muslim women's strategies of engagement in sport from recreational to Olympic levels, as will be illustrated in the section 'Tensions for Muslim women in modern sport'.

Tensions for Muslim women in modern sport

The interface of Islam and modern sport can create a contested space where values and preferences for bodily actions and behaviours differ. Most notably for Muslim women athletes, differences in political, social and cultural context determine their ability to negotiate their religious and sporting identities (Hamzeh and Oliver 2010). For example, some women are free to engage in faith-based choices regarding their participation in sport, others may be less free in situations where political Islam or political secularism can remove choices from individuals. For example, Ruqaya Al-Ghasara (Bahrain) chose to compete in the 2008 Beijing Olympics in a specially designed outfit that she wanted to wear to meet her Islamic needs (Al-Ansari 2011). Many sports manufacturers, such as Nike, are working to find ways to meet such growing needs of Muslim women with specially designed fabrics that facilitate religious observance and freedom of movement. This private choice for religious freedom by some Muslim women, however, becomes a public symbol of adherence, which can create tensions for those who see the hijab (headscarf) as an affront to religious neutrality (Comité Atlanta+ 2011). Other Muslim women, such as Moroccan athletic champions like Nezha Bidouane, view competing in Western sports dress as unproblematic. For them, their faith is internalized and private. Competing, winning and continuing to contribute at the highest international sports level is a respected and highly honoured lifetime achievement, supported by family, community and country (El-Faquir 2011). For 'Zeynap', who is Turkish, her international sporting career required enforced removal of head and body covering to meet the secular sport competition laws of her Muslim majority country. This created much personal conflict because to achieve her potential success as an athlete she had to renegotiate her identity as a Muslim (Koca and Hacisoftaoglu 2011).

Differences also exist for those Muslim women requiring sex-segregated sports spaces. Examples of all-female sporting championships include the Islamic Women's Games in Iran held in 1993, 1997, 2001 and 2005, with the support of the president of the IOC (Jahromi 2011), and the Gulf Council Countries Women's Championships that started in 2008 (Al-Sinani and Benn 2011). Some Muslim women regard such opportunities as a 'safe-space' in which to protect their religious and sporting identities (Ahmad 2011). Others view such provision as a symbol of political Islam, used to oppress women and a practice that needs to be stopped because it perpetuates sexism and the exclusion of women from mainstream sport opportunities and rewards (Comité Atlanta+ 2011). While some Muslim women feel able to participate in mixed-sex events if their bodies are suitably covered, other Muslims see no clash between their faith and sporting identities, as illustrated above with Nezha Bidouane (the Moroccan champion). Hence, the ways in which Muslim women are situated influence their abilities and preferences for sporting participation. Can sporting structures accommodate the clear need for flexibility in pursuit of inclusion?

Evidence from sport policies and regulations indicates that International Sport Federations in the Olympic Movement can be including or excluding Muslim women. Examples of recent high profile cases outlined below often bring negative media exposure to Muslim women, fuel Islamophobia and ignore the effects on the highly skilled sports women victimized in such actions.

Hijab and football

There were controversies and contradictions in 2010 and 2011 over the International Football Association's (FIFA) ban of the Iranian women's football teams for wearing the hijab (head covering). The reason for the ban was that the hijab contravened Law 4: 'The basic compulsory equipment must not have any political, religious or personal statements' (FIFA Laws of the Game 2010/2011, p. 20). In 2010, the ban by FIFA meant the Iranian women's Youth Football Team could not compete in the Inaugural Summer Youth Olympic Games (August 2010). Iran is an Islamic country where all women are required by law to wear the hijab in public spaces, including in sport arenas. After protests, FIFA lifted the initial ban and the Iranian team was allowed to play in the Games in Singapore. A compromise was reached with officials by replacing the hijab with caps. According to FIFA President Sepp Blatter, this constituted a new set of clothing that would not break the laws of the game (Degun 2010, Mackay 2010). On 3 June 2011, FIFA again banned the Iranian women's football team because of their dress code in a pre-Olympic match held in Jordan. The FIFA hijab ban has been described as an example of 'gendered Islamophobia' in sport (Zine 2006, Ahmad 2011), a strategy that excludes many Muslim women from international sports competition. The ban raises many complex questions over power, politics of international sport, public–private faith and individual human rights.

Overlapping layers of discrimination are evident in FIFA's ban, impacting negatively on many Muslim women around the world. It contradicts inclusion and anti-discrimination claims. It coerces women to deny their faith and to adopt identical dress codes if they want to participate in top level football. Intransigent dress policy forms one strategy in the ongoing drive for a 'global sports monoculture' (Donnelly 1996 cited Wamsley 2004, p. 239). In critiquing Olympism, the Olympics and the globalization of modern sports, Wamsley (2004) describes sports monoculture as problematic. There will be winners and losers in FIFA's decision but discriminating policies are socially constructed and therefore possible to change. The Sport Association of Arab Women with members in 22 Arab countries is just one group contesting FIFA's ban by pointing out the effects of the ban on many Muslim women worldwide (open letter to FIFA president, www.iapesgw.org).

Body modesty and sport dress code, negative and positive change

Other international sport governing bodies' dress code policies have provided a specific site for gender and religious discrimination. In 2011, the Badminton World Federation tried to mandate the wearing of short skirts by all women to increase the 'attractiveness of the sport'. This was rescinded after opponents pointed out the sexist nature of the move as well as its potential to exclude some women for religious and cultural reasons (Longman 2011). In contrast, the International Weightlifting Federation (IWF) announced, on 29 June 2011, the addition of 'unitards' that cover arms and legs to their dress code regulations in order to open more opportunities for Muslim women. Head covering had always been allowed by the IWF (www.iwf.net). The Federation Internationale de Gymnastique (FIG) also allows the unitard in contrast to previous regulations which stipulated a leotard (FIG 2009–2012 Code of Points for Women's Artistic Gymnastics). These moves are positive, although the figure-hugging nature of 'unitards' would remain problematic to some Muslim women.

The most extreme example of exclusionary uniform policy belonged to beach volleyball. Dress code used to be restricted to brief bikinis (maximum 6 cm on side of hip) for women but the governing body now allows shorts or a one-piece swimsuit (Federation International de Volleyball rules 2009–2012). These changes do not eliminate the difficulty for those Muslim women who want to cover arms and legs and wear looser fitting clothes that conceal the body outline. The collective power of women was seen in Chennai, India, in 2008 when the International Volleyball Association was forced to relax its rules during the first World Beach Volleyball championships. The Indian women's team refused to adopt the official dress code and officials were forced to accept their Islamically acceptable dress. The change was made in Chennai to respect the religious, cultural and ethical sentiment of the country (Kala 2008). With more awareness, knowledge and understanding, sport policymakers and organizers could foresee and avoid such tensions. This dress code appears to align itself more closely to the exploitation or sexploitation of women's bodies than sport functionality (Brackenridge 2001, Australian Sport Commission 2010). While in gymnastics, the aesthetic judgements require visibility of body outline, there are no such limitations for dress code in beach volleyball so greater flexibility is possible. What would be so problematic about allowing track suits? Unequivocally, dress code policies of international sport governing bodies can determine the inclusion or exclusion of Muslim women.

Ramadan and Olympic Games 2012

Current tensions for Muslim athletes in the Olympic Movement can relate to wider Islamic cultural requirements, such as Ramadan. The announcement of dates for the 2012 London Olympics generated some controversy when it was realized by Muslims that Ramadan, the holy month for Muslims, which normally requires followers to fast between sunrise and sunset, falls in the middle of the event. Joseph (2006) claimed this would put an anticipated 3000 Muslim competitors at a disadvantage. Responses varied from those who claimed such a decision was insensitive and ridiculous to others who believed that it was not problematic because there would be ways for Muslim athletes to comply with religious requirements and participate in the Olympics with dispensation from religious leaders. Certainly it has raised debates about disadvantage to Muslim athletes and disregard of religious needs. It would be difficult to conceive, from a Western viewpoint, of an Olympic Games programmed to span Christmas Day, or to what extent objections would relate to contravening of religious respect or the expected holiday period.

The complex interface of Islamic and Olympic sport cultures creates a web of influences on experiences of Muslim sports women. According to Donnelly (1996), the Olympic Movement forms a 'global sports monoculture' that can lose sight of where meaning is created and lived in everyday lives: '... delimiting how people come to understand sport, how they participate in it, actively rendering alternative sports forms irrelevant or even unthinkable' (Wamsley 2004, p. 240). The above discussion highlights the disadvantaged position of many Muslim sports women and raises important questions for policymakers in modern sport who seek to avoid compromising the equality and anti-discrimination principles of the Olympic Charter.

Secular versus religious values: is there an impasse?

The rhetoric of the IOC's Olympic Charter (IOC 2010, p. 11) appears to contradict the realities recounted above, for example, Fundamental Principles of Olympism paragraphs 4 and 5 state the following:

- The practice of sport is a human right. Every individual must have the possibility of practising sport, without discrimination of any kind and in the Olympic spirit, which requires mutual understanding with a spirit of friendship, solidarity and fair play.
- Any form of discrimination with regard to a country or a person on grounds of race, religion, politics, gender or otherwise is incompatible with belonging to the Olympic Movement.

These equality and anti-discrimination policies build on universal human rights and are embedded in sport policy from national to international levels. The Western worldview of universal human rights has been criticized for its lack of cultural understanding, sensitivity to difference, obvious compromises and contradictions (Kennedy 2008, Waljee 2008):

... the *Olympic Charter* invokes the practice of sport as a human right and one of the Fundamental Principles of the Olympic movement, but ... proceeds to define the limits of inclusion – and exclusion – defining who is permitted to belong, and who will be officially recognized by the IOC. (Wamsley 2004, p. 234)

For example, there is a list of 'Olympic Sports' recognized by the IOC and yet there are many other sports that fall outside of the Olympic family. There are sport organizations and international bodies that are officially recognized 'insiders' or 'outsiders'. In terms of the mainstream Olympic Movement, the globalized commercial and economic power of the Olympic Movement ensures that the sports and athletes who are included are advantaged and those excluded are disadvantaged. For example, the British Muslim women's team attending the 2005 Islamic Women's Games in Tehran did not receive any government sponsorship for training or travel, and attracted only limited or sensationalist media coverage, yet the Muslim vote was courted by senior officials to gain the 2012 Olympics in London and many promises were made about an inclusive legacy (Bee 2005, Muslim News 2005, Syed 2005, Benn and Ahmad 2006). Can the Olympic Movement compromise and embrace religious difference or is there an impasse between secular and religious values in the sport arena that can only conflict and result in tensions?

Critics of the Olympic Movement rarely seize on secular versus religious values, and the potential for irreconcilable difference in orientation. While Coubertin (1935 cited in Roesch 1979) seems to make claim for Olympism as a religion and the 'religio athletae', Roesch argues that the '... pseudo-cultic' expressions of Olympism, consciously created by Coubertin, do not qualify Olympism (or sport) as a religion:

The individual athlete, no matter what his religion, denomination or ideology, lives and acts according to his religious conviction as a Christian, Moslem, Buddist, Jew and so on ... 'Olympism' can't take the place of that. (Roesch 1979, pp. 199–200)

It is not a new phenomenon for the Olympic Movement to ignore athletes' religious needs. Crucially, for example, it was founded in the late nineteenth century in Europe when Christianity and sport were closely aligned. Problems were illustrated in the film 'Chariots of Fire', which dramatized Eric Liddell's refusal, on religious grounds, to run a race on a Sunday in the 1924 Olympics (Parry 2007).

More recently, Islam has grown as a world faith, and global interest in the lives of Muslim people has accelerated. This is partly due to growing visibility, revivalist Islam and the increasing attention to Islamophobia in Western societies, often fuelled by media hype, fear and lack of understanding (Fekete 2008). Can sport provide a space in international understanding, education, peace and development that addresses such fears and differences? Here, the present writers argue that the difference between secular and divinely inspired belief does not, sui generis, preclude the possibility for a meaningful universal social philosophy, but would need to embrace value differences. There is a need for caution where conflicting values meet and people's preconceptions about life and meaning are challenged. Wamsley's (2004, p. 242) advice, following his critique of Olympism, was that '... if we are really prepared or motivated to take on the challenges (of striving for peace and understanding through sport), we would best start with an honest engagement with the people around us'. Engaging in those realities, as cited in this article, is essential to addressing any confrontation between secular and religious values and any engagement requires understanding of the importance of religious belief and related religious dispositions towards the body in the twenty-first century.

Two paths to the same goal

The 'Accept and Respect' declaration and 'Atlanta+' strategies are advocacy paths to the same goal for improved inclusion of Muslim women in sport. They are examined here because they illustrate the contested debates regarding Muslim women and sport. They adopt oppositional paths to persuading sport policymakers to change policies and practices. Atlanta+ is a group of feminists led by a French lawyer, that has lobbied at each Olympic Games since the Atlanta Games, to persuade the IOC to ban male competitors from Islamic countries that deny women the chance to compete. Their latest document *London 2012, 7 Impéritifs* (Comité Atlanta+ 2011) is addressed to the IOC and London 2012 organizers and two of the seven imperatives, aimed specifically at the issue of Muslim women and sport, are used here to illustrate their current strategy. 'Accept and Respect' is an international declaration to improve the inclusion of Muslim women in sport, produced under the auspices of a non-governmental organization, the International Association of Physical Education and Sport for Girls and Women (IAPESGW, www.iapesgw.org). It is one strategy formulated in response to the request of Muslim women members to help counter international, negative stereotyping and challenges for them in sport. The Consensus Declaration has seven clauses and was one outcome of a seminar week hosted by Sultan Qaboos University, Oman (2008) focused on *Improving opportunities for Muslim women in sport*. Participants included Muslims and non-Muslims from 14 countries, academics and practitioners (including an Islamic Studies scholar) from Europe, Africa, the Middle East and Far East. The Declaration is intended to persuade sport policymakers to be flexible and recognize the diverse needs of Muslim women in different situations internationally (www.iapesgw.org, Benn and Koushkie 2008).

'Accept and Respect' acknowledges the importance of faith in the lives of Muslim women and the range of ways in which their faith can influence preferences for participation in sport. The first clause recognizes Islam as an 'enabling religion', framing the Declaration in the knowledge that there is nothing in the holy scriptures that denies women's participation in sport, a key foundation to improving opportunities for Muslim women. The Declaration focuses on respecting women's *choices* in a world where both state and sport policy can coerce. The need for greater sensitivity towards individual agency was advocated. For example, the preference for sex-segregated spaces, uncommon in Western models of competition, was recognized, and the need for more modest clothing than some international sport governing bodies currently allow, in order to improve inclusion of Muslim women around the world (Benn and Ahmad 2006, Dagkas *et al.* 2011).

Two 'Accept and Respect' declaration clauses state the following:

- We recommend that people working in the sport and education systems *Accept and Respect* the diverse ways in which Muslim women and girls practise their religion and participate in sport and physical activity, for example, choices of activity, dress and gender grouping.
- We urge international sport federations to show their commitment to inclusion by ensuring that their dress codes for competition embrace Islamic requirements, taking into account the principles of propriety, safety and integrity.

These 'Accept and Respect' clauses stand in stark contrast to Atlanta+'s *London 2012, 7 Impéritifs* (Comité Atlanta+ 2011), which uses text and cartoons to call on the IOC and London 2012 Olympics organizers to

- ensure neutrality by banning the wearing of religious symbols and
- to stop supporting separate games for women which institutionalize sexual segregation in sport.

Cartoons used to support these calls include one depicting a covered Muslim woman athlete running while being stoned by Muslim men; another depicts a Muslim man shouting the word 'indecent' at a covered Muslim woman swimmer who has bare feet. The authors suggest that neither the Atlanta+ text nor the cartoons are helpful to many Muslim women or Muslim/non-Muslim understanding. The cartoon strategy misrepresents and demonizes gender relations in Islam, reinforcing negative stereotypes of life in Muslim communities and exacerbating divides between Islam and the West. In whose interests do such cartoons work? How can Muslim sports women move forward with such stereotypical depictions of them that deny the real diversity of their situations worldwide? What effects do such cartoons have on different viewers and whose purpose do they serve? In addition, the text recommending banning of the hijab and support for women-only sporting environments leaves many Muslim sports women with no possibility of participation in sport at any level. This is not only an issue for Muslim majority countries since increasing migration has led to the establishment of separate Muslim women's sport associations to offer safe-spaces for minority countries in European countries, for example, the Muslim Women's Sport Foundation in the United Kingdom.

The contrast in approaches illustrates the polarized views that exist in the contested area of making space for Muslim women in sport. The framework for 'Open and Closed' views of Islam (Runnymede Trust 1997) allows deeper reflection on these opposing paths. 'Accept and Respect' is premised upon an open view of Islam; works co-operatively with Muslim and non-Muslim women seeking solutions to inclusion in diverse situations internationally; is based on advocacy for accepting and respecting the choices of Muslim women; and recognizes faith-based and political Islam as enabling and constraining of women's choices for sport participation. In contrast, Atlanta+ has produced a document for London 2012 that depicts closed views of Islam that fuel negative stereotyping, are confrontational, ridicule gender relations in Islamic communities and purport coercion of all Muslim women into the dominant global monoculture of modern sport. The document is reactive, for example, in suggesting Ruqaya Al-Ghasara, who competed in Beijing Games in 2008 for Bahrain (as mentioned earlier in this article), should have been banned for wearing religious dress. The approach recognizes political Islam that can be coercive to some women who would choose not to wear Islamic dress, but not political secularism that forces some Muslim women, such as Zeynap (as mentioned earlier in this article), to deny Islamic requirements in order to conform to sporting regulations. The document denies, or treats as irrelevant, faith-based Islam, embodied faith and the reality that some Muslim women choose to adopt Islamic practices as a prerequisite for sport participation. Perhaps with the best of intentions for removing what radical Western feminists may see as gender discrimination, the Atlanta+ pathway does nothing to help the IOC and sporting bodies to meet anti-discrimination commitments on the basis of religion.

The authors' suggest that the 'Accept and Respect' pathway for working with Muslim women and being prepared to negotiate appropriate provision in relation to participants' situations are most likely to succeed in improving opportunities for Muslim girls and women in sport-related activities. The approach, based on evidence of global diversity in the realities of Muslim sports women, is for seeking solutions between universals and cultural relativity. It lies in the area of 'situated ethics', seeking what 'ought to be' in a time and place to foster greater inclusion (Henry 2007). Adopting such an approach would continue the shift in sporting culture towards more conducive participation environments that recognize and respond to the power of religious belief and its effect on preferred body practices for some Muslim women. Indeed, the recent *Olympia European Charter of Women's Rights in Sport* (UISP 2011) can only be achieved through this path since it purports '... the right to participate in sport in a safe environment that preserves human dignity ... for all including those from different social and ethnic backgrounds'. Such a discourse of social inclusion, in an increasingly multi-ethnic Europe, means solutions to challenges, such as those presented in this article, must continue to be sought.

Conclusion

In conclusion, through this article the authors have challenged the equality rhetoric/reality gap regarding issues of religion and diverse expressions of faith for Muslim women in the sporting arena. Focus has been on tensions, successes and challenges for Muslim women at the interface of Islamic culture and the Olympic Movement. With globalization, the increase in diasporic communities and the rising politicization of Islam, the issues are equally pertinent across Islamic and non-Islamic countries. Those who should engage in inclusion debates are the stakeholders: participants, politicians, policymakers, sports entrepreneurs and the providers of facilities, events and opportunities at every level. There is a need to recognize points of conflict and then negotiate resolutions for compromise. With responsibility for sport policymaking lying predominantly in Western secular countries, it is perhaps not surprising that attention to religion and religious needs has been missing. In a multicultural, multi-faith England, on the eve of the 2012 Olympic Games, stakeholders cannot ignore the constant processes of sociocultural change or the challenges and opportunities these bring. This moment should bring increased motivation to seek intercultural understanding and continued moves beyond the rhetoric towards inclusive sporting realities for all.

The authors call for the Olympic Movement and all sport policymakers to 'Accept and Respect' the voices and choices of Muslim women in sport and to make safe-spaces for their inclusion in line with principles of non-discrimination on the grounds of gender and religion, enshrined in the Olympic Charter. In addition to responding to requests for changes in sport policy and practice in order to be more inclusive of different values, the authors propose using Olympism and its international Education programme to critically engage young people in analysing the complexities of the principles of the Olympic Charter, for example, on notions of 'universal ethical principles', 'sport as a human right' and 'discrimination'. It is important to problematize these notions as scholars increasingly challenge the appropriateness of 'Western' yardsticks to decree global values and parameters for justice. This is especially the case when they deny, or treat as inferior, cultural preferences which differ from mainstream, dominant views (Houlihan 2003, Damkjaer 2004, Girginov and Parry 2005, Waljee 2008). Key questions that need to be asked are: 'Whose values count?', 'Whose values are marginalized?', 'In whose interests are policies and regulations made?', 'Who is advantaged and who is disadvantaged?', 'How do marginalized groups overcome discrimination?' and 'How can we use sport for peace and development if we do not first understand the people around us and how they live their lives?'

The research referenced in this discursive article offers insights into the lives of Muslim women athletes in all their diversity, and therefore provides a springboard for anyone interested in broadening understanding of the topic. There has to be fluidity in the search for a more inclusive way forward if sport is to retain its global influence. Olympism, the

Olympic Movement and the Olympic Games can all contribute if they continually seek positive ways to be inclusive in policy and practice:

> Olympism is not just an abstract ideal. Embodied in the actual Olympics . . . are the opportunities to realize a sense of global, post-national belonging . . . . It allows, however temporarily, for wider solidarities to be produced and new senses of self to be formed. The fact that such a politics remains indeterminate is all the more reason to see Olympism as a possible site for progressive forms of intervention. (Carrington 2004, p. 97)

References

Ahmad, A., 2011. British Muslim female experiences in football: Islam, identity and the hijab. *In*: D. Burdsey, ed. *Race, ethnicity and football: persisting debates and emergent issues*. London: Routledge, 101–116.

Al-Ansari, M., 2011. Women in sports leadership in Bahrain. *In*: T. Benn, G. Pfister, and H. Jawad, eds. *Muslim women and sport*. London: Routledge, 79–91.

Allen, C. and Nielsen, J.S., 2002. *Summary report on Islamophobia in the EU after 11 September 2001*. England: European Monitoring Centre on Racism and Xenophobia, Centre for the Study of Islam and Christian-Muslim Relations, Department of Theology, University of Birmingham.

Al-Sinani, Y. and Benn, T., 2011. The Sultanate of Oman and the position of girls and women in physical education and sport. *In*: T. Benn, G. Pfister, and H. Jawad, eds. *Muslim women and sport*. London: Routledge, 125–137.

Asad, T., 1993. *Genealogies of religions*. Baltimore, MD: John Hopkins University Press.

Australian Sport Commission, 2010. *Sexploitation* [online]. Available from: http://www.ausport.gov. au/participating/women/issues/sexploitation [Accessed 28 October 2010].

Bale, J. and Christensen, M., eds., 2004. *Post-Olympism? Questioning sport in the twenty-first century*. Oxford: Berg.

Bee, P., 2005. The veil is slowly lifting for Muslim women athletes. *The Guardian Newspaper, Sport Supplement*, 11 Oct, p. 9.

Benn, T., 2009. Muslim women in sport: a researcher's journey to understanding 'Embodied faith'. In recreation sport and social change in sustainable community development. *Bulletin 55, International Council for Sports Science and Physical Education (ICSSPE)* [online]. Available from: http://www.icsspe.org/bulletin/drucken_194bb68c.php.html [Accessed 25 January 2012].

Benn, T. and Ahmad, A., 2006. Alternative visions: international sporting opportunities for Muslim women and implications for British youth sport. *Youth & policy*, 92, 119–132.

Benn, T., Dagkas, S., and Jawad, H., 2011b. Embodied faith: Islam, religious freedom and educational practices in physical education. *Sport, education and society*, 16 (1) 17–34.

Benn, T. and Koushkie, M., 2008. Increasing global inclusion of Muslim girls and women in physical activity. *ICSSPE bulletin*, 54, 22–24.

Benn, T., Pfister, G., and Jawad, H., 2011a. *Muslim women and sport*. London: Routledge.

Brackenridge, C., 2001. *Spoilsports: understanding and preventing sexual exploitation in sport*. London: Routledge.

Carrington, B., 2004. Cosmopolitan Olympism, humanism and the spectacle of 'race'. *In*: J. Bale and M. Krogh Christensen, eds. *Post-Olympism? Questioning sport in the twenty-first century*. Oxford: Berg, 81–97.

Comité Atlanta+, 2011. *London 2012 – 7 impéritifs, ligue du droit* [online]. Paris: International des femmes. Available from: http://www.ldif.asso.fr [Accessed 1 April 2011].

Dagkas, S., Koushkie, M., and Talbot, M., 2011. Reaffirming the values of physical education, physical activity and sport in the lives of young Muslim women. *In*: T. Benn, G. Pfister, and H. Jawad, eds. *Muslim women and sport*. London: Routledge, 13–24.

Damkjaer, S., 2004. Post-Olympism and the aestheticization of sport. *In*: J. Bale and M. Christensen, eds. *Post-Olympism? Questioning sport in the twenty-first century*. Oxford: Berg, 211–230.

Degun, T., 2010. *Exclusive: blatter delighted to see Iran compete in Youth Olympic Games following hijab controversy* [online]. Available from: http://www.insidethegames.biz/youth-olympics/ singapore-2010/10282 [Accessed 25 October 2010].

Donnelly, P., 1996. Prolympism: sport monoculture as crisis and opportunity. *Quest*, 48, 25–42.

El-Faquir, F., 2011. Women in sport in North Africa: voices of Moroccan athletes. *In*: T. Benn, G. Pfister, and H. Jawad, eds. *Muslim women and sport*. London: Routledge, 236–248.

Esposito, J.L. and Mogahed, D., 2007. *Who speaks for Islam? What a billion Muslims really think*. New York: Gallup Press.

FIFA Laws of the Game, 2010–2011. Available from: http://www.fifa.com/mm/document/affederation/generic/81/42/36/lawsofthegame_2010_11_e.pdf [Accessed 25 January 2012].

Fekete, L., 2008. *Integration, Islamophobia and civil rights in Europe*. London: Institute of Race Relations.

Garrett, R., 2004. Gendered bodies and physical identities. *In*: J. Evans, B. Davies, and J. Wright, eds. *Body, knowledge and control: studies in the sociology of physical education and health*. London: Routledge, 140–156.

Girginov, V. and Parry, J., 2005. *The Olympic games explained*. Oxford: Routledge.

Hamzeh, M.Z. and Oliver, K., 2010. Gaining research access into the lives of Muslim girls: researchers negotiating *muslimness*, modesty, *inshallah,* and *haram*. *International journal of qualitative studies in education*, 23 (2), 165–180.

Hargreaves, J., 1994. *Sporting females: critical issues in the history and sociology of women's sport*. London: Routledge.

Hargreaves, J., 2000. *Heroines of sport: the politics of difference and identity*. London: Routledge.

Henry, I., 2007. *Transnational and comparative research in sport: globalisation, governance and sport policy*. London: Routledge.

Houlihan, B., ed., 2003. *Sport and society*. London: Sage.

International Olympic Committee, 2010. *Olympic charter*. Switzerland: Lausanne.

Jahromi, K., 2011. Physical activities and sport for women in Iran. *In*: T. Benn, G. Pfister, and H. Jawad, eds. *Muslim women and sport*. London: Routledge, 109–124.

Joseph, C., 2006. Muslims anger as London Olympics clash with Ramadan [online]. *Mail Online*, 14 Oct. Available from: http://www.dailymail.co.uk/news/article-410439/Muslims-anger-London-Olympics-clash-Ramadan.html [Accessed 25 January 2012].

Kala, B., 2008. *Indian girls refuse to play in bikinis; beach volleyball authorities relax dress code* [online]. Available from: http://www.topnews.in/indian-girls-refuse-play-bikinis-beach-volleyball-authorities-relax-dress-code-253487 [Accessed 26 October 2010].

Kennedy, D., 2008. The International Human Rights Movement: part of the problem? *Harvard human rights journal* [online], 15 (Spring). Available from: http://www.law.harvard.edu/students/orgs/hrj/iss15/kennedy.shtml [Accessed 25 January 2012].

Koca and Hacisoftaoglu, 2011. Religion and the state – the story of a Turkish elite athlete. *In*: T. Benn, G. Pfister, and H. Jawad, eds. *Muslim women and sport*. London: Routledge, 198–210.

Longman, J., 2011. Governing group ends controversial dress code. D2. *New York Times* [online], 30 May. Available from: www.nytimes.com/2011.05/30/sport/badminton-group-kills-controversial-dress-code-rules.html [Accessed 20 July 2011].

Mackay, D., 2010. *Exclusive: FIFA lift Olympic dress ban in Iranian women's team* [online]. Available from: http://www.insideworldfootball.biz [Accessed 25 October 2010].

Muller, N., ed., 2000. *Pierre de Coubertin 1863–1937: Olympism, selected writings*. Lausanne: International Olympic Committee.

Muslim News, 2005. British Muslims urge Muslim Countries to back London Olympic bid. *Muslim News* [online], 5 July. Available from: http://www.muslimnews.co.uk/news/news.php?article=9482 [Accessed 6 November 2005].

Parry, J., 2007. Sport, ethos and education. *In*: J. Parry, S. Robinson, N. Watson, and M. Nesti, eds. *Sport and spirituality, an introduction*. London: Routledge, 186–200.

Pfister, G., 2000. Contested her-story: the historical discourse on women in the Olympic movement in (2000). *In*: *Pre-Olympic congress sports medicine and physical education, international congress on sport science*, 7–13 September 2000, Brisbane, Australia.

Pfister, G., 2003. Women and sport in Iran: keeping goal in the hijab? *In*: I. Hartmann-Tews and G. Pfister, eds. *Sport and women: social issues in international perspective*. London: Routledge, 207–223.

Pfister, G., 2010. Outsiders: Muslim women and Olympic games – barriers and opportunities. *The international journal of the history of sport*, 27 (16–17), 1–33.

Powell, J.T., 1994. *Origins and aspects of Olympism*. Champaign, IL: Stripes.

Richardson, R., 2004. *Islamophobia: issues, challenges and action*. A report by the Commission on British Muslims and Islamophobia. Stoke-on-Trent: Trentham Books.

Roesch, H.-E., 1979. Olympism and religion. *International Olympic academy proceedings*, 19, 192–205.

Ruel, M., 1982. Christians as believers. *In*: J. Davies, ed. *Religions and religious experience*. London: Academic Press, 9–32.

Runnymede Trust, 1997. *Islamophobia – a challenge to us all*. London: Runnymede Trust.

Segrave, J.O. and Chu, D., eds., 1988. *The Olympic games in transition*. Champaign, IL: Human Kinetics.

Shilling, C., 2008. *Changing bodies: habit, crisis and creativity*. London: Sage.

Syed, M., 2005. Muslim women leading gentle revolution with a football. *The Times Newspaper, Sport Section*, 21 Sep, p. 76.

UISP, 2011. The Olympia European charter of women's rights in sport [online]. Presented to the European Parliament in Brussels, 24 May 2011. Unioné Italiana Sport Pertuti. Available from: www.olympiaproject.net/?p=187 [Accessed 20 July 2011].

Waljee, A., 2008. Researching transitions: gendered education, marketisation and Islam in Tajikistan. *In*: S. Fennell and M. Arnot, eds. *Gender education and equality in a global context*. London: Routledge, 87–101.

Wamsley, K., 2004. Laying Olympism to rest. *In*: J. Bale and M. Christensen, eds. *Post-Olympism? Questioning sport in the twenty-first century*. Oxford: Berg, 231–240.

Zine, J., 2006. Unveiled sentiments: gendered Islamophobia and experiences of veiling among Muslim girls in a Canadian Islamic school. *Equity and excellence in education*, 39 (3), 239–252.

Policy transfer, regeneration legacy and the summer Olympic Games: lessons for London 2012 and beyond

Jon Coaffee

Centre for Urban and Regional Studies, University of Birmingham, Birmingham, UK

The hosting of major sporting events, often linked to elite sports development systems, has become a key determinant of urban and state promotion as well as related policy objectives, notably around enhancing levels of physical activity, and stimulating the social, economic and environmental regeneration of host cities – commonly now referred to as 'legacy'. What is noticeable about such major event bidding documents and subsequent market analysis and government rhetoric regarding the rationale for, and likely successes of, hosting major sporting events is the adoption of a set of uncritical but standardized justifications regarding the benefits that such events will bring to the host community and nation. Commonly, it is argued that such legacy will ensue simply because it has been evident at prior events around the globe. Within this context and with specific reference to the summer Olympiad to be held in London in 2012, this article unpacks some of the difficulties that occur when mega-event policy is transferred, often uncritically from city to city and nation to nation. After situating this article within the context of ongoing political science debates regarding the efficiency and efficacy of 'policy transfer', especially within recent and contemporary UK sports policy context, this article focuses upon how a number of paradoxes have emerged through attempts to deliver Olympic legacy that highlights a number of shortcomings, especially with regard to financial and democratic accountability, and the likelihood of regeneration legacies that benefit local people.

We can provide a legacy – a sporting legacy, not just the regeneration of this particular part of London, but a sporting legacy for the UK that is very important.

Former UK Prime Minister Tony Blair, 16 June 2005
(BBC Sport 2005)

Introduction

The hosting of major sporting events, often linked to the development of elite sports development systems, has become a key determinant of selected urban areas acquiring status and developing as a 'global' city, and/or of nations asserting a perceived superiority through enhanced sporting success (Riordan 1999, Sassen 2000, Gratton and Henry 2001, Gold and Gold 2010). As is also well documented, the acquisition of the right to host major sporting competitions is often sought for other related policy objectives, notably around enhancing levels of physical activity (and related health and well-being objectives) of the population, stimulating employment opportunities, reducing social exclusion and enhancing the physical, social, economic and environmental regeneration of host cities (Scottish Executive 2000, Social Exclusion Unit 2001, Sport England 2001, Coulter 2007). This latter concern with urban regeneration is now playing a significant role in what is commonly referred to as 'legacy' – a relatively recent addition to the lexicon of required phrases and actions in any (successful) bidding document for major sporting events. As Gold and Gold (2010) note in relation to *Olympic Cities*, legacy emerged as a core Olympic Games outcome for the host city and nation in the mid-1990s, although it was first used in a nondescript way in the 1956 Melbourne bid documents (p. 4). Legacy as noted by them, has now become 'the touchstone' by which politicians and municipal managers judge the cost and benefits of biding to stage major sporting events (pp. 2–3). Moreover, as host cities are selected and pre-Games preparation starts in earnest, the rhetoric of legacy promises plays an important function as the justification for a range of disruptions and cost increases. Legacy, in this context, is thus often asserted as 'fact' of what will happen, whereas in reality, it is based on a set of loose assumptions about what will hopefully occur many years in the future.

This article is concerned with the question of: why increasingly leaders of cities and nations are deciding to bid to host major sporting events with the expectation of such legacy, while the risks of doing so are so high, especially in financial terms? And, why is it that established policy models which emphasize the importance of such event hosting, more often than not, transferred from different contexts, are adopted without adequate critique or reflection? What is noticeable about major event bidding documents, and subsequent market analysis and Government rhetoric regarding the rationale for, and likely legacy successes of hosting major sporting events is the adoption of a set of almost uncritical, but standardized, justifications and perceived benefits that such events will bring. In other words, such events, it is argued, will be beneficial simply because it has been evident at prior events, around the globe (albeit hosted in different contexts) as such a 'magic formula' exists, which if copied, will ensure success in terms of winning the race to host such events and also in delivering an array of benefits to the host city and nation. As Gold and Gold (2010, p. 6) note, there is a tendency with regard to (Olympic) legacy to 'accent the positive' which . . . 'may prove to be rhetoric, given the numerous instances when inadequate and overambitious planning, poor stadium design, the withdrawal of sponsors, and heavy cost overruns have bequeathed legacies of debt and environmental damage'.

Within this context, and with specific reference to the summer Olympiad to be held in London in 2012, this article unpacks some of the difficulties that ensue when mega-event strategies – often as part of an overarching national sports policy model – are transferred, often uncritically, from city to city and nation to nation. Given the breadth of this area, the article focuses on what this means for the interface between sporting and urban policy models and for regeneration legacy implications. To do this, the article is divided into four sections. First, the article is situated within the context of ongoing political science debates regarding the efficiency and efficacy of 'policy transfer'. Here, the focus is placed on the tendencies for policy communities to be blinkered to the deficiencies of established policy models, especially with regard to the hosting of major events or the construction of mega-projects. Second, the article connects to a stream of work around the positive and negative implications of sporting mega-project construction and mega-event hosting. Here, examples of prior summer Olympic Games are used to illustrate the risks urban authorities and national Governments take when deciding to develop a mega-events strategy. Thirdly, using a series of UK Sport strategy documents and the evolving pre-Games experience of London as the host city for the summer Olympic Games of 2012, this article critiques the model of Olympic legacy London is trying to develop. This section particularly focuses upon how a number of paradoxes have emerged though attempts to deliver a sustainable summer Olympiad which highlight a number of shortcomings in the adopted 'policy model', especially with regard to financial and democratic accountability, and the likelihood of regeneration activities that benefits local people. This article concludes by reflecting upon the transfer of mega-event policy, and questioning why city and state leaders are still keen to bid to host major sporting events given the financial (and other) risks involved.

Policy transfer and sports policy

Although neither a new process nor without critique (James and Lodge 2003) in the past 15 years, a vast array of analysis has been undertaken in the political sciences, social policy and international studies regarding how public policies are transferred, diffused and reassigned in different international and socio-political contexts. This has been driven by the increased internationalization of public policy-making (Parsons, 1996). Moreover, importance has been placed on how 'lesson learning', often from best practice examples, is increasingly seen as an integral part of policy-making, policy implementation and ultimately, a key contributor to policy learning (see, e.g. Rose 1993, Dolowitz and Marsh 1996, Stone 2004, Bulmer *et al.* 2007). Although couched in differential terminologies and with slightly differing academic interpretations across disciplines, policy transfer can broadly be defined as 'the occurrence of, and processes in, the development of programmes, policies, institutions, etc. within one political and/or social system which are based upon the ideas, institutions, programmes and policies, emanating from other political and/or social systems' (Dolowitz *et al.* 2000, p. 3, cited Johnston 2005, p. 73).

Such a recycling of policy models is almost exclusively conveyed as beneficial, and commonly leads to a convergence of policy in particular fields of interest (Dolowitz *et al.* 2000, Evans 2010). However, as Johnston (2005, p. 73) has argued the transference of policy 'is often applied prescriptively or "pulled off the shelf" and mapped uncritically into a particular organisational landscape without due care'. Her analysis of how local governments adopt policy priorities from elsewhere highlights the fundamental (and often flawed) assumptions underlying the positive benefits to be derived from 'emulating' policies from other places: namely that the 'borrowing' institution will appropriately graft the policy onto local contingencies and do so in an appropriate timescale. However, what is clear is that such policy transference is often 'hasty and messy' (Mamadouh *et al.* 2002, p. 5) and inappropriately applied to local context, with policy-makers failing to appreciate 'the importance of adapting "foreign" models before implementing them' despite claiming to understand that this was required (Dolowitz 2000, p. 1). Furthermore, in trying to better understand this process Dolowitz and Marsh (2000) suggested three factors/processes at play which may help explain why policy failure can occur from policy transference: first, uninformed transfer, where the receiving institution has limited or incomplete information about the context and governance arrangements in the originating setting/country; second, incomplete transfer, where intentionally or unintentionally important elements of the form and structure of the policy are not transferred to the new setting and third, and perhaps of most relevance to this article, inappropriate transfer, where 'insufficient attention may be paid to the differences between economic, social, political and ideological context in the transferring and borrowing country' (Dolowitz and Marsh 2000, p. 17).

This set of factors/processes implies a strong role for agency in decision-making about the appropriateness of particular polices. Clearly, though, as globalization gathers pace and the visibility of potential policy transfers increases, there are also more structural features that are assisting the convergence of particular policy dynamics. Increasingly, policy ideas are being 'sold' or promoted internationally by agency coalitions and global networks, which are progressively more influential in shaping the direction of policy. As Stone (2004, p. 547) noted, some 'suggest that transfer is more the outcome of structural forces; that is driven by industrialisation, globalisation or regionalisation forcing a pattern of increasing similarity in economic, social and political organisation between countries'. International organizations such as the United Nations and World Trade Organization, or non-state actors (what Dolowitz and Marsh 1996, p. 345, referred to as policy transfer entrepreneurs), transnational think tanks, consultancies or foundations, increasingly exert influence on policy transfer processes and become *de faco* 'transfer agents' in the 'transnationlization of policy', including sports policy (Stone 2004).

The transfer and standardization of sports policy and mega-events

Although, majority of the literature surrounding policy transfer and 'lesson learning' tends to focus upon the emulation of political ideas and/or public service delivery, these core issues and implications have applicability across an expansive range of public policy areas. Given the focus of this article, the forthcoming discussion focuses on ideas of policy transfer as they pertain to sports policy and major events, with particular reference to the Olympic Games.[1] Here, the concern is with how, as Houlihan (2009, p. 52) notes 'a well established infrastructure of global sports institutions focused on event organising', are impacting differentially upon individual countries.

Recent and ongoing work of the evolution of elite sports policy in advanced economies has highlighted the propensity for policy transfer, over the last 40 years, to be driven through policy networks that operate on supranational levels (Houlihan 2009). This appears to be particularly the case with elite sports development policy that has evolved in many countries, such as the United Kingdom, Australia and Japan, based significantly on sports systems that developed in the former Soviet Union and East Germany (Houlihan *et al.* 2010; see also Grix 2008). Moreover, as Green (2007) noted, in a comparative study of policy transfer of elite sporting development, this is often focused upon enhancing Olympic medal success and is in part legitimated through a generalized discourse as to the performance benefits of prioritizing elite sports policy. As such Oakley and Green (2001, p. 91)[2] referred to 'common approaches to the problems of enhancing elite sports [indicating] . . . a growing trend towards the homogenisation of elite sports development'.

In a not dissimilar way Houlihan *et al.*'s (2010), study of policy learning between China and the United States with regard to elite basketball development shows how China has attempted to emulate an American 'NBA' model of elite sports in order to rapidly enhance the quality of its coaches and players. They argued that this was undertaken, as much policy transfer is, due to pressure to achieve a 'quick fix', and adopt a proven model of success in order to excel in this sport at the 2008 Beijing Olympics. They also highlighted tensions that emerged due to significant socio-political, language and ideological differences and how this impacted upon the ability to transpose a full-blown US model into China's sports system without alteration.

More generally, the focus on an emerging 'model' for elite sports development in many advanced nations has often led to heavy investment in new training methods, coaching, talent identification and development and sports science facilities, particularly for Olympic sports, as well as a reduced focus on mass participation approaches to sport and physical activity (for elite sport 'models', see Dennis and Grix (2012)).[3] However, emerging models of elite sports development are also often premised on the promise of the hosting of major sporting events, and through this mechanism, to encourage greater levels of sporting activity among the general population and leave a lasting legacy benefit in terms of high-class facilities and overall contribution to economic development and urban regeneration.[4] Moreover, such positive pronouncements of major event benefits are increasingly institutionalized in local/national and international governance systems, with major sporting organizations such as International Federation of Association Football (FIFA) and the International Olympic Committee (IOC), asserting their power through insistence on specific 'conditions' being met by the host city. For example, Rule 2, Article 14 of the Olympic Charter notes that part of the IOC's mission is 'to promote a positive legacy from the Olympic Games to the host cities and host countries'. It does this in part by giving the host cities access to the IOC's Olympic Games Knowledge Management service that comprises a vast amount of technical information and reports on previous Olympic experiences from which local urban mangers can 'draw from the lessons that previous cities have learned and adapt them to their own, specific context' (IOC 2011, p. 1). However, as noted in the following section, this urban legacy is not without critique.

The mega-project paradox

In recent years, the concept of the urban mega-project has generated much attention among academics and policy-makers alike as a key part of standardized entrepreneurial strategies deployed by urban leaders to develop and promote their cities and regions.[5] In *Great Planning Disasters*, Hall (1980) charted how large planning projects turn out to be disasters, attributing this tendency to two key variables – overestimation of demand and underestimation of cost (Coaffee and Johnston 2007). Hall drew attention to the fact that cost escalation for such planning projects are typically around 50%, further arguing that what he refers to as 'the art of imaginative judgement' will only be alleviated once more effective and transparent forecasting of projected trends is undertaken (p. 250).[6]

More recent work on the costs and benefits of planning mega-projects has taken Hall's basic premise and expanded it to take account of differing social, economic and political contexts, as well as emphasizing the different spatial aims and outcomes of projects such as highlighting the 'place promotion' benefits of, for example, conventions and major cultural and sporting events (e.g. Roche 2000). Further examples can also be drawn from recent research in America. For instance, Altshular and Luberoff (2003) in *The Changing Politics of Urban Mega-Projects* identified the shifts in American urban policy that have led to the recent boom in mega-projects, paralleling this to a similar impulse in the 1950s and 1960s linked to ideas of urban 'boosterism' and local 'growth machines' (Molotch 1976, Logan and Molotch 1987). In so doing, they, like Hall, stressed the large-scale cost escalation that many projects in both eras suffered from. Likewise, Flyvbjerg *et al.* (2003) provided a detailed expose of the development of a number of large-scale infrastructural projects and how the concept of risk acceptance has been central to mega-project development. On the one hand, they argued that in recent years the mega-project has become a 'new political and physical animal', that such projects have 'witnessed a steep increase around the world in ... magnitude, frequency and geographical spread' (ibid., 136) and have been financed by 'a mixture of national and supranational government, private capital and development banks' (ibid., 3). On the other hand, they also threw into stark relief the fact that such projects commonly have a calamitous history of cost overrun. In this context, (Flyvbjerg *et al.* 2003, p. 3) a central pillar of enquiry was the mega-project paradox:

> At the same time, as many more and larger infrastructure projects are being proposed and built around the world, it is becoming clear that many such projects have strikingly poor performance records in terms of economy, environment and public support.

They argued that the main cause of the paradox was 'inadequate deliberation about risk and the lack of accountability in the project decision making process' (ibid., 6).

Taken together, this aforementioned work allows four key themes to emerge as being central to the planning of the contemporary mega-project, which can then be applied to critique the modern Olympic Games. First, it is commonly argued that the impacts of such projects are, within reason, priceless due to their place promotional benefits. This argument ignores the significant risk of municipal bankruptcy and long-term government debt – often leading to higher local taxes – that can ensue. Second, for decades, mega-projects have received dubious costing that have lacked realism, underestimated financial contingency and significantly undervalued safety and environmental costs. In short, 'megaprojects often come draped in the politics of mistrust' (Flyvbjerg *et al.* 2003, p. 5). Third, initiators and managers of mega-projects often present their projects to the public in terms of supposed legacy benefits to the environment and society, as well as with regard to citywide and regional economic and employment growth. These 'benefits', however, are routinely exaggerated. As Coaffee and Johnston (2007, p. 141) note, 'there are widespread and recurrent accusations that such projects have been partially funded or had their cost overruns met by massaging "mainstream" public service budgets. In this sense, megaprojects can be seen to exacerbate social disadvantage and inequality'. Fourth, the governance of massive public expenditure on mega-projects often lacks financial and democratic accountability, with such projects often being associated with the development of so-called 'pro-growth regimes' and the subsequent closure of local politics to local citizens. This can be viewed as inculcating strategies that selectively favour elite capital interests, mobilize their resources to realize state capacity via partnerships, and do so through interventions aligned with their policy preferences at the urban scale (see, e.g. McGuick 2004).

The foregoing analysis has highlighted the characteristics that have plagued the development of urban mega-projects. Their proliferation and transfer across space and time, therefore, may seem surprising, but they have undoubted value as spectacle and promotional tools. This property undoubtedly helps to explain why the number of cities seeking to develop such projects has expanded greatly in recent years. Using this conceptual frame, the following section seeks to throw light on the relationship between such ideas of policy and project emulation, and bidding for and ultimately hosting the Olympics Games – a competitive race that has become increasingly popular in recent decades. As Roche (2000, p. 150) highlighted this, 'Olympic city bidding game' has expanded in scope since the 1990s with many more cities willing to bid for the right to host the Games. For example, since the race to host the 1992 Games (eventually awarded to Barcelona) where five other cites (Amsterdam, Belgrade, Birmingham, Brisbane and Paris) bid, the number of cites spending vast resources seriously considering bidding, or actually submitting a bid to host the summer Games, has been unprecedented. As the popularity of the bidding process has increased, so too has its standardization in terms of, for example, how it is run, the timetable of activities, necessary security infrastructure, media requirements and the promised legacy benefits such as urban valorization and enhanced sporting participation among the populace. In highlighting, the 'utterly standardized' nature of the modern Olympiad, Roche (2000, p. 135) referred to what he terms the 'Olympic city theme park', which can be viewed as the epitome of uncritical transfer of policy ideas on an international stage. In line with the ideas of the mega-project paradox, the ensuing section questions: why it is that there is an unparalleled interest in hosting such mega-sporting events when the risks involved in doing so are so high?

The shadow of Olympic legacy

The typical rhetoric emanating from recent Olympic cities draws particular attention to the positive 'legacy' elements particularly around regeneration (including the boost in sporting participation rates), inward investment, place promotion and tourism. Taking this perspective, hosting an Olympics is seen as a once in a lifetime opportunity for a city to rebrand and remake itself in the new globalized era (see, e.g. Dunn and McGuirk 1999). As Andranovich *et al.* (2001, p. 113) noted, utilizing examples from the US Olympics in Los Angeles (1984), Atlanta (1996) and Salt Lake City (2002), a 'mega-event strategy' is 'a new and potentially high risk strategy for stimulating local economic growth', but is seen as beneficial due to the high-media profile and tourism boom that is expected to occur, although the European Tour Operators Association believe this unlikely to be the case in 2012.

However, such a positive portrayal of expected legacy should be counterbalanced by more critical 'voices' that have questioned the very logic and justification for the hosting of such mega-events (Coaffee and Johnston 2007). Notably, commentators have routinely illuminated the social and economic dangers associated with being an Olympic city, especially with regard to the risk of municipal bankruptcy, and the dubious legacy impact in terms of the post-event underuse of venues and infrastructure (ibid.). A number of recent examples from Summer Olympiads illustrate these concerns.

By awarding the 1976 Summer Games to Montréal, the IOC wanted to show that a smaller city could successfully stage the Games. However, the mayor of Montreal saw the Games as an opportunity to develop a series of 'grand projects'. The construction of these monumental Olympic projects was, however, beset by political corruption, mismanagement, labour disputes, inflation and heightened security costs. The Games proved to be a financial disaster for the City that financed a huge building boom and spent then an enormous figure of around $1.5 billion representing a five-fold increase in original estimates. Debts for this Olympiad were only finally paid off (through higher taxes) in 2006.

Even the apparently most successful Games in terms of urban renewal – Barcelona – are not without critique. As Coaffee and Johnston (2007, p. 143) noted, 'the 1992 Barcelona Olympics, was a celebrated exemplar of urban rejuvenation linked to major sporting events, from which a "Barcelona Model" or "cult of Catalonia" has emerged which urban policy makers still blindly follow hoping for similar gains'. Others too questioned the equity of the associated Olympic development strategies that led to the privileging of a pro-growth agenda aimed at a global political-economic audience, while severely disadvantaged areas of Barcelona were largely unaffected (Garcia-Ramon and Albert 2000).

The summer Games in both Sydney (2000) and Athens (2004) provide examples of tangible attempts by urban authorities to follow the model of Olympic-led regeneration that was successful in Barcelona and to project themselves to the world as a vibrant 'global city'. However, ex-post analysis of these Games has highlighted the overestimation of projected benefits and financial mismanagement. As Coaffee and Johnston (2007, p. 143) noted, 'the 2000 Sydney Games had to be "bailed out" by the National Government to allow all the construction to take place and the predicted long term "Barcelona style" tourist boom failed to materialise'. Moreover, in the post-games period, many of the sporting facilities were underutilized, creating a burden on the taxpayer estimated at $46 m (£19.6 m) per year (see also Demos 2005). Lenskyj (2002) also highlighted how the 2000 games had 'serious shortcomings' in a number of socio-economic areas concluding that there was:

> ... extensive secrecy and obfuscation on the part of Olympic and government officials. In the absence of thorough and accurate financial, social and environmental impact assessment – and

in the general euphoria surrounding the 'best ever Olympics' – they are unlikely to engage in any serious post-Game initiatives that will benefits all … residents. (p. 231)

Similar pronouncements were also made after the 2004 Athens Games that doubled in cost from an estimated $4 billion to nearer $8 billion. Moreover, as Coaffee (2007, p. 157) noted, 'in regeneration terms, whereas the 2004 Games left a legacy of significant infrastructure improvements in terms of trams, suburban railways and metro extensions it has also left behind a collection of semi-redundant sporting venues and significant debt, which due to underestimated costs, the Athenian population will be paying back for years to come'.

Overall, the legacy of Olympic Games hosting is not universally positive with such mega-event strategies often suffering from conflicts over the predicted and actual cost of such projects, the transparency of related planning, decision-making processes and, ultimately, about the appropriateness of risk management protocols utilized by those in charge of such schemes (see, e.g. Whitson and Horne 2006). The spectre of Olympic-related regeneration and economic growth was, however, one that the UK Government and those in charge of elite sports development were keen to embrace at the turn of the new Millennium.

The growth in importance of major events in UK sports policy

In the United Kingdom, the development and standardization of elite sports policy, and the drive towards the hosting of major events, exhibit many of the characteristics of policy transfer. This in part can also be attributed to the far greater integration of sports policy with other social and economic policy as part of a general trend in cross-cutting policy development. At national level, over the past 15 years, the untapped potential of sports and recreation has moved from the periphery to the centre of government thinking with sport becoming more influential to public policy-making at all spatial scales (Houlihan and White 2002, Coaffee and Shaw 2005). Notably, as a result of the restructuring of UK Government services following the 1997 election of the New Labour Government, the Department of Culture, Media and Sport (DCMS) was established to rationalize the delivery of mainstream sports and cultural services.[7]

As part of this process of modernization, part of a larger process of reorganization that begun in the early 1990s, the former British Sports Council was re-engineered into two blocs to reflect the traditional approaches of 'sport for all' and enhancing 'sporting excellence' on the world stage: firstly, Sport England – with a remit to improve the existing community sports system, enhance and sustain participation levels in physical activity, and to identify sports talent – and secondly, UK Sport with a role to enhance elite sports performance and develop a coherent policy to attract major sporting events to the United Kingdom. It is the genesis of UK Sport and its evolving mega-events strategy (discussed below) that sowed the seeds of London's Olympic bid in 2003.

In 1999, a series of policy and evaluation documents emerged from UK Sport under the collective banner *Major Events – a 'Blueprint' for success* (UK Sport 1999a). These documents argued that a lack of leadership, vision and a joined-up approach were seen as fundamental reasons why the United Kingdom had found it so difficult to win the rights to hold major events, despite a series of bids being submitted (Birmingham's failed Olympics bid for the 1992 Summer Games and Manchester's unsuccessful efforts to attract the 1996 and 2000 Summer Games, are exemplars of this). The document, quoting a House of Commons National Heritage Committee Report (1995), noted that:

... unless Britain does coordinate the multitudinous and sometimes apparently conflicting organisations that are involved, and it is given a clear focus, then our country is unlikely to be successful in any bid for which there is fierce competition. (UK Sport 1999b, p. 1)

Sir Rodney Walker, then Chairman of UK Sport, further highlighted the vision that the United Kingdom had to develop to win, and subsequently deliver, major sporting events to the nation:

> UK Sport has developed a blueprint for Major Events that is relevant to and can be owned by all the major stakeholders. This structured approach to every angle of event planning and management will involve all the United Kingdom's key players in the events industry and ensure that when the UK bids, it has the nation's firm commitment. If that is the case, then our bids will be taken seriously and will be seriously competitive. (UK Sport 1999a, frontispiece)

The resultant guides within the *Major Events – a 'Blueprint' for success* publication (on developing strategy, policy, economic viability and environmental guidance – UK Sport 1999b–f) were published as part of this compendium and dealt with the key dimensions of major event bidding, gleaned from what was deemed to be successful international best practice, and sought to set out a strategic framework for winning future bids. Particular emphasis was placed on attracting so-called 'mega' events, such as the Summer Olympics. There was also prominence given to the long-term impact of such events on society and economy, and upon ensuring that facilities developed for such events did not have costly repercussions for host communities. This latter point, relating to the idea of 'legacy' was articulated in terms of 'optimizing public benefit':

> ... money will only be invested in events that reap significant sporting, economic, social and cultural benefits and avoid unnecessary duplication of competition facilities. (UK Sport 1999b, p. 4)

At this time, the evidence base for justifying (economically) the pursuit of major events was also emerging (UK Sport 1999g,h), although guidance also noted that decisions made over initially bidding for such events was 'often perceived as being controversial', was not an 'exact science', and, as such, evolving UK sports policy was pragmatically aiming at 'determining when to bid for the right event at the right time and place and understand the legacies that these events are likely to leave long after the closing ceremony has taken place' (UK Sport 1999e, p. 16).

Policies surrounding attempts to host major sports events in the United Kingdom continued to evolve in the noughties. In 2002, the landmark *Game Plan* sports strategy document (DCMS 2002) reinforced the desire of the United Kingdom to attract major events but, similarly to UK Sport, argued that 'there should be a more cautious approach to hosting these events' reflecting uncertainty over evaluating likely impacts (p. 12) and that 'historically, there has been poor investment appraisal, management and co-ordination for some of these events' (p. 29):

> Understandably, the failure to win the bid to stage the FIFA 2006 Football World Cup, the loss of staging rights to the 2005 World Athletics Championships and the lengthy deliberations over the construction of an English National Stadium focused attention on sporting events and major facilities. However, the recent Commonwealth Games in Manchester were regarded as a success and an example of what could be achieved. (p. 30)

As such it was argued that a mega-events 'centre of expertize' should be established within DCMS to evaluate the processes involved in creating a winning bid at 'each stage of the event lifecycle: bidding, delivery and evaluation' (p. 17) alongside 'a long term strategy which sets out those mega-events which the Government will consider supporting over the next 20 years' (ibid.). Part of the rationale for the establishment of this centre was to provide concrete justification – quantifiable evidence – for the claimed benefits attributed to the hosting of major events that should be considered alongside, the often, exorbitant costs.

In relation to the previous discussion in this article on international policy transfer, *Game Plan* also drew on both historic and contemporary evidence from summer Olympiads as to the cost and benefits accrued from major event hosting, and included the following table (p. 67). This table (see Table 1) highlighted the different ways in which Summer Olympics between 1984 and 2000 had been funded by a combination of public and private resources as well as hinting at positive regeneration legacies.

It was further recognized that more intangible benefits, such as place promotion and the creation of local 'cultural capital' as a result of enhanced volunteer training, should also be considered alongside this cost–benefit calculation. As *Game Plan* noted, 'the message is not: 'don't invest in mega events'; it is rather: 'be clear that they appear to be more about celebration than economic returns' (*Game Plan*, p. 66).[8] *Game Plan* also noted that 'there is little evidence that hosting events has a significant influence on participation' (p. 75).

Table 1. Commentary on recent summer Olympics (from *Game Plan*).

Year	Location	Finance (US$ in bn) (1995)	% Public	Comments
1984	Los Angeles	<0.5	0	LA sole bidder – low-cost games
				Mainly modernization of existing facilities rather than new build
				Financial surplus used to fund youth sports
1988	Seoul	~2.5	46	Large investment in facilities
				New urban development undertaken
1992	Barcelona	~11	38	Most expensive games ever
				Major new urban infrastructure development
				Increased city tourism and recognition
1996	Atlanta	~2	15	Historically under-utilized stadia
				Some urban redevelopment
				Some new sports facilities, but mainly existing
				Mainly modernization of existing facilities rather than new build
2000	Sydney	~2.5	~30	Games deemed 'a success'.
				Tourism down
				NSW significant debt overhang
				Currently underutilized stadia

The particular approach that was being evolved by UK Sport, through DCMS, was one that had a demonstrable urban regeneration legacy at its core, reflecting the approach recently operationalized in Manchester's sports-led regeneration approach for the 2002 Commonwealth Games, itself mirrored upon the 1992 Barcelona Olympic experience. In the Manchester case, facilities built for the 2002 Commonwealth Games were 'seen as part of a wider vision for regeneration, with sustainable after-use of venues being seen as a priority' (*Game Plan*, p. 68).[9] In the case of Barcelona, the expenditure on regeneration legacy and spatial improvement accounted for 83% on the total investment in the Games with the remaining 17% for the sporting element (Coaffee 2007, Gold and Gold 2010).

In sum, *Game Plan*, developing prior UK Sport thinking, was implicitly setting out a case for the UK bidding to host the 2012 Summer Olympics – a process that begun in 2003.

Playing (or paying) to win?

In May 2003, announcing the United Kingdom's intention to put London forward as a host for the 2012 Summer Olympics, the Secretary of State for Culture, Media and Sport pointed to the regenerative and participatory potential of the Games, noting that 'the Olympics are not just the greatest show on earth. They will help to revitalise East London,' and 'will inspire and enthuse a generation of young people' (BBC Sport 2003). A decisive selling point of the London 2012 bid was the comprehensive plans proposing the regeneration of East London and an associated renewed transport infrastructure. As the candidature file stated, 'by staging the Games in this part of the city, the most enduring legacy of the Olympics will be the regeneration of an entire community for the direct benefit of everyone who lives there' (CF2012 2004, p. 19). Particular emphasis was given to how London might learn lessons from the Barcelona 1992 Olympic experience, particularity with regard to the reuse of brownfield land, urban design, tourist growth and employment enhancements, and transfer some of their policy and practices to the United Kingdom. As preparations for the 2012 Games have progressed, regular visitations from London have been made to Barcelona to facilitate such policy learning. To cite an Olympic Delivery Agency representative after one such visit in 2006:

> I think we can learn a lot from what Barcelona achieved in terms of urban regeneration ... We want to learn from what Barcelona got right and use this experience to ensure London 2012 is not only the best Games ever, but also provides real and lasting benefits for generations to come.

However, drawing on the concept of the 'mega-project paradox' introduced earlier in this article, the successful London bid and subsequent efforts to get London ready for games-time, have subsequently occurred against a background of opaque costing and governance processes with tender estimates and construction costs which, it might be argued, are typical of other mega-projects in that they are 'highly systematically and significantly deceptive' (Flyvbjerg *et al.*, ibid., p. 20). In the case of the London Olympics, the initial bidding-time cost estimate to host the Games of around £3 billion are, at the time of writing, now estimated to be in the order of £9–£10 billion reflecting the totally unrealistic initial cost projections. In November 2006, only 16 months after London won the right to host the Games in July 2005, expenditure had already spiralled. The cost of constructing the showpiece Olympic Park area, containing the main events venues had risen by 40% and security budgets had increased four-fold. The Government's official opposition argued that the budget had gone 'disas-trously wrong' and that the Government had 'failed to disclose the true cost of VAT, contingency building cost inflation, and security, much of which was entirely predictable at the time of the bid' (BBC News 2006). Indeed, in November 2007, the Public Accounts Committee (PAC) in the House of Commons argued that costs had been 'grossly underestimated' and that the Government had left itself 'financially exposed' (BBC News 2007). Likewise, in April 2008, a further PAC report (House of Commons 2008) argued that initial costs were 'entirely unrealistic' with the committee's chairman arguing that 'ministers and officials had underestimated the true cost in order to win government and public support for the bid' (Kelso 2008). Later that year, and in the midst of the global economic downturn, the then Olympics Minster hinted that the long-term viability (legacy) of the overall Olympic project was in doubt given the budget for the 2012 games had risen to nearly £9.5 billion since Britain won the bid in July 2005, £6 billion of which is coming directly from the Government. She noted that 'had we known what we know now, would we have bid for the Olympics? Almost certainly not' (cited in Property Week 2008).

Moreover, since winning the rights to host the 2012 Summer Games evidence has grown that culture and arts provision, and associated lottery grants, are also being adversely affected by the ongoing and significant Olympic 'overspend' – what one opposition Member of Parliament referred to as an 'Olympic smash-and-grab raid on lottery funds' (Holmes 2007). For example, as the Director of the National Theatre, argued[10]:

> There is a spectacular lack of logic in using money earmarked for the arts to plug the holes in the Olympics bills ... Pulling the carpet out from under them and nobbling their money is undermining the future of our major arts institutions.[11]

Moreover hundreds of small businesses that existed on or around the Olympic Park site were evicted in the summer of 2007 in an apparent reversal of official rhetoric, which argued that the Games would leave a legacy of growth and local employment (Raco and Tunney 2010). As noted in the candidate file, the Games would supposedly lead to the:

> ... creation of wider employment opportunities and improvements in the education, skills and knowledge of the local labour force in an area of very high unemployment. The nature and range of those skills will enable residents of the Lower Lea Valley to have a stake in the economic growth of their region and begin to break the cycle of deprivation in the area. (CF2012 2004, p. 25)

The emphasis of the Government's sports policy model was also changing around this time. In 2008, DCMS replaced *Game Plan* with a new national sports strategy – *Playing to Win*, which its name suggested, continued to emphasize elite sports development that had been at the heart of previous policy.

> This plan ... sets out a vision for sports to 2012 and beyond. It suggests a shared goal to unite around – maximising English sporting success by expanding the pool of talent in all sports. In short, more coaching and more competitive sports for all young people. (DCMS 2008, p. ii)

While *Game Plan* was, and arguably still is, the most comprehensive sports policy document produced by UK Government to date, *Playing to Win* set out a much shorter and broader vision for sports development, which re-emphasized a pre-existing focus upon enhancing the UK standing in the 2012 Olympics medal table as well as drawing on the opportunities presented by being an Olympic nation:

As Olympic host nation, we have a moment in time to set a new level of ambition for sports and change permanently its place in our society. It's an era of unprecedented opportunity. (ibid.)

Everyone involved in the running of sports in this country has a responsibility to translate our Olympic host nation status into a legacy for generations to come. (ibid., p. 5)

However, paradoxically there is a particular concern over the impact of Olympic cost overruns on community-based sports – seen as one of the areas that would benefit most from the Olympics. As the Chief executive of the Central Council for Physical Recreation noted in response to a reported £100million cut in Sport England's budget in 2007: 'If there is to be a real legacy of increasing participation in sport, it seems ironic, if not perverse, for money to be taken away from community sport to fund the Olympics' (cited in Culf and Higgins 2007). Indeed, approaching the 2012 Games some have suggested that the anticipated participation legacy promise is unlikely to emerge despite unprecedented public investment (Gibson 2011). A Sport England Active People survey conducted in 2011 noted that in many sports participation rates are declining rather than increasing as the Games draw near with nearly 60% of the population doing little or no exercise (cited in ibid.). Moreover, the available evidence from outside of London does not support the contention that mega-events automatically lead to enhanced levels of participation among the general public. Veal's (2003) study on the 2000 summer Games in Sydney's and Mori's (2004) survey in the aftermath of the 2002 commonwealth games in Manchester, United Kingdom, both showed that participation in many sports declined in the post-Games period.

Conclusions

In the last 40 years, a strong interest has developed around the potential of sport-led mega-events to renew and regenerate cities and regions through infrastructure development and associated increases in sporting participation rates, inward investment and tourism. Today, such impacts, commonly referred to in terms of 'legacy' are promised to local and national communities by politicians keen to attract major sporting events, especially the Summer Olympics, to a particular location. Legacy is projected as a universal positive and as an almost certain outcome of event hosting, rather than as what might hopefully occur. Ideas of what constitutes legacy are also increasingly subject to the process of policy transfer that is seen to operate at an international scale and which has led to the adoption of a 'blueprint' for many aspects of summer Games development. Often such blueprints have been adopted uncritically by would-be Olympic hosts, and designated Olympic cities, and embedded within national (elite) sports policy models. The influence of supranational policy networks and 'transfer agents', in this case IOC criteria, especially around issues of regenerative legacy, are now also strongly framing the model of how urban authorities can expect to renew vast tracts of land and enhance mass participation in sport and physical activity, while improving their standing in the medals table at their home Olympics. Overall, this relates to (Dolowitz and Marsh 2000, p. 17) notion of 'inappropriate transfer' where not enough attention is paid to the contextual differences between the 'transferring' and 'borrowing' countries.

However, as demonstrated in this article, the hosting of Olympic Games and the development of legacy is far from a universal positive for a city and its people, and many shadows remain in the process related to a situation where such mega-event strategies are increasingly encouraged against a background of opaque costing and unaccountable governance processes. The assertion in UK Sport's blueprint (1999a) that legacy should be about 'optimizing public benefit' appears to be difficult to deliver. Ahead of London 2012 sporting participation rates are declining, not increasing, and there are widespread concerns, real or imagined, that funding dedicated for grassroots sport is being diverted from lottery 'good causes' to help fund the Olympic overspend. But, we should perhaps not be surprised by this. History tells us that such mega-event strategies are often risky and that through the process of policy transference mistakes often get repeated rather than corrected. But ultimately, as Gratton *et al.* (2001, p. 36) highlighted, hosting mega-sporting events are now often considered to be worth the risk by governing regimes primarily for place promotional purposes:

> Increasingly sports events are part of a broader strategy aimed at raising the profile of a city and *therefore success cannot be judged on simply a profit and loss basis.* …Often the attraction of events is linked to a re-imaging process … is invariably linked to strategies of urban regeneration and tourism development. (emphasis added)

Notes

1. The aim here is to outline the broad issues surrounding sports-based policy transfer. For a more detailed analysis of this phenomena in relation to elite sports development in advanced economies, see Houlihan *et al.* (2010).
2. Cited in Houlihan (2009, p. 54).
3. For example, Houlihan (2005, p. 181) suggested that, in specific relation to UK sport policy, there appears to have been a retreat from the 'sport for all' policy discourse to 'one which emphasises the demonstration effects of elite success as catalyst for increasing participation' (see also Green 2004, Collins 2010).
4. The justification given by Government's for wishing to host major sporting events often cuts across a number of different policy priorities but are often hybridized under the banner of legacy. In this article the focus is upon the legacies associated with urban regeneration that includes the impact of economic developments and infrastructure upgrading as well as less tangible impacts such as enhanced sporting participation rates.
5. Elements of this section draw from a variety of written work by the author on the relationship between, policy transfer, risk and mega-events (see, e.g. Coaffee and Johnston 2007).
6. The most dramatic example given is that of the Sydney Opera House, which opened in 1973 and where the cost of construction was no less than fifteen times greater than the figure specified in the initial budget.
7. See Coaffee (2008) for a more detailed description.
8. It should however be noted that some Summer Games are seen as successful in economic terms. According to the IOC (2010, p. 3/4), 10 years after the 1996 Games in Atlanta, a USD 5 billion economic impact had been shown and 'more than USD 1.8 billion in hotels, office buildings, high-rise residential buildings and entertainment venues had risen in the downtown area … (and) Atlanta had nearly 280 more international businesses than prior to the Games'.
9. *Game Plan* also justified its approach to major sport development projects through examples of a series of sport stadium developments which had been spatially planned to deliver regenerative benefits to the local community. Drawing on examples provided by the Commission for Architecture and the Built Environment, *Game Plan* cited a number of examples of the regeneration benefits associated with the relocation of professional football clubs (p. 31). Moreover, it was argued that a flexible planning system was vital to such success: 'if regeneration is intended as an explicit pay-off from hosting a mega-event, then it must underpin the whole planning process to ensure that maximum benefit is achieved for the investment' (p. 67). These developments utilized planning legislation called section 106 agreements – a type of planning obligation which can be used by local planning authorities following the granting of planning permission (normally major developments) to secure community infrastructure in order to meet the needs of residents in new developments, or to mitigate the impact of new developments on existing facilities.
10. Cited in Culf and Higgns (2007).
11. This reallocation of cultural funding has been made possible, or at least easier, by the strategic alignment of culture-related funding streams when the DCMS was established in 1997 under attempts to modernize government and develop more holistic and integrated polity (Coaffee 2008).

References

Altshular, A. and Luberoff, D., 2003. *Mega-projects: the changing politics of urban public investment.* Washington, DC: Brookings Institution.

Andranovich, G., Burbank, M., and Heying, C., 2001. Olympic cities: lessons learned from mega-event politics. *Urban affairs*, 23 (2), 113–131.

BBC News, 2006. Cost of 2012 Olympics 'up £900m', *BBC News* [online], 21 November. Available from: http://news.bbc.co.uk/1/hi/6167504.stm [Accessed 21 November 2006].

BBC News, 2007. 2012 Olympics budget 'on track', *BBC News* [online], 10 December. Available from: http://news.bbc.co.uk/1/hi/uk_politics/7135824.stm [Accessed 1 February 2008].

BBC Sport, 2003. Blair backs Olympic bid. Available from: http://news.bbc.co.uk/sport1/hi/other_sports/3029851.stm [Accessed 15 May 2003].

BBC Sport, 2005. Bid vital for kids. Available from: http://news.bbc.co.uk/sport1/hi/other_sports/olympics_2012/4098660.stm

Bulmer, S., *et al.*, 2007. *Policy transfer in European Union governance: regulating the utilities.* London: Routledge.

Candidate file 2012. 2004. London 2012, London.

Coaffee, J., 2007. Urban regeneration and the Olympic experience. *In*: J.R. Gold and M. Gold, eds. *Olympic cities: urban planning, city agendas and the world's games, 1896 to the present.* London: Routledge, 150–164.

Coaffee, J., 2008. Sport, culture and the modern state; emerging themes in stimulating urban regeneration in the UK. *International journal of cultural policy*, 14 (4), 377–397.

Coaffee, J. and Johnston, L., 2007. Accommodating the spectacle. *In*: J.R. Gold and M. Gold, eds. *Olympic cities: urban planning, city agendas and the world's games, 1896 to the present.* London: Routledge, 138–149.

Coaffee, J. and Shaw., T., 2005. The liveability agenda: new regionalism, liveability and the untapped potential of sport and recreation. *Town planning review*, 76 (2), i–v.

Coalter, F., 2007. *A wider social role for sport: who's keeping the score?* London: Routledge.

Collins, M., 2010. From "sport for good" to "sport for sport's sake" – not a good move for sports development in England? *International journal of sport policy*, 2 (3), 367–379.

Culf, A. and Higgins, C., 2007. Arts leaders turn on Jowell over Olympics: call for Commons debate on cuts. *The Guardian* [online], 23 April. Available from: http://www.guardian.co.uk/society/ [Accessed 23 April].

DEMOS, 2005. *After the gold rush – a sustainable Olympics for London.* London: Demos/IPPR.

Dennis, M. and Grix, J., 2012. *Sport under communism. Behind the East German 'Miracle'.* Basingstoke: Palgrave.

Department of Culture, Media and Sport (DCMS), 2002. *Game Plan: a strategy for delivering government's sport and physical activity objectives.* London: DCMS.

Department of Culture, Media and Sport (DCMS), 2008. *Playing to win: a new era for sport.* London: DCMS.

Dolowitz, D.P., *et al.*, 2000. *Policy transfer and British social policy: learning from the USA.* Buckingham: Open University Press.

Dolowitz, D. and Marsh, D., 1996. Who learns from whom: a review of the policy transfer literature. *Political studies*, 44 (2), 343–357.

Dolowitz, D. and Marsh, D., 2000. Learning from abroad: the role of policy transfer in contemporary policy making. *Governance*, 13 (1), 5–24.

Dunn, K.M. and McGuirk, P., 1999. Hallmark events. *In*: R. Cashman and A. Hughes, eds. *Staging the Olympics – the events and its impact.* Sydney: University of New South Wales Press, 18–34.

Evans, M., 2010. *New directions in the study of policy transfer.* London: Routledge.

Flyvbjerg, B., Bruzelius, N., and Rothengatter, W., 2003. *Megaprojects and risk: an anatomy of ambition.* Cambridge, MA: Cambridge University Press.

Garcia-Ramon, M.D. and Albet, A., 2000. 'Pre-Olympic and post-Olympic Barcelona, a model for urban regeneration today? *Environment and planning A*, 32, 1331–1334.

Gibson, O., 2011. London legacy promises fail to prevent decline in sports participation, *The Guardian*, 8 December, p. 7.

Gold, J.R. and Gold, M., eds., 2010. *Olympic cities: urban planning, city agendas and the world's games, 1896 to the present.* 2nd ed. London: Routledge.

Gratton, R., Dobson, N., and Shibi, S., 2001. The role of major sports events in the economic regeneration of cities. *In*: C. Gratton and I. Henry, eds. *Sport in the city – the role of sport in economic and social regeneration*. London: Routledge, 78–89.

Gratton, C. and Henry, I., 2001. *Sport in the city – the role of sport in economic and social regeneration*. London: Routledge.

Green, M., 2004. Changing policy priorities for sport in England: the emergence of elite sport development as a key policy concern. *Leisure studies*, 23 (4), 365–385.

Green, M., 2007. Policy transfer, lesson drawing and perspectives on elite sport development systems. *International journal of sport management and marketing*, 2 (4), 426–441.

Grix, J., 2008. The decline of mass sport provision in the German democratic republic. *International journal of the history of sport*, 25 (4), 406–420.

Hall, P., 1980. *Great planning disasters*. London: Weidfeld and Nicolson.

Holmes, P., 2007. *House of Commons debates arts and heritage funding (Olympics)*, 6 June.

Houlihan, B., 2005. Public sector sport policy: developing a framework for analysis. *International review for the sociology of sport*, 40 (2), 163–185.

Houlihan, B., 2009. Mechanisms of international influence on domestic elite sports policy. *International journal of sports policy*, 1 (1), 51–69.

Houlihan, B., Tan, T.C., and Green, M., 2010. Policy transfer and learning from the west: elite basketball development in the people's republic of China. *Journal of sport and social issues*, 34 (1), 4–28.

Houlihan, B. and White, A., 2002. *The politics of sport development – development of sport of development through sport*. London: Routledge.

House of Commons, Committee of Public Accounts (HCCPA), 2008. *The budget for the London 2012 Olympic and paralympic games: 14th report of the session 2007–08*. London: HMSO.

International Olympic Committee (IOC), 2010. *Factsheet – legacies of the games – update January 2010*. Lausanne: IOC.

International Olympic Committee, 2011. *Olympic charter*. Lausanne: IOC.

James, O. and Lodge, M., 2003. The limitations for 'policy transfer' and 'lesson drawing' for public policy research. *Political studies review*, 1, 179–193.

Johnston, L., 2005. 'Waking up the sleeping giant': change management, policy transfer and the search for collaboration. *Public policy and administration*, 20, 69–88.

Kelso, P., 2008. Parliament and public misled over Olympics budget, say MPs. *The Guardian* [online], 22 April. Available from: http://www.guardian.co.uk/politics/2008/apr/22/tessajowell.olympics2012 [Accessed 23 April 2008].

Lenskyj, H., 2002. *Best Olympics ever? The social impacts of Sydney 2000*. New York: SUNY Press.

Logan, J.R. and Molotch, H., 1987. *Urban fortunes*. Berkeley, CA: University of California Press.

Mamadouh, V., De Jong, M., and Lalenis, K., 2002. An introduction to institutional transplantation. *In*: M. De Jong, K. Lalenis, and V. Mamadouh, eds. *The theory and practice of institutional transplantation: experiences with the transfer of policy institutions*. The Netherlands: Kluwer Academic Publishers, 1–18.

McGuick, P.M., 2004. State, strategy, and scale in the competitive city: a neo-Gramscian analysis of the governance of global Sydney. *Environment and planning A*, 36, 1019–1043.

Molotch, H., 1976. The city as growth machine: towards a political economy of place. *American journal of sociology*, 82 (2), 309–332.

Oakley, B. and Green, M., 2001. The production of Olympic champions: international perspectives on elite sport development system. *European journal of sport management*, 8, 83–105.

Parsons, D.W., 1996. *Public policy: an introduction to the theory and practice of policy analysis*. Cheltenham: Edward Elgar Publishing.

Property Week, 2008. Olympics Minster wishes UK had not bid. Available from: http://www.propertyweek.com/news/olympics-minister-wishes-uk-had-not-bid/3127615.article [Accessed 14 November 2008].

Raco, M. and Tunney, E., 2010. Visibilities and invisibilities in urban development: small business communities and the London Olympics 2012. *Urban studies*, 47 (10), 2069–2091.

Riordan, J., 1999. The impact of communism on sport. *In*: J. Riordan and A. Krueger, eds. *The international politics of sport in the twentieth century*. London: Spon Press.

Roche, M., 2000. *Mega-events and modernity: Olympics and expos in the growth of global culture*. London: Routledge.

Rose, R., 1993. *Lesson drawing in public policy: a guide to learning across time and space*. Chatham, NJ: Chatham house.

Sassen, S., 2000. The global city: strategic site/new frontier. *American studies*, 41 (2-3), 79–95.

Scottish Executive Central Research Unit, 2000. *The role of sport in regenerating deprived areas*. Edinburgh: Scottish Executive.

Social Exclusion Unit, 2001. Report *of policy action team 10 arts and sport*. London: DCMS.

Sport England, 2001. *Sport and regeneration – Planning Bulletin – Issue 10*, September.

Stone, D., 2004. Transfer agents and global networks in the 'transnationalization' of policy. *Journal of European public policy*, 11 (3), 545–566.

UK Sport, 1999a. *Major events – a blueprint' for success (compendium pack)*. London: UK Sport.

UK Sport, 1999b. *Major events – a blueprint' for success*. London: UK Sport.

UK Sport, 1999c. *A UK strategy*. London: UK Sport.

UK Sport, 1999d. *A UK policy*. London: UK Sport.

UK Sport, 1999e. *Major events – the economics*. London: UK Sport.

UK Sport, 1999f. *Practical environmental guidelines*. London: UK Sport.

UK Sport, 1999g. *The economic impact of major sports events*. London: UK Sport.

UK Sport, 1999h. *The economic impact of sports events: guidance document*. London: UK Sport.

Whitson, D. and Horne, J., 2006. Underestimated costs and overestimated benefits? Comparing the outcomes of sports mega-events in Canada and Japan. *Sociological review*, 54 (s2), 72–89.

Index

Anti-doping: Policy and Governance

Edited by Barrie Houlihan and Mike McNamee

The book addresses a series of key aspects of contemporary anti-doping policy. At the broader philosophical level, questions are asked about whether the scale of anti-doping activity and the intrusiveness of anti-doping policy in the lives of athletes is proportionate to the problem of doping. Aspects of existing anti-doping practice are also explored at the level of transnational organisations such as the EU and WADA and also at the level of the personal choices that need to be made by athletes and doctors in relation to doping control. Other contributions examine the complex issue of assessing the extent of doping and also understanding the factors that motivate athletes to use performance-enhancing drugs.

This book was published as a special issue of the *International Journal of Sport Policy and Politics*.

Barrie Houlihan is Professor of Sport Policy at Loughborough University, Visiting Professor at the Norwegian School of Sport Sciences and editor of the *International Journal of Sport Policy and Politics*.

Mike McNamee is Professor of Applied Ethics at Swansea University and is editor of the journal *Sport, Ethics and Philosophy*.

Mar 2013: 246 x 174: 160pp
Hb: 978-0-415-81408-9
£85 / $145

Related titles from Routledge

Women's Football in the UK

Continuing with Gender Analyses

Edited by Jayne Caudwell

This book examines the complex ways in which girls and women experience football cultures in Britain. It extends current debate surrounding women and football (namely, how gender has functioned to shape women's experiences of playing the game), by focusing on organisational, administrative and coaching practices, alongside the particular issues surrounding sexuality, ethnicity and disability (not only gender).

The book analyses football and gender to reveal the subtle forms of discrimination that persist. It is important to highlight the many challenges and transformations made by girls and women but more importantly to consider the ways power continues to operate to devalue and undermine girls and women involved in the game. The UK-based authors make use of their recent research findings to offer critical debate on girls' and women's current experiences of British football cultures. Overall the book reveals the present day complexities of marginalisation and exclusion.

This book was published as a special issue of *Sport and Society*.

Jayne Caudwell is Senior Lecturer in Sport Studies at the University of Brighton, UK.

Sep 2011: 246 x 174: 168pp
Hb: 978-0-415-56087-0
£85 / $145

Available from all good bookshops